enVisionmath2.0

Volume 1B Topics 4-7

Authors

Randall I. Charles
Professor Emeritus
Department of Mathematics
San Jose State University
San Jose, California

Jennifer Bay-Williams
Professor of Mathematics Education
College of Education and Human Development
University of Louisville
Louisville, Kentucky

Robert Q. Berry, III
Associate Professor of Mathematics Education
Department of Curriculum, Instruction and Special Education
University of Virginia
Charlottesville, Virginia

Janet H. Caldwell
Professor of Mathematics
Rowan University
Glassboro, New Jersey

Zachary Champagne
Assistant in Research
Florida Center for Research in Science, Technology, Engineering, and Mathematics (FCR-STEM)
Jacksonville, Florida

Juanita Copley
Professor Emerita, College of Education
University of Houston
Houston, Texas

Warren Crown
Professor Emeritus of Mathematics Education
Graduate School of Education
Rutgers University
New Brunswick, New Jersey

Francis (Skip) Fennell
L. Stanley Bowlsbey Professor of Education and Graduate and Professional Studies
McDaniel College
Westminster, Maryland

Karen Karp
Professor of Mathematics Education
Department of Early Childhood and Elementary Education
University of Louisville
Louisville, Kentucky

Stuart J. Murphy
Visual Learning Specialist
Boston, Massachusetts

Jane F. Schielack
Professor of Mathematics
Associate Dean for Assessment and Pre K-12 Education, College of Science
Texas A&M University
College Station, Texas

Jennifer M. Suh
Associate Professor for Mathematics Education
George Mason University
Fairfax, Virginia

Jonathan A. Wray
Mathematics Instructional Facilitator
Howard County Public Schools
Ellicott City, Maryland

Mathematicians

Roger Howe
Professor of Mathematics
Yale University
New Haven, Connecticut

Gary Lippman
Professor of Mathematics and Computer Science
California State University, East Bay
Hayward, California

ELL Consultants

Janice R. Corona
Independent Education Consultant
Dallas, Texas

Jim Cummins
Professor
The University of Toronto
Toronto, Canada

Reviewers

Debbie Crisco
Math Coach
Beebe Public Schools
Beebe, Arkansas

Kathleen A. Cuff
Teacher
Kings Park Central School District
Kings Park, New York

Erika Doyle
Math and Science Coordinator
Richland School District
Richland, Washington

Susan Jarvis
Math and Science Curriculum Coordinator
Ocean Springs Schools
Ocean Springs, Mississippi

Savvas Learning Company LLC, 15 East Midland Avenue, Paramus, NJ 07652

ISBN-13: 978-0-328-93063-0
ISBN-10: 0-328-93063-6
6 22

TOPIC 4 Subtraction Facts to 20: Use Strategies

Essential Question: What strategies can you use while subtracting?

During the day, the sun appears to move across the sky.

At night, the sun is gone and the moon and stars appear.

Why do objects in the sky appear to move? Let's do this project and learn more.

Math and Science Project: Pattern of Day and Night

Find Out Talk to friends or relatives about how day and night changes on Earth. How do day and night change as the Earth turns?

Journal: Make a Book Draw pictures of the day sky and the night sky. In your book, also:

- Draw objects that appear in the day and night skies.
- Write subtraction problems about objects that appear in the sky.

Name ____________________

Review What You Know

Vocabulary

1. Circle the number that is 4 **fewer** than 8.

10

6

4

0

2. Circle the **doubles-plus-1 fact.**

3 + 7 = 10

8 + 0 = 8

3 + 4 = 7

6 + 6 = 12

3. Circle the **doubles-plus-2 fact.**

4 + 5 = 9

3 + 5 = 8

2 + 5 = 7

2 + 2 = 4

Subtraction Stories

4. Molly has 6 goldfish. She gives 3 goldfish to Nick.

How many goldfish does Molly have now?

Write an equation to show the difference.

____ − ____ = ____

5. Katie has 7 stamps. She gives 2 stamps to Jamie.

How many stamps does Katie have now?

Write an equation to show the difference.

____ − ____ = ____

Parts and Whole

6. Write the parts and the whole for 9 − 1 = 8.

Whole: ____

Part: ____

Part: ____

My Word Cards

Study the words on the front of the card. Complete the activity on the back.

A-Z Glossary

related facts

$2 + 3 = 5$

$5 - 2 = 3$

fact family

$3 + 5 = 8$

$5 + 3 = 8$

$8 - 3 = 5$

$8 - 5 = 3$

My Word Cards

Use what you know to complete the sentences.
Extend learning by writing your own sentence using each word.

A group of related addition and subtraction facts is called a

____

_______________.

If a subtraction fact and an addition fact have the same whole and the same parts, they are called

____

_______________.

Name ____________________

Lesson 4-1
Count to Subtract

I can ...
subtract using a number line.

I can also use math tools correctly.

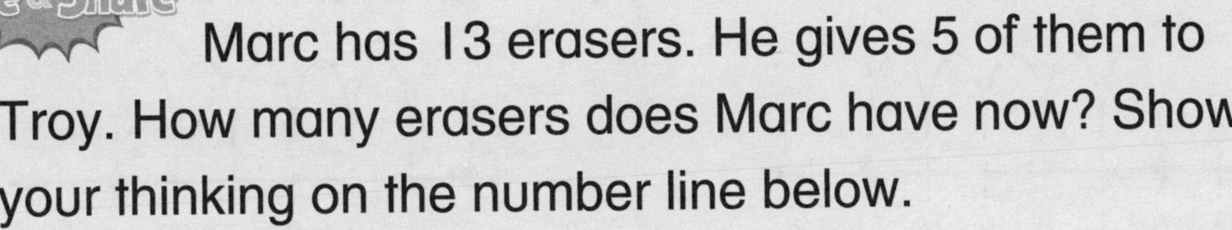

Solve & Share Marc has 13 erasers. He gives 5 of them to Troy. How many erasers does Marc have now? Show your thinking on the number line below.

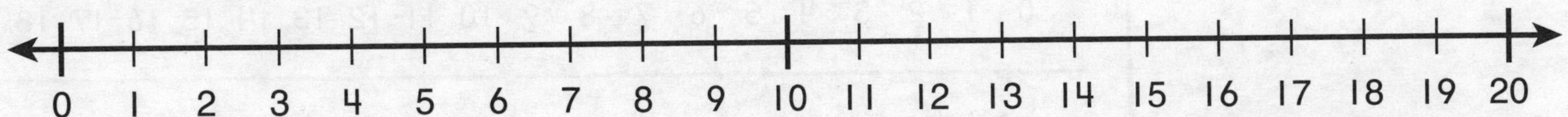

Marc has ____ erasers now.

You can count back or count on to subtract.

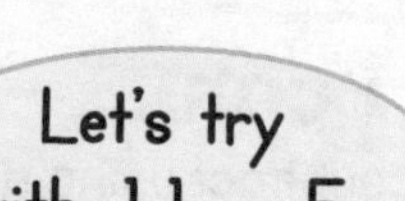

You can count back on a number line to subtract 11 – 5.

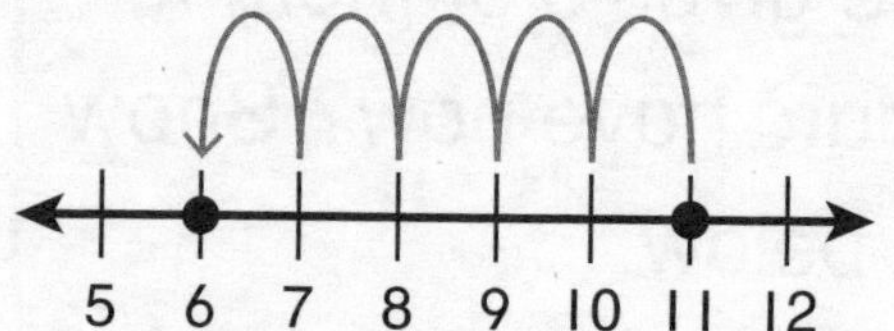

I start at 11 and count back 5.
$11 - 5 = 6$

You can also count on to subtract 11 – 5 on a number line.

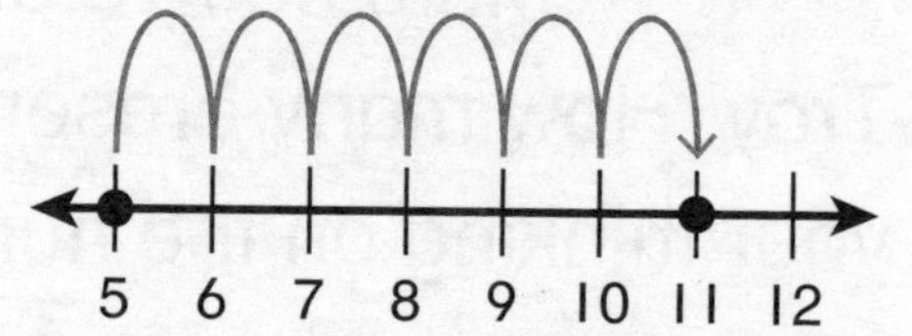

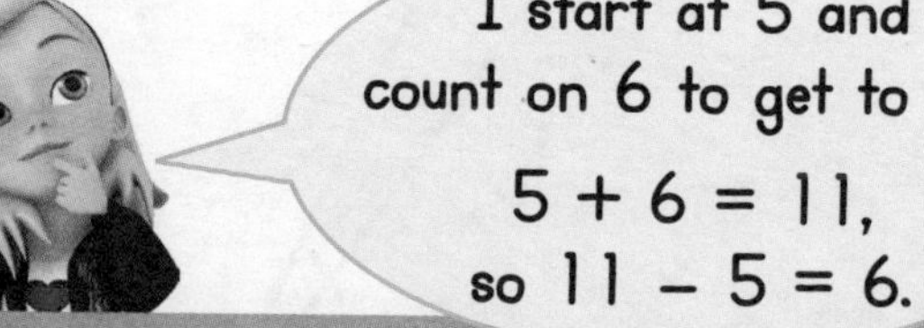

I start at 5 and count on 6 to get to 11.
5 + 6 = 11,
so 11 – 5 = 6.

Do You Understand?

Show Me! How can you use a number line to solve 9 – 5?

Guided Practice

Use the number line to count back or count on and find the difference.

1. $11 - 3 =$ 8

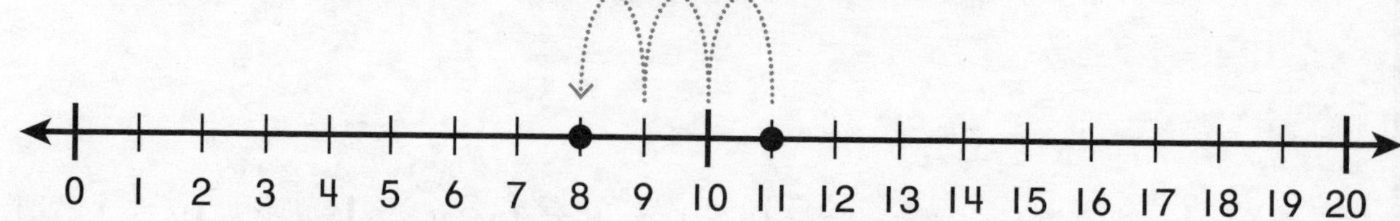

2. ___ $= 15 - 6$

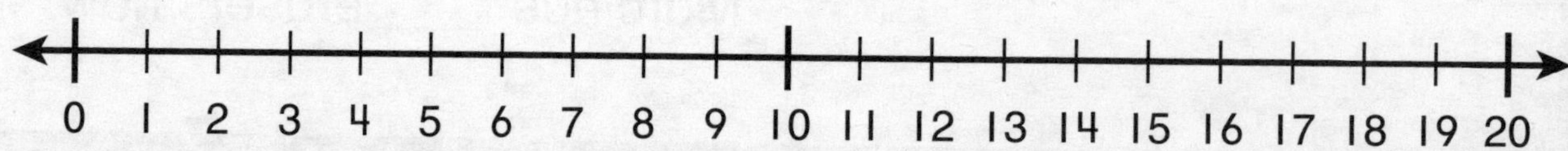

Name ____________________

Tools Assessment

Independent Practice Use the number line to count back or count on and find the difference. Show your work.

3. $11 - 6 =$ ___

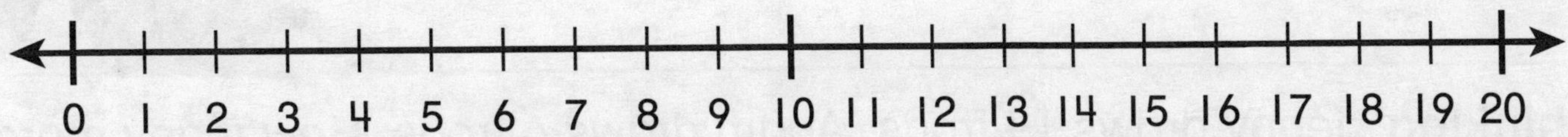

4. ___ $= 7 - 7$

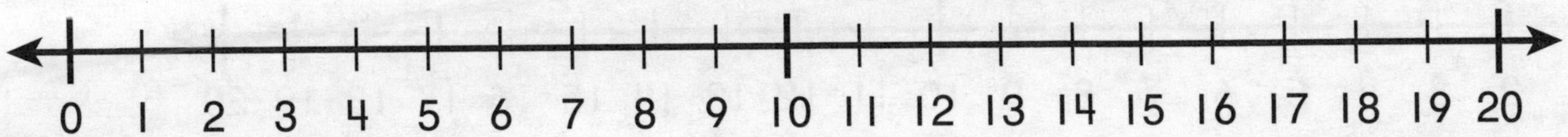

5. $15 -$ ___ $= 7$

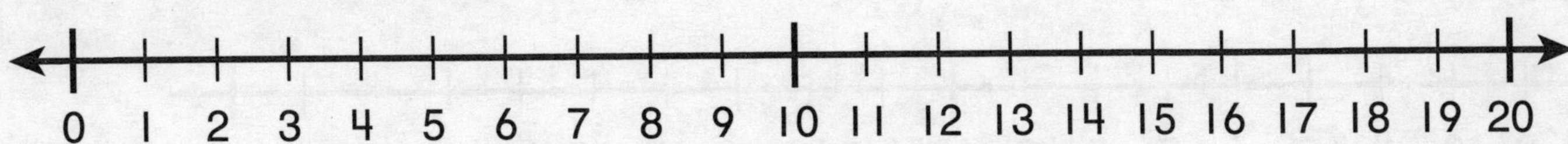

Problem Solving Solve the problems below.

6. **Use Tools** David finds 16 − 7 on a number line. Write where David starts. Write how many he counts back. Then write the difference.

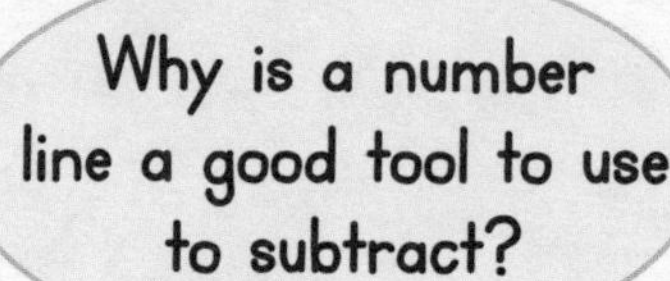

Why is a number line a good tool to use to subtract?

Start at ____.

Count back ____.

16 − 7 = ____

7. **Higher Order Thinking** Jenny draws 14 frogs. Adam draws 6 frogs. How many more frogs does Jenny draw than Adam? Use the number line to show how you can count back or count on to solve. Then write an equation to show the problem.

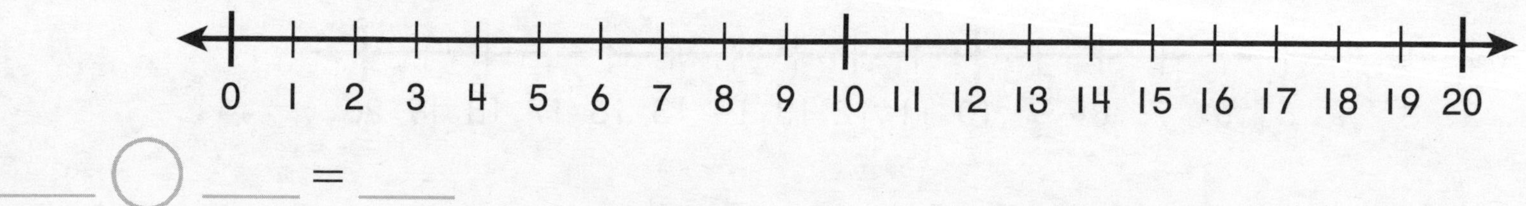

____ ◯ ____ = ____

8. **Assessment** Use the number line to find the difference. Show your work.

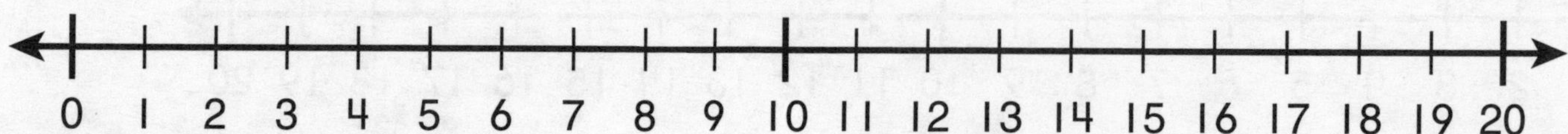

15 − 9 = ____

Name ___________________________

Help Tools Games

Homework & Practice 4-1
Count to Subtract

Another Look! You can count back on a number line to subtract.

12 − 5 = ?

Start at the number you are subtracting from.
Count back the number that you are subtracting.

I started at 12.
Then I counted back 5.
I ended at 7.

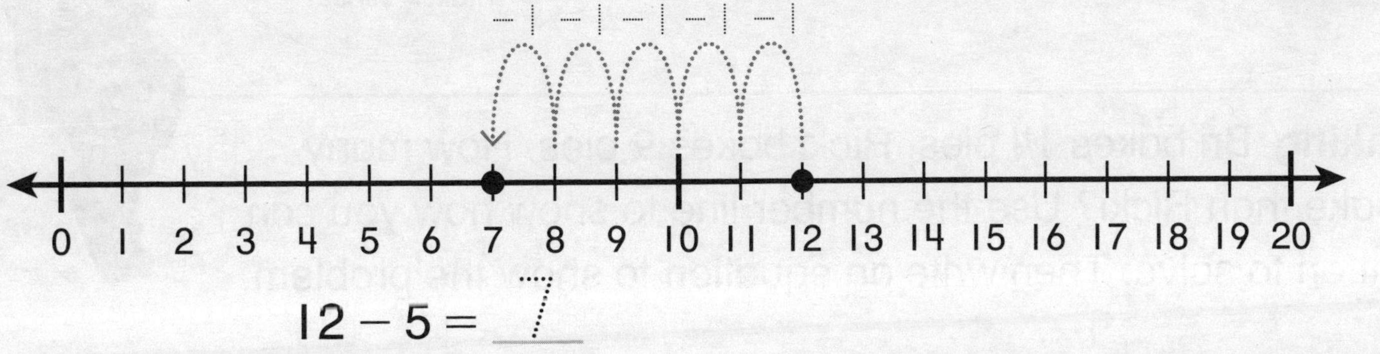

12 − 5 = 7

HOME ACTIVITY Draw a number line and label it 0-20. Give your child a subtraction fact, such as 11 − 4. Ask, "How can you use counting back to subtract?" Have your child use the number line to show counting back to subtract 4 from 11. Repeat with other subtraction facts.

Use the number line to count back or count up and find the difference.

1. 13 − 8 = ____

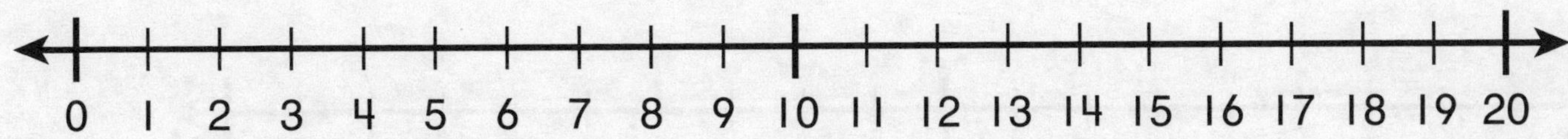

Solve the problems below.

2. **Make Sense** Patty finds 11 − 4 on a number line. Where does she start? How many does she count back? Then write the difference.

Start at ____.

Count back ____.

11 − 4 = ____

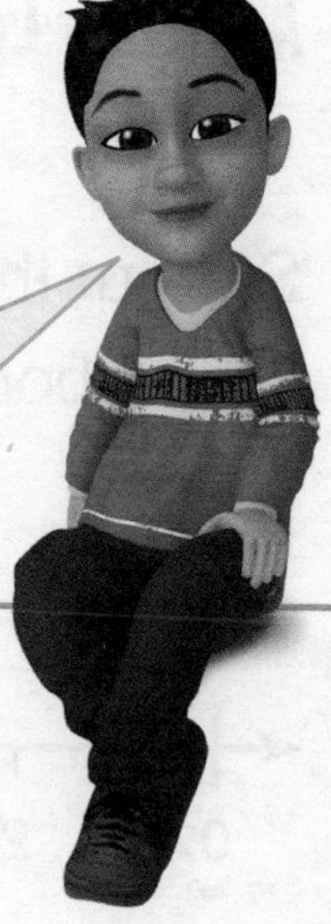

How can you check that your solution makes sense?

3. **Higher Order Thinking** Bri bakes 14 pies. Ricki bakes 9 pies. How many more pies did Bri bake than Ricki? Use the number line to show how you can count back or count on to solve. Then write an equation to show the problem.

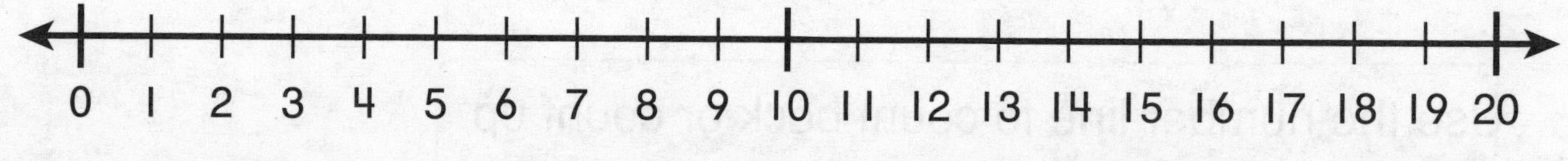

____ ◯ ____ = ____ ____ more pies

4. **Assessment** Use the number line to find the difference. Show your work.

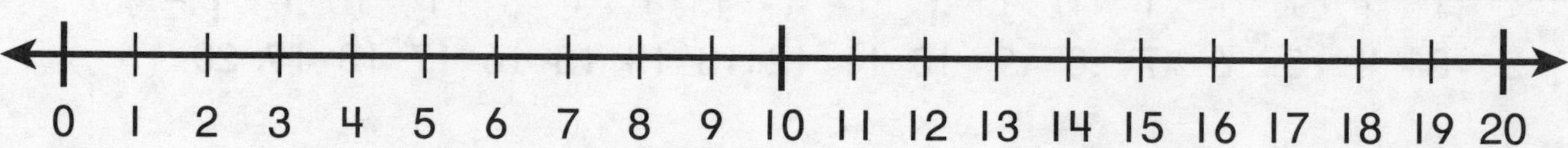

13 − 8 = ____

Name ______________________

Lesson 4-2
Make 10 to Subtract

I can ...
make subtraction easier by making 10 to subtract.

I can also make math arguments.

Solve & Share

How can thinking about 10 help you find the answer to the subtraction fact $13 - 7$?

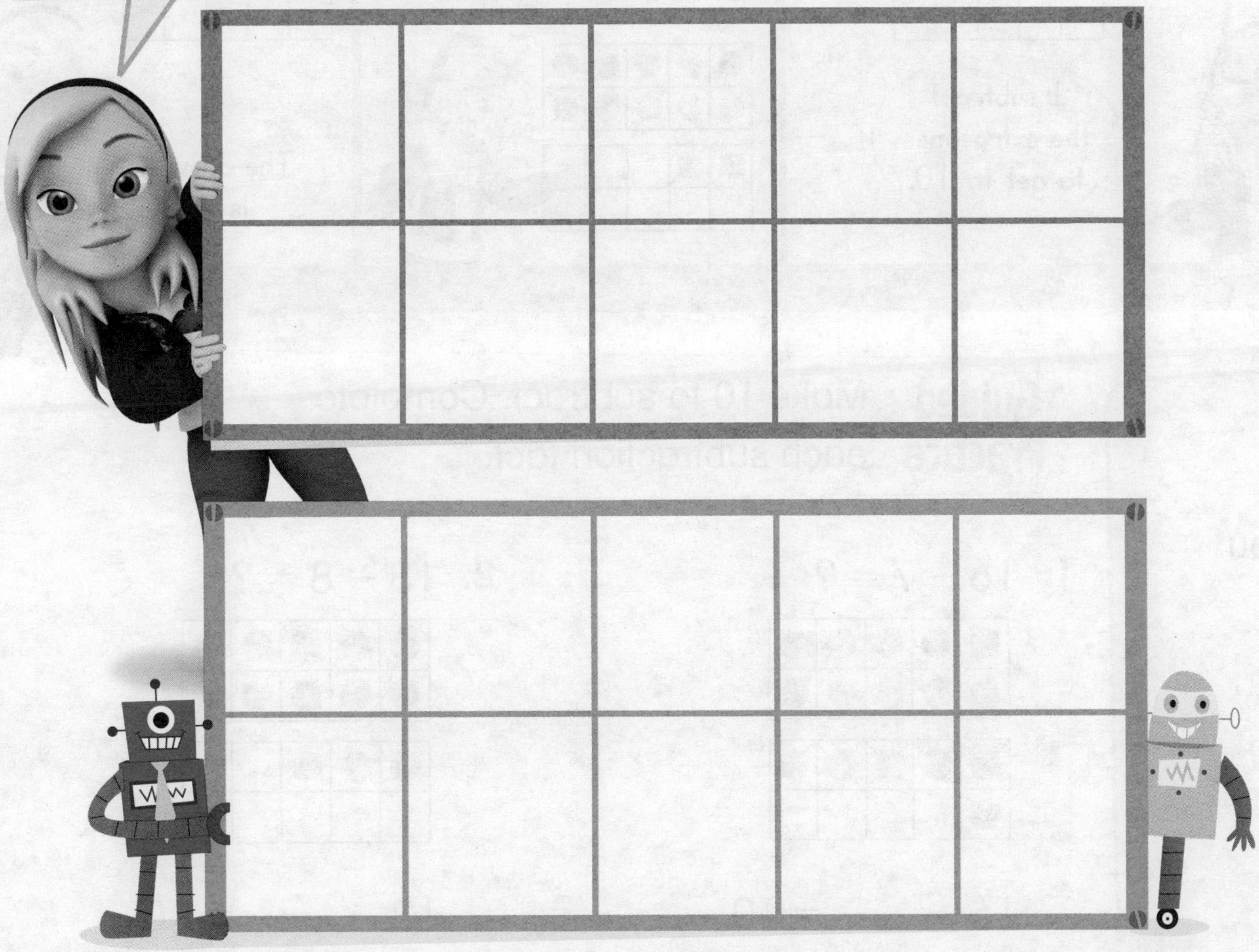

____ − ____ = ____

You can make 10 to help you subtract.

$12 - 5 = ?$

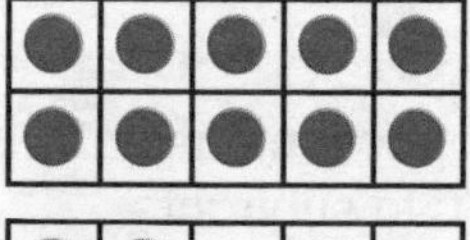

Subtract 2 to get to 10.

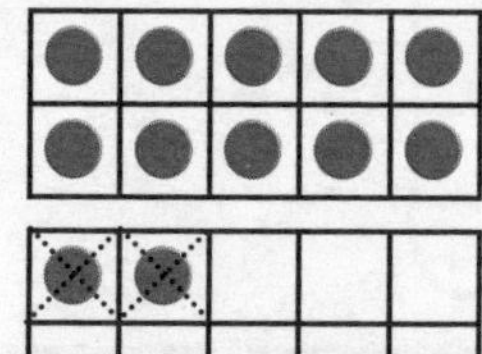

Subtract 3 more because $5 = 2 + 3$.

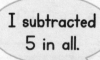

There are 7 left.

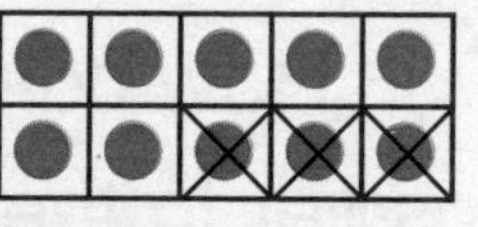
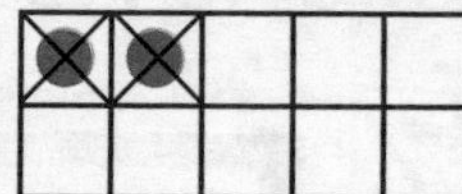

Do You Understand?

Show Me! How can finding $14 - 4$ help you find $14 - 6$?

Guided Practice

Make 10 to subtract. Complete each subtraction fact.

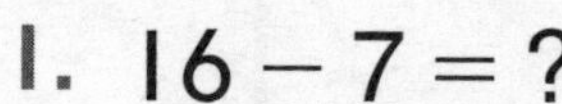

1. $16 - 7 = ?$

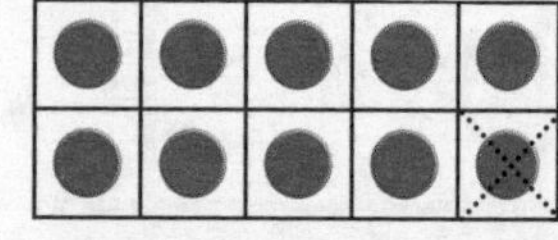
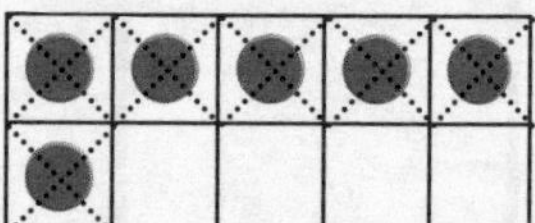

$16 -$ 6 $= 10$

$10 -$ 1 $=$ 9

So, $16 - 7 =$ 9.

2. $13 - 8 = ?$

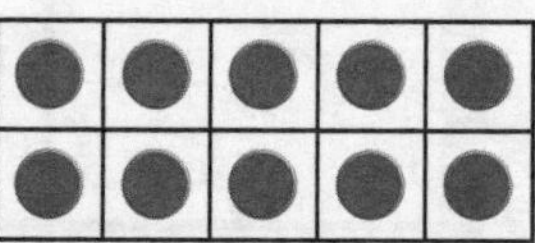
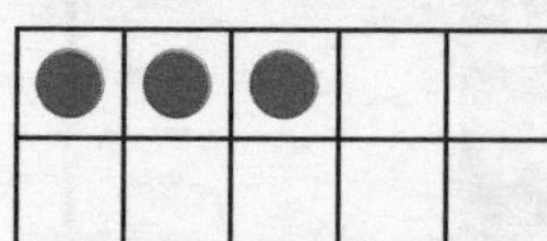

$13 -$ ____ $= 10$

$10 -$ ____ $=$ ____

So, $13 - 8 =$ ____.

Name ______________________

Independent Practice

Make 10 to subtract. Complete each subtraction fact.

3. 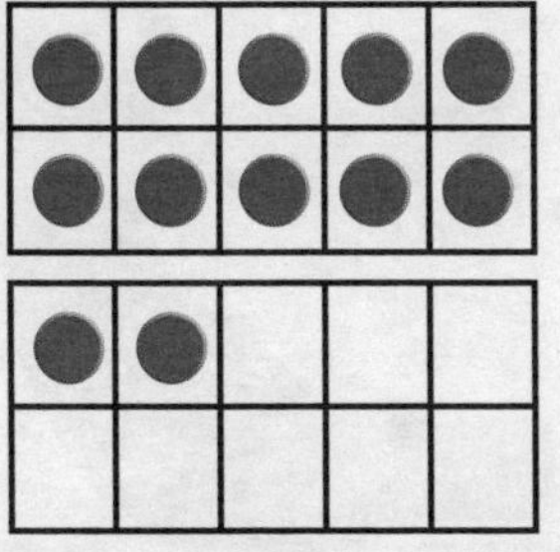

$12 - 4 =$ ____

4. 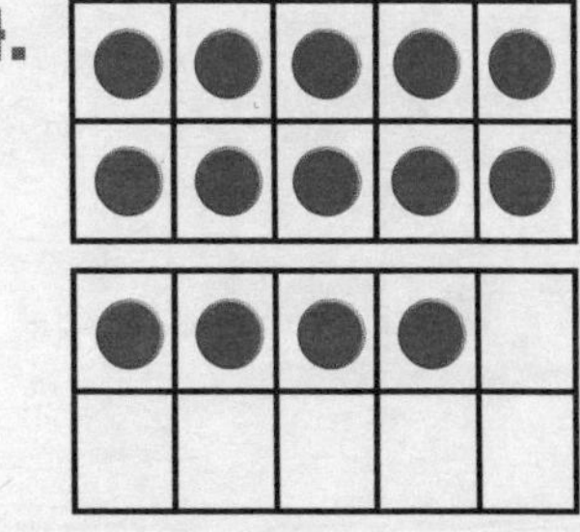

$14 - 6 =$ ____

5. 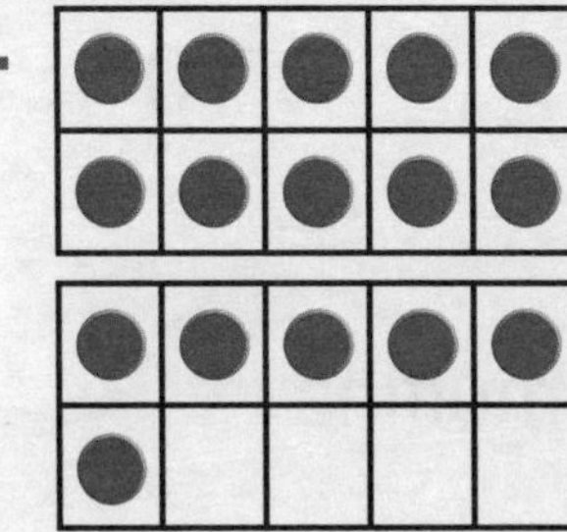

$16 - 9 =$ ____

6. 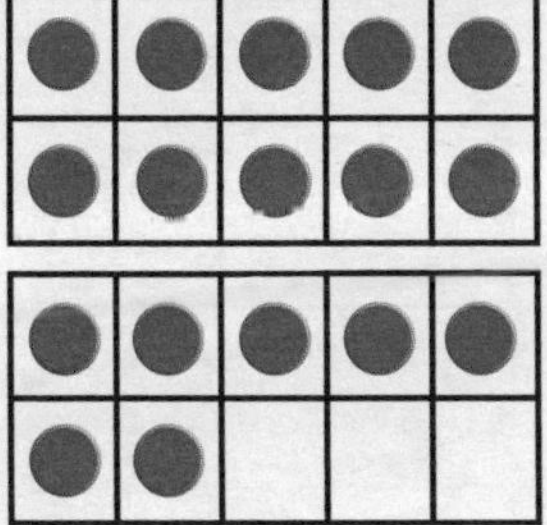

$17 - 8 =$ ____

7. 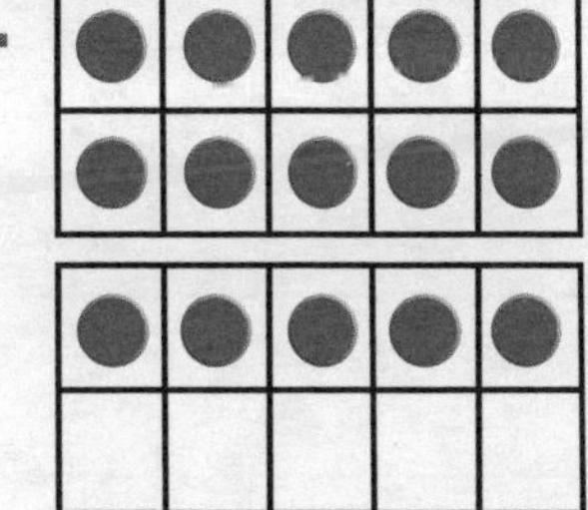

$15 - 7 =$ ____

8. 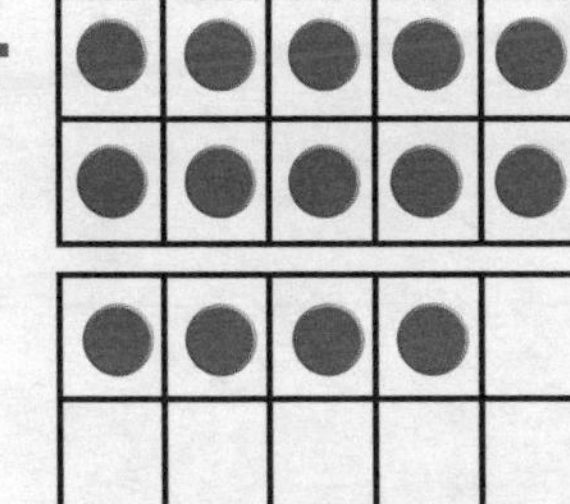

$14 - 9 =$ ____

Draw counters in the ten-frames to show your work.

9. **Number Sense** Show how you can make 10 to find $13 - 6$.

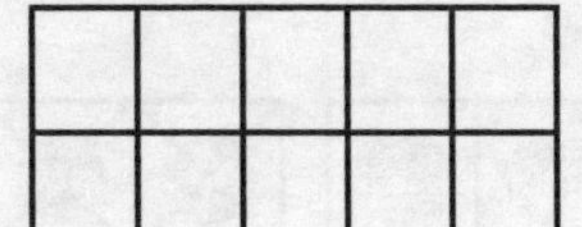

$13 - 6 =$ ____

Problem Solving Solve each problem below.

10. Use Tools Kyle bakes 12 muffins. His friends eat 6 muffins. How many muffins are left? Make 10 to subtract.

$12 - \_\_\_ = 10$

$10 - \_\_\_ = \_\_\_$

___ muffins

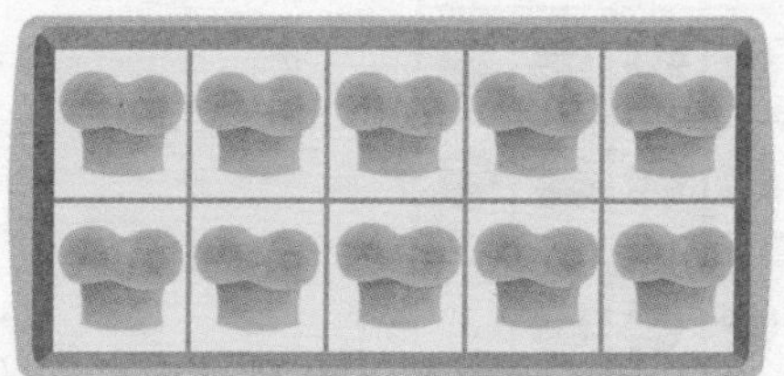

11. Higher Order Thinking Zak makes 10 to solve $12 - 5$ by changing the problem to $12 - 2 - 3$. How does Zak make 10?

____

____

____

12. Assessment Match the pair of ten-frames with the correct pair of equations that show how to solve by making 10.

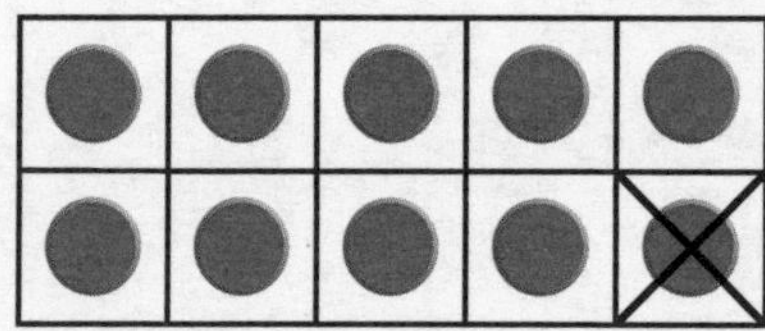

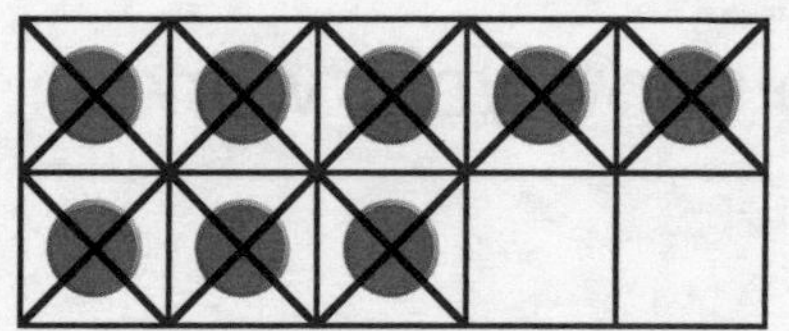

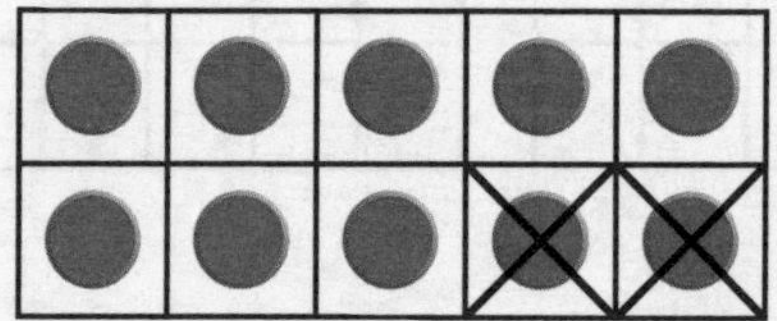

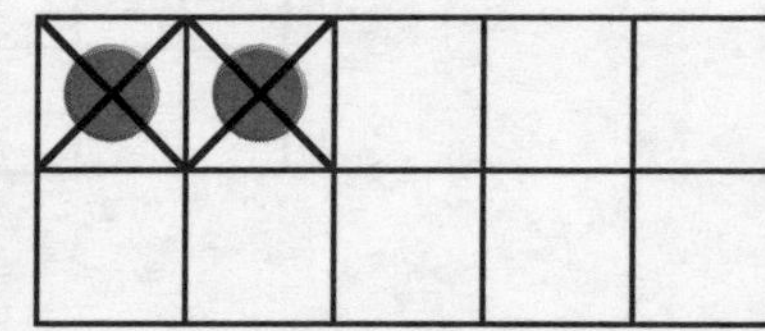

$12 - 2 = 10, \ 10 - 2 = 8$

$12 - 3 = 9, \ 9 - 1 = 8$

$18 - 8 = 10, \ 10 - 1 = 9$

$18 - 8 = 10, \ 10 - 2 = 8$

Name ____________________

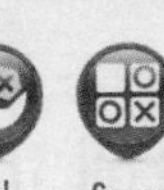

Homework & Practice 4-2
Make 10 to Subtract

Another Look! Breaking numbers apart to make 10 can make it easier to subtract.

13 − 4 = ?

First, take away 3 to make 10.

13 − 3 = 10

Then, take away 1 more because you need to subtract 4 in all.

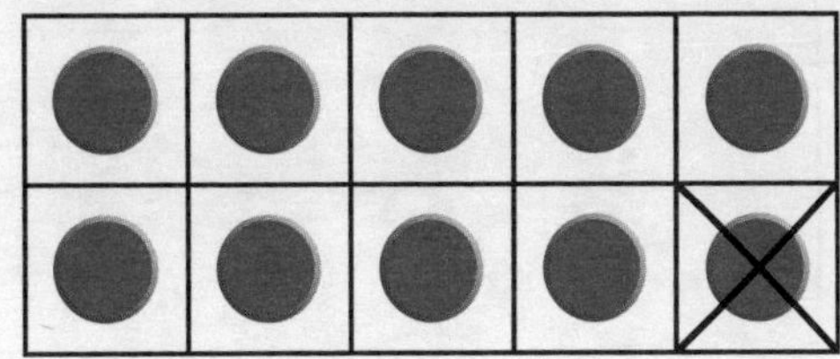

10 − 1 = 9

13 − 4 is the same as 13 − 3 − 1.

13 − 4 = 9

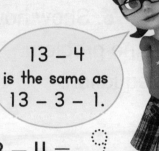

HOME ACTIVITY Write 12 − 7 = ? on a piece of paper. Have your child use small objects to find the difference. Tell your child to make a 10 to subtract: by adding on to get 10 or by subtracting to get 10. Have your child explain each step of the process as he or she solves the problem.

Make 10 to subtract.
Complete each subtraction fact.

1.

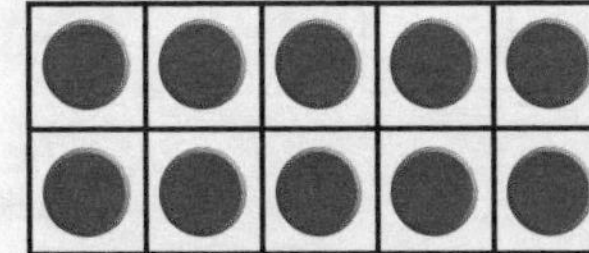

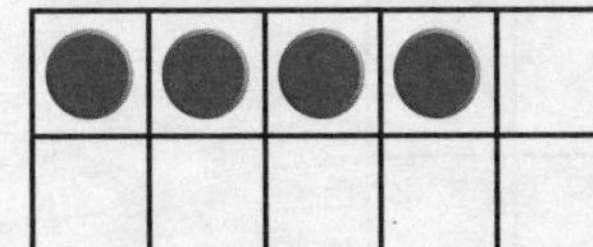

14 − 5 = ____

2.

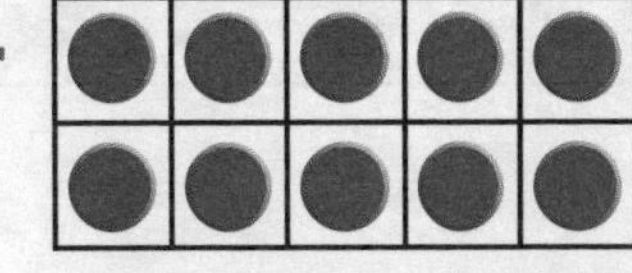

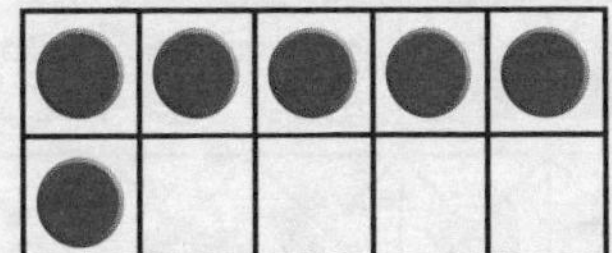

16 − 7 = ____

3.

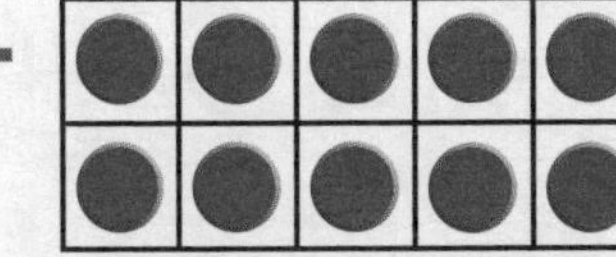

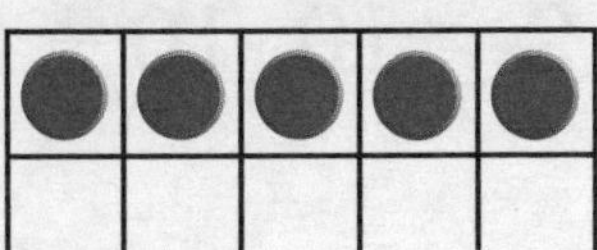

15 − 8 = ____

Make 10 to help you find the missing number in each problem.

4. Algebra

$5 = 12 - \_\_\_\_$

5. Algebra

$\_\_\_\_ - 6 = 8$

6. Algebra

$15 - \_\_\_\_ = 7$

7. Higher Order Thinking Write a story problem for 15 − 6. Show how to make 10 to solve the problem. Then complete the equation.

$15 - 6 = \_\_\_\_$

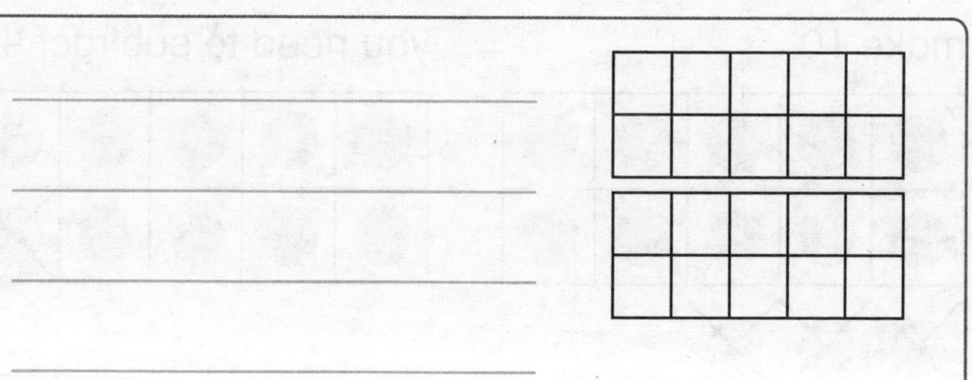

8. Assessment Match the pair of ten-frames with the correct pair of equations that show how to solve by making 10.

$17 - 7 = 10,\ 10 - 2 = 8$

$12 - 2 = 10,\ 10 - 4 = 6$

$12 - 2 = 10,\ 10 - 5 = 5$

$17 - 8 = 9,\ 9 - 1 = 8$

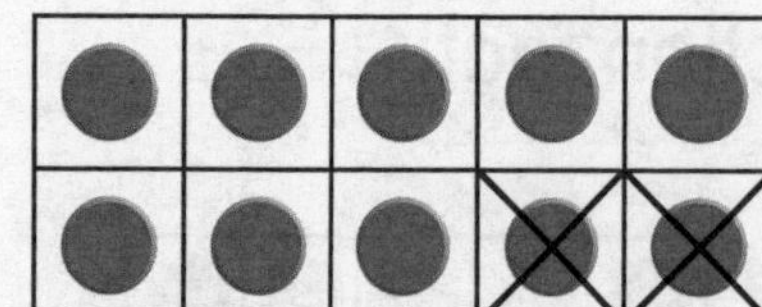

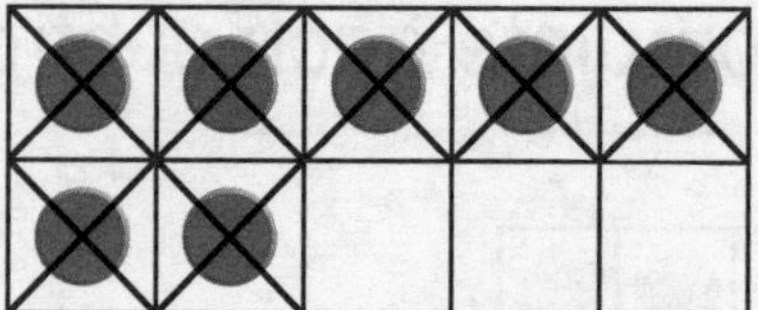

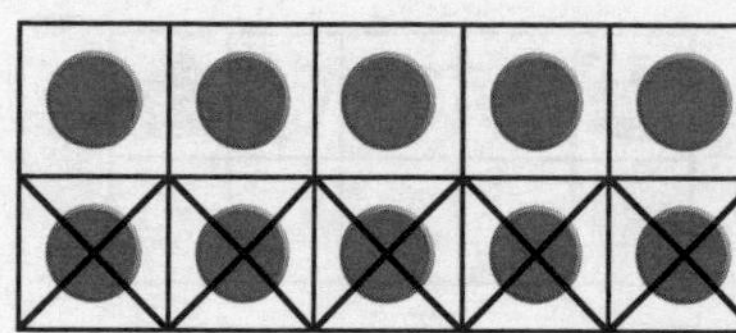

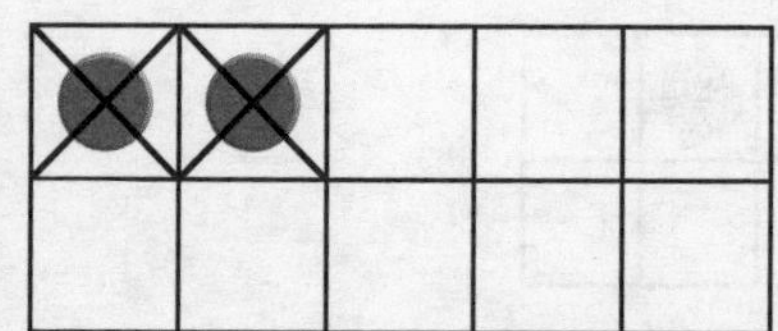

Name ____________________

Lesson 4-3

Continue to Make 10 to Subtract

I can ...
count on to subtract using 10 as a landmark.

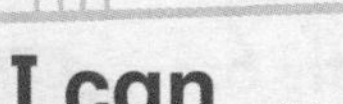

I can also make math arguments.

Solve & Share Emily counts on to find 11 − 7. She makes 10 while counting. Use counters and the ten-frames to explain what Emily could have done.

11 − 7 = ____

Counting on to make 10 can help you subtract.

14 − 6 = ?

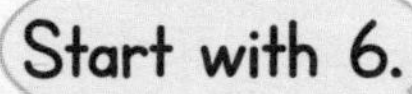

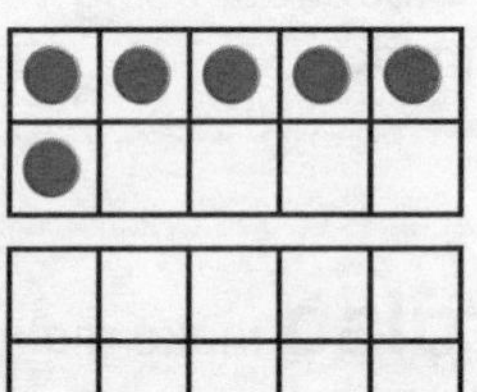

Add 4 to make 10.

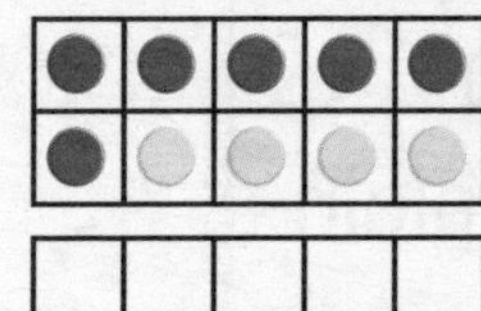

6 + 4 = 10

I add 4 to 6 to make 10.

Add 4 more to make 14.

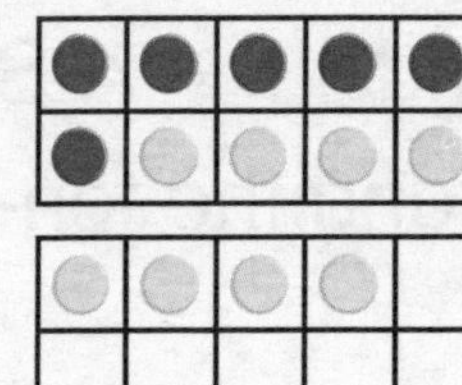

10 + 4 = 14

How many did you count on?

6 + 4 + 4 = 14

6 + 8 = 14

I added 8 to 6 to make 14. So, 14 − 6 = 8.

Do You Understand?

Show Me! How can counting on to make 10 help you find 15 − 8?

Guided Practice

Subtract. Count on to make 10. Complete the facts.

1. 13 − 9 = ?

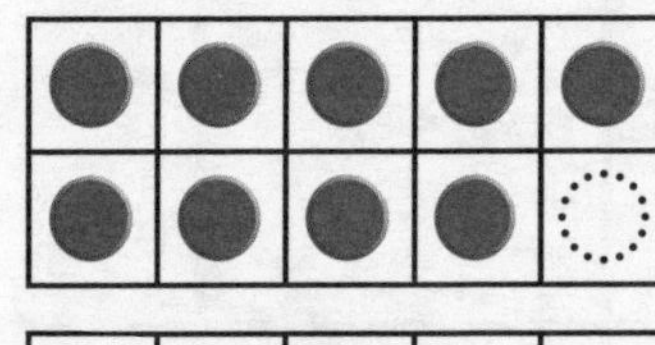

9 + 1 = 10

10 + 3 = 13

9 + ___ = 13, so

13 − 9 = ___.

Name ____________________

Independent Practice

Subtract. Count on to make 10. Show your work.

2.

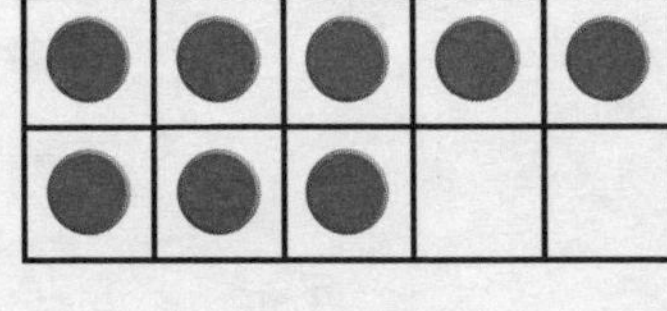

8 + ____ = 10

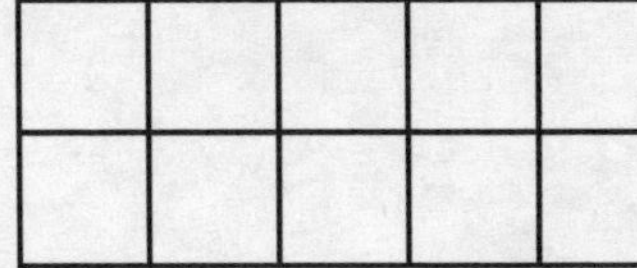

10 + ____ = 12

8 + ____ = 12, so 12 − 8 = ____.

3.

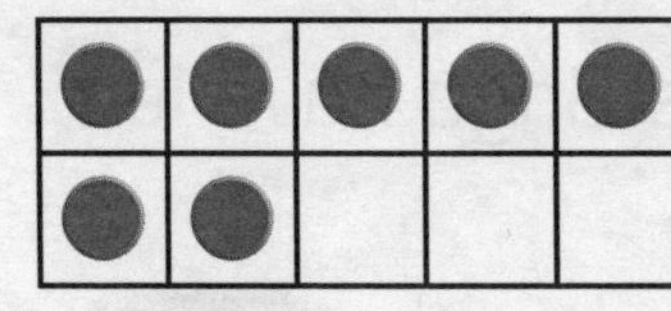

7 + ____ = 10

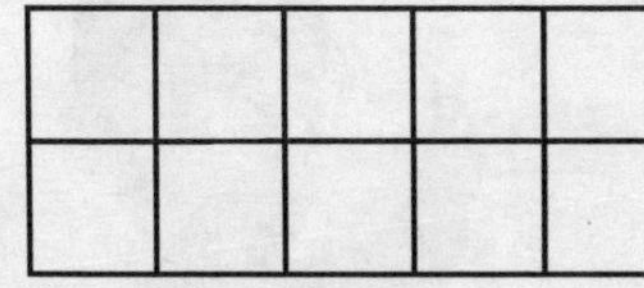

10 + ____ = 15

7 + ____ = 15, so 15 − 7 = ____.

4.

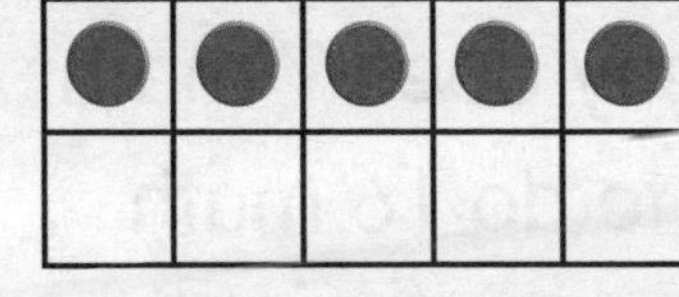

5 + ____ = 10

10 + ____ = 14

5 + ____ = 14, so 14 − 5 = ____.

5.

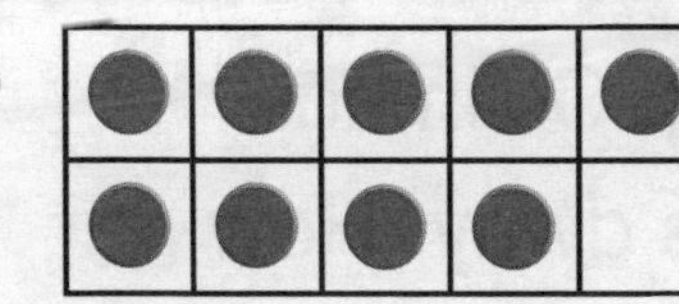

9 + ____ = 10

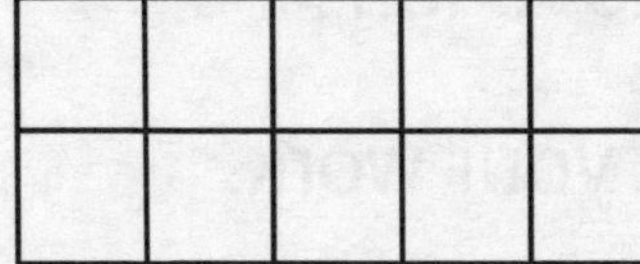

10 + ____ = 16

9 + ____ = 16, so 16 − 9 = ____.

6. Math and Science Hoshi watches either the sunrise or sunset for 13 days. She watches sunsets for 5 of the days. How many of the days did Hoshi watch sunrises? Make 10 to help you solve.

5 + ____ = 10

10 + ____ = 13

5 + ____ = 13, so 13 − 5 = ____.

Problem Solving Solve the problems below.

7. Make Sense Sage has 13 stickers. She gives 7 to her brother.

How many stickers does Sage have left?

What's my plan for solving the problem?

Sage has ____ stickers left.

8. Higher Order Thinking Colin has 12 toys. He gives 9 toys away. How many toys does Colin have left?

Make 10 to solve. Show your work.

____ ◯ ____ = ____

Colin has ____ toys left.

9. Assessment Shay does 7 math problems. She has to do 16 math problems in all. How many problems does Shay have left to do?

Which equations show how to make 10 to solve the problem?

Ⓐ $16 - 7 = 9$

Ⓑ $7 + 3 = 10, 10 + 6 = 16$

Ⓒ $7 + 3 = 10, 10 + 7 = 17$

Ⓓ $9 + 7 = 16$

Name ______________________

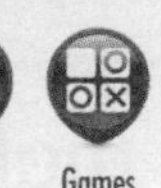

Homework & Practice 4-3

Continue to Make 10 to Subtract

Another Look! Counting on to make 10 can help you subtract.

16 − 7 = ?

You added 3 and then 6 more.
3 + 6 = 9. You added 9 in all.
So, 16 − 7 = 9.

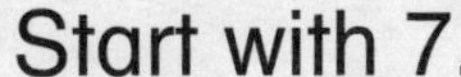

Start with 7.

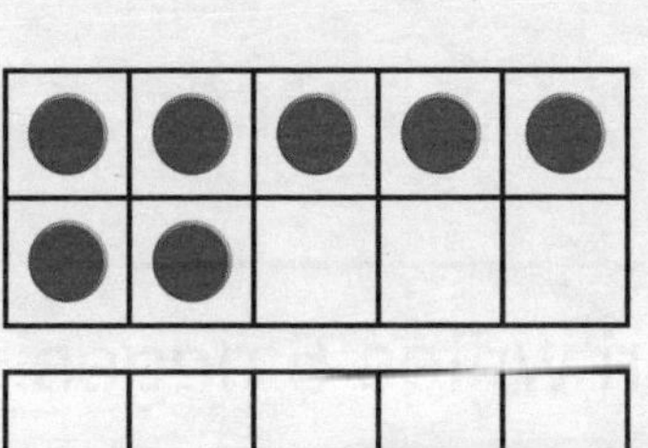

Add 3 to make 10.

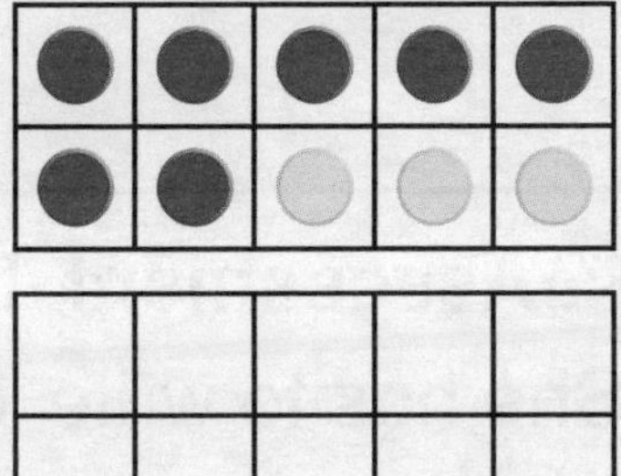

Then add 6 more to make 16.

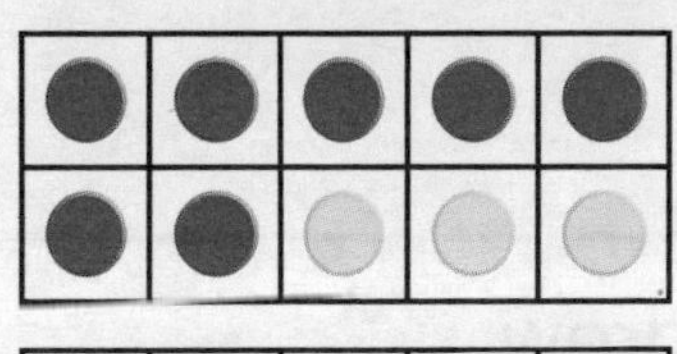

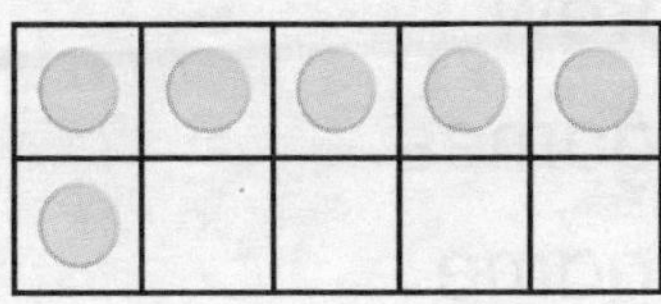

HOME ACTIVITY Give your child a subraction fact, such as 14 − 5. Ask how many you need to add to 5 to make 10. Then ask your child how many you need to add to 10 to get to 14. Ask your child to tell you how many he or she counted on in all. Repeat with different subtraction facts.

Subtract. Count on to make 10. Show your work.

1. 17 − 8 = ?

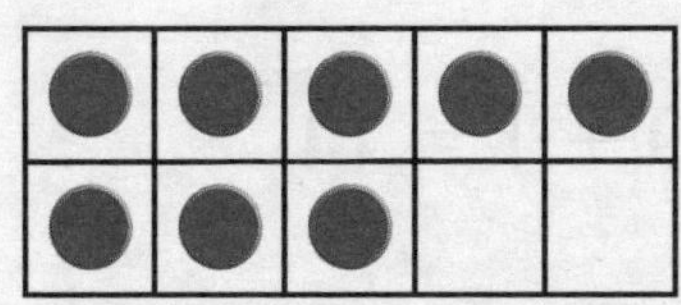

8 + ____ = 10

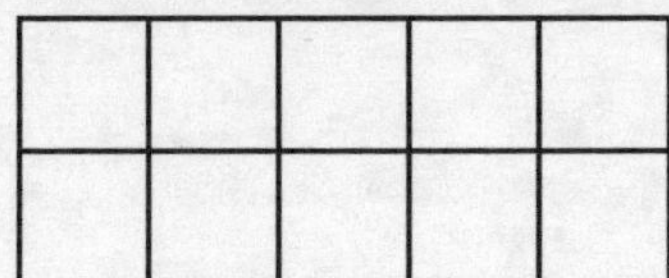

10 + ____ = 17

8 + ____ = 17, so

17 − 8 = ____.

Digital Resources at SavvasRealize.com

Subtract. Count on to make 10. Show your work.

2. 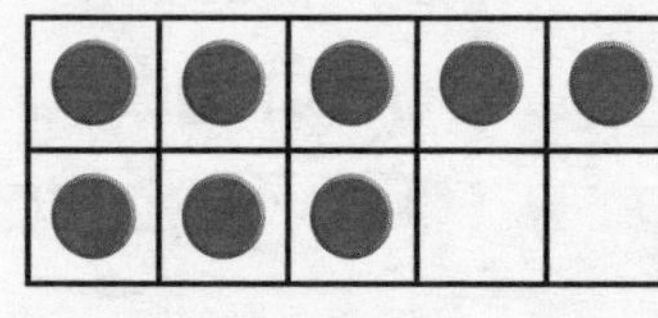

8 + ____ = 10

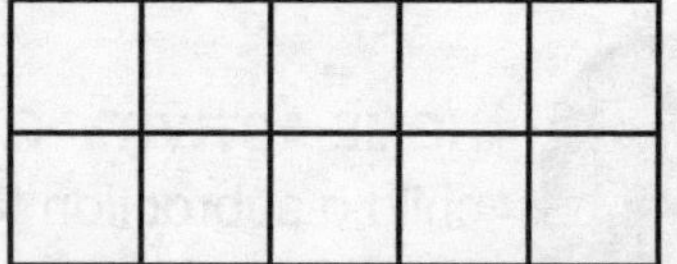

10 + ____ = 13

8 + ____ = 13, so 13 − 8 = ____.

3. 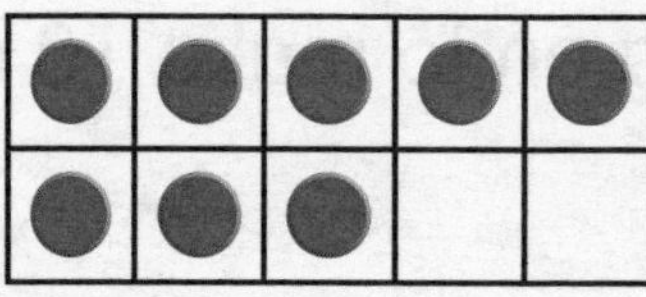

8 + ____ = 10

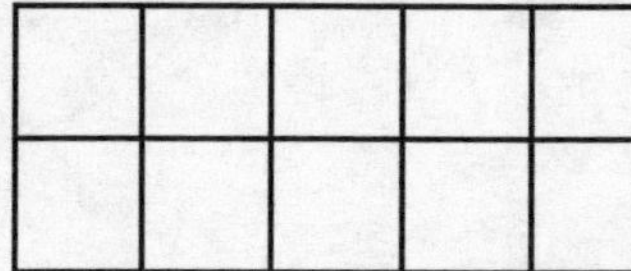

10 + ____ = 15

8 + ____ = 15, so 15 − 8 = ____.

4. **Higher Order Thinking** Andrew makes 11 saves in 2 soccer games. He made 8 saves in the first game. How many saves did Andrew make in the second game?

Make 10 to solve. Show your work.

____ ◯ ____ = ____

Andrew made ____ saves.

5. **Assessment** Dori writes 5 pages. She has to write 11 pages in all. How many pages does Dori have left to write?

Which equations show how to make 10 to solve the problem?

Ⓐ 5 + 5 = 10, 10 + 2 = 12

Ⓑ 11 + 5 = 16

Ⓒ 5 + 5 = 10, 10 + 1 = 11

Ⓓ 10 + 5 = 15

Name ___________________________

Lesson 4-4

Fact Families

Solve & Share

Can you write 2 addition and 2 subtraction facts that use the numbers 8, 9, and 17? Use cubes to help you.

I can ... make addition and subtraction facts using the same three numbers.

I can also look for patterns.

___ + ___ = ___ ___ − ___ = ___

___ + ___ = ___ ___ − ___ = ___

Write 2 addition facts for this model.

9 + 6 = 15

15

6 + 9 = 15

Add the parts in any order.

You can also write 2 subtraction facts.

15

15 − 6 = 9

Subtract 1 part from the whole.

Subtract the other part from the whole.

15

15 − 9 = 6

These are **related facts**. They are a **fact family**.

9 + 6 = 15
6 + 9 = 15
15 − 6 = 9
15 − 9 = 6

Do You Understand?

Show Me! How are 15 − 6 = 9 and 15 − 9 = 6 related?

Guided Practice

Write the fact family for each model.

1. 14

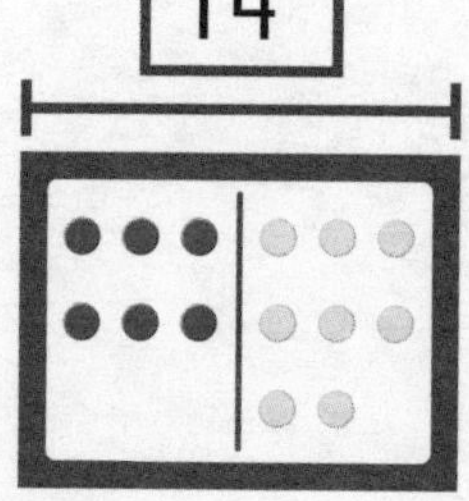

14 = 6 + 8
14 = 8 + 6
8 = 14 − 6
6 = 14 − 8

2. 16

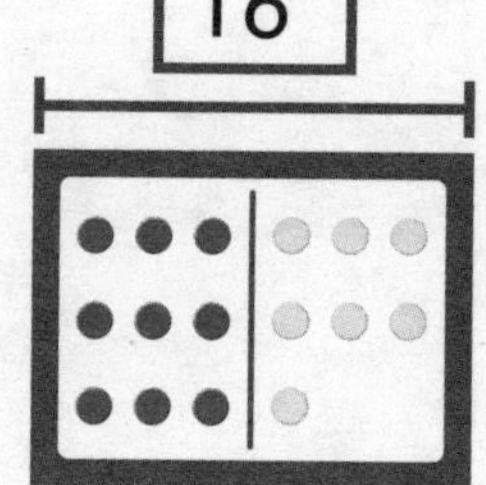

___ + ___ = ___
___ + ___ = ___
___ − ___ = ___
___ − ___ = ___

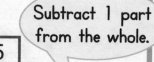

Name ______________________

Tools Assessment

Independent Practice

Write the fact family for each model.

3.

___ + ___ = ___

___ + ___ = ___

___ − ___ = ___

___ − ___ = ___

4.

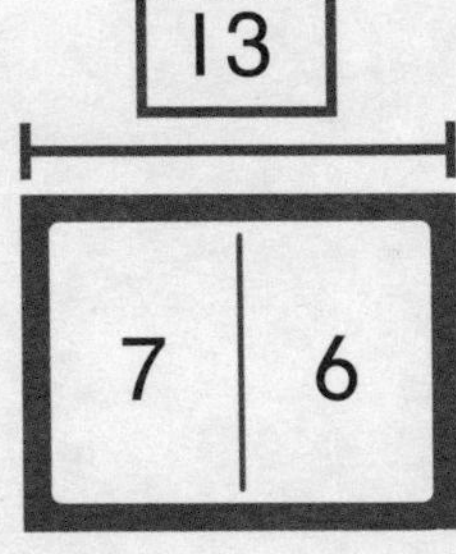

___ = ___ + ___

___ = ___ + ___

___ = ___ − ___

___ = ___ − ___

5.

12

4 | 8

___ + ___ = ___

___ + ___ = ___

___ − ___ = ___

___ − ___ = ___

6. Number Sense Are the following equations a fact family? Explain your answer.

$9 + 5 = 14$

$15 - 5 = 10$

$4 + 4 = 8$

$15 = 6 + 9$

____

____

____

____

What is the whole?
What are the parts?

Problem Solving Solve the problems below.

7. **Look for Patterns** Pat arranged the counters below. Write the fact family for the set of counters.

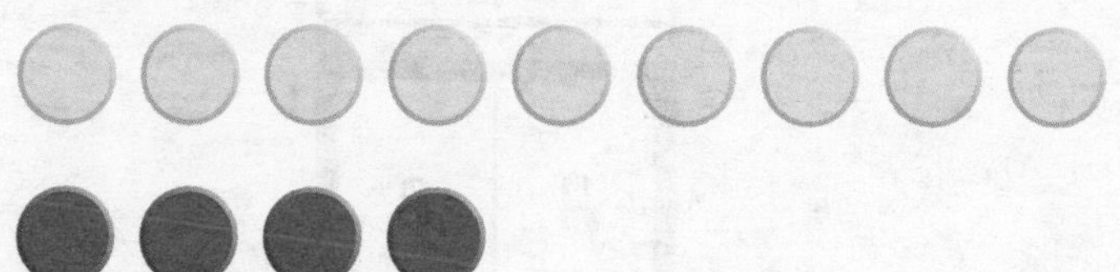

____ = ____ + ____

____ = ____ + ____

____ = ____ − ____

____ = ____ − ____

8. **Higher Order Thinking** Write an equation to solve the problem below. Then write 3 related facts to complete a fact family.

Tanya has 8 stickers. Miguel gave her 5 more. How many stickers does Tanya have in all? ____ stickers

____ ◯ ____ = ____

____ ◯ ____ = ____

____ ◯ ____ = ____

____ ◯ ____ = ____

9. **Assessment** Write a fact family to match the picture of the yellow robots and green robots.

____ + ____ = ____

____ + ____ = ____

____ − ____ = ____

____ − ____ = ____

Name ______________________

Help Tools Games

Homework & Practice 4-4

Fact Families

Another Look! You can use models to make a fact family.

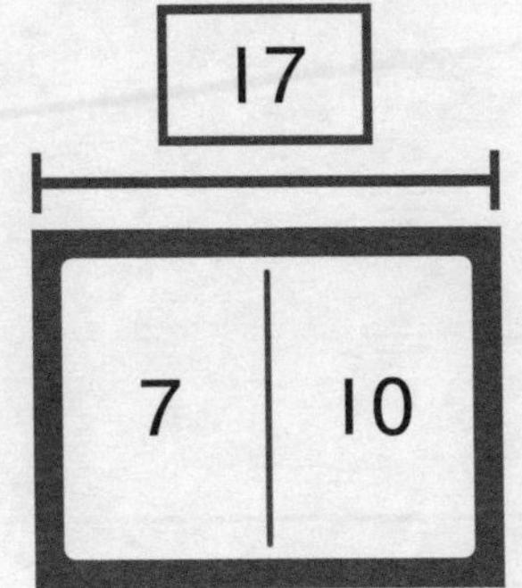

7 + 10 = 17
10 + 7 = 17
17 − 10 = 7
17 − 7 = 10

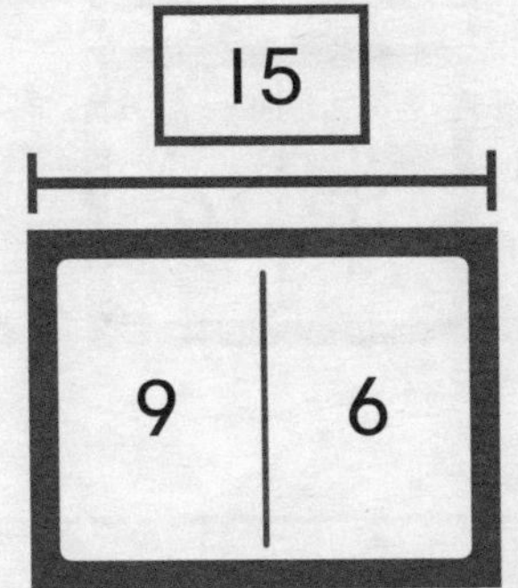

9 + 6 = 15
6 + 9 = 15
15 − 6 = 9
15 − 9 = 6

HOME ACTIVITY Write an addition problem, such as 9 + 4 = ? Have your child find the sum and write the related addition fact. (4 + 9 = 13) Then ask your child to write the 2 related subtraction equations to complete the fact family. (13 − 9 = 4 and 13 − 4 = 9) Continue wilh several other fact families.

Write the fact family for each model.

1.

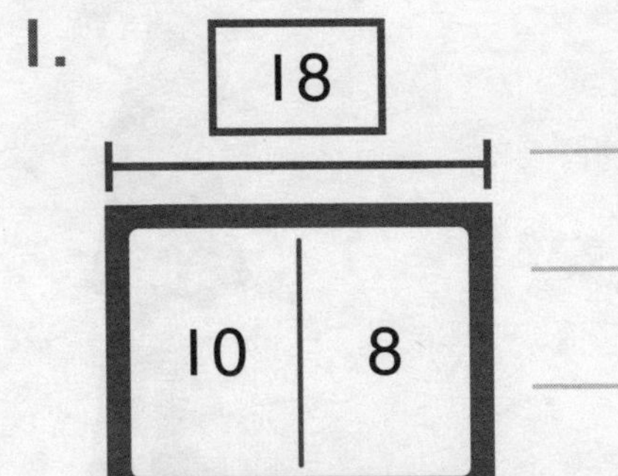

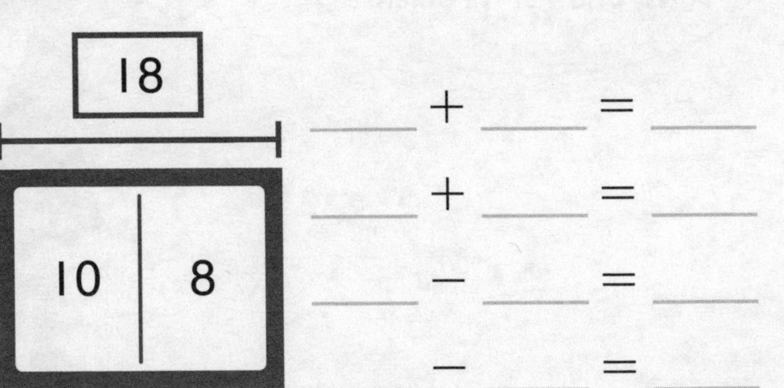

___ + ___ = ___
___ + ___ = ___
___ − ___ = ___
___ − ___ = ___

2.

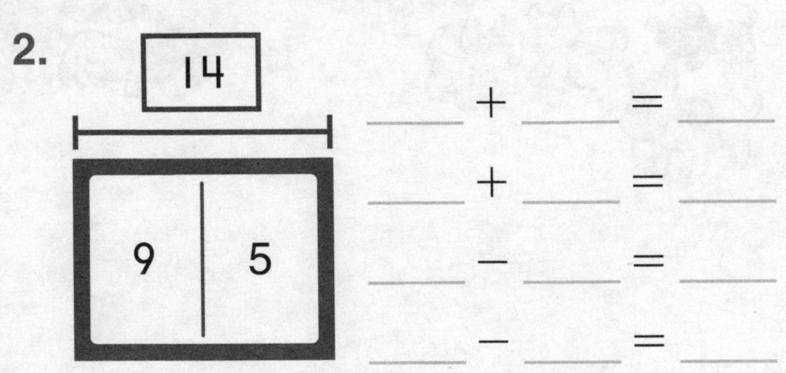

___ + ___ = ___
___ + ___ = ___
___ − ___ = ___
___ − ___ = ___

Write the fact family for each model.

3. 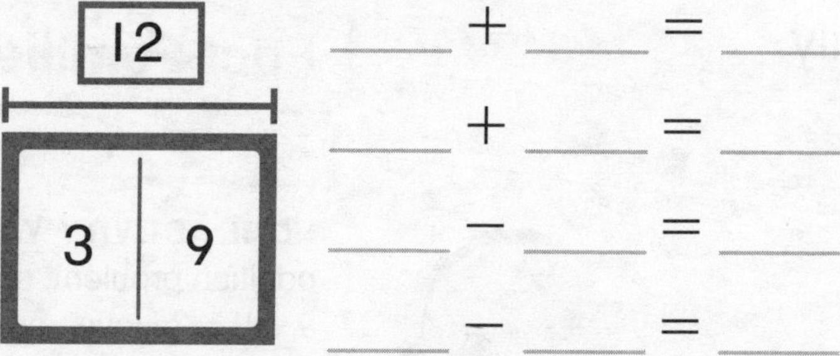

___ + ___ = ___

___ + ___ = ___

___ − ___ = ___

___ − ___ = ___

4. 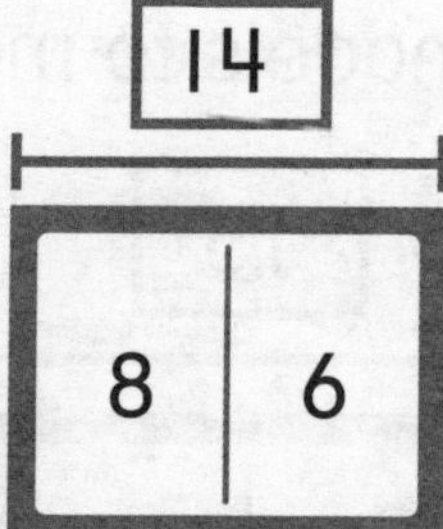

___ + ___ = ___

___ + ___ = ___

___ − ___ = ___

___ − ___ = ___

5. **Higher Order Thinking** Circle the 3 numbers that make up a fact family. Write the fact family.

5   7   8   4   13

___ + ___ = ___

___ + ___ = ___

___ − ___ = ___

___ − ___ = ___

6. **Assessment** Write a fact family to match the picture.

How does the solution to one problem help you solve another problem?

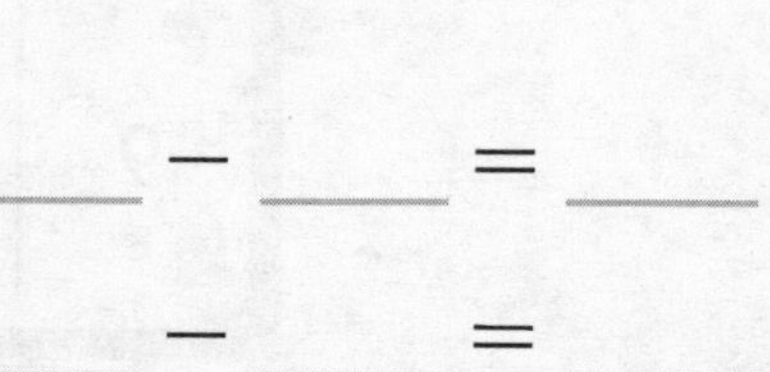

___ + ___ = ___

___ + ___ = ___

___ − ___ = ___

___ − ___ = ___

Name ______________________________

Lesson 4-5

Use Addition to Subtract

I can ...
use addition facts to find subtraction facts.

I can also model with math.

Solve & Share

$12 - 9 = ?$

How can you use a related fact to help you find the difference? Write the related addition and subtraction facts. Use counters to help you.

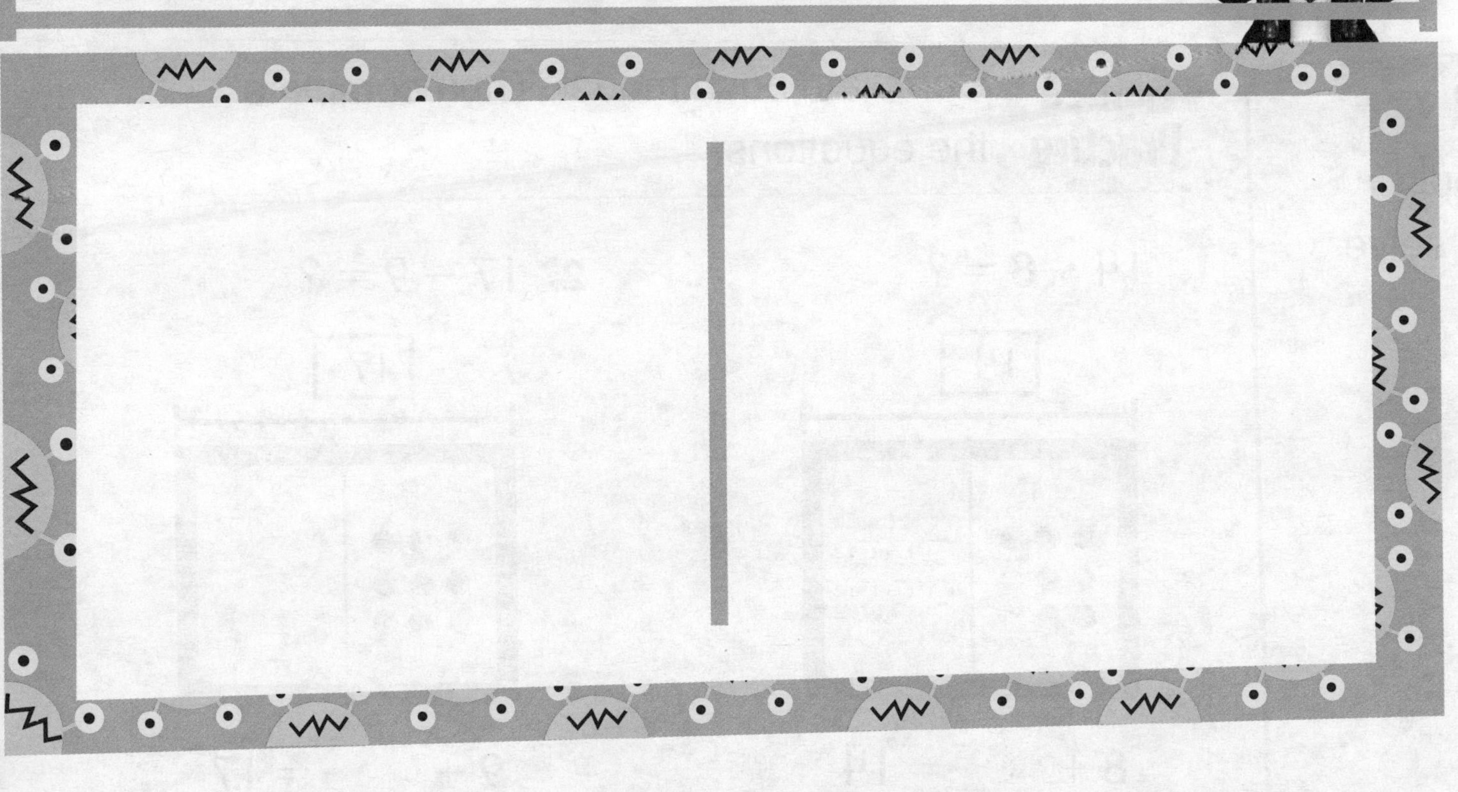

____ + ____ = ____   ____ − ____ = ____

$13 - 8 = ?$

Use addition to help you subtract.

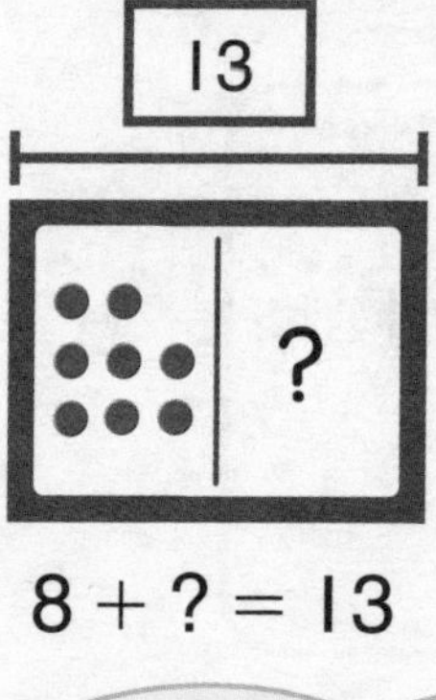

$8 + ? = 13$

What can I add to 8 to make 13?

Model the addition fact.

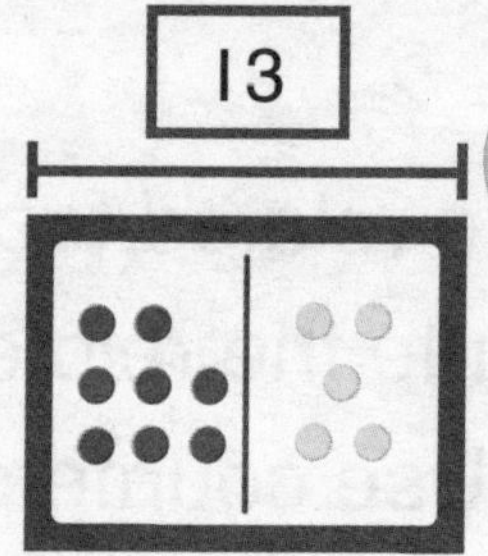

The missing part is 5.
8 + 5 = 13, so
13 − 8 = 5.

Do You Understand?

Show Me! How could you use addition to solve $16 - 9$?

Guided Practice

Complete each model. Then complete the equations.

1. $14 - 8 = ?$

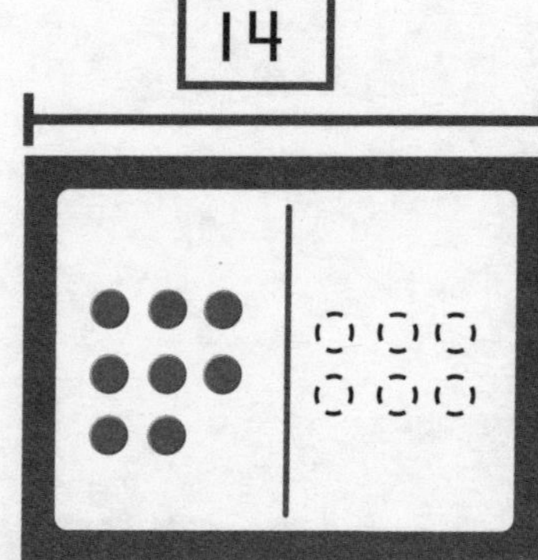

$8 + \underline{6} = 14$

$14 - 8 = \underline{6}$

2. $17 - 9 = ?$

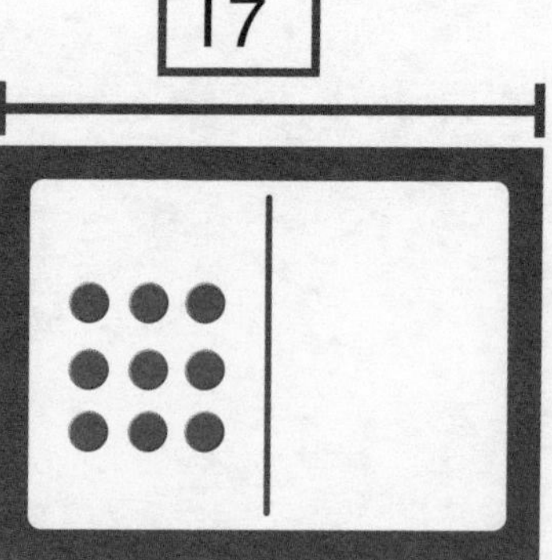

$9 + \_\_\_ = 17$

$17 - 9 = \_\_\_$

Name ___________________________________

Independent Practice

Complete each model. Then complete the equations.

3. 13 − 9 = ?

9 + ____ = 13

13 − 9 = ____

4. 20 − 10 = ?

10 + ____ = 20

20 − 10 = ____

5. 15 − 7 = ?

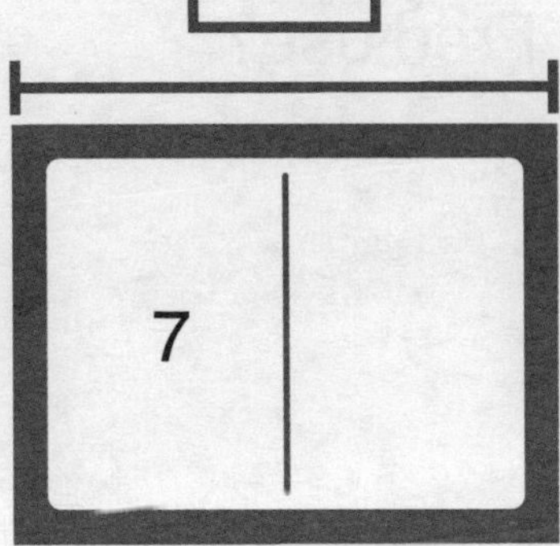

7 + ____ = 15

15 − 7 = ____

Draw the missing shape for each problem.

6. Algebra

If ● + ■ = ▲,

then ▲ − ■ = ____ .

7. Algebra

If ▬ − ▮ = ▮,

then ____ + ▮ = ▬.

Problem Solving Write a related addition and subtraction fact to help you solve each problem.

8. **Generalize** There are 17 robot parts in a box. Fred uses some of the parts. Now there are 8 left. How many parts did Fred use?

____ parts

____ + ____ = ____

____ − ____ = ____

9. **Generalize** Maria invites 10 friends to her party. 3 cannot come. How many friends will be at Maria's party?

____ friends

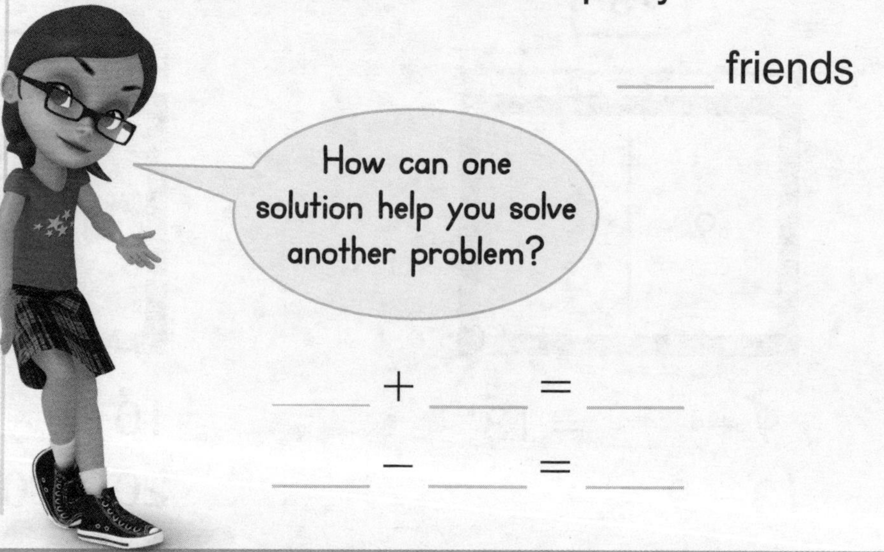

How can one solution help you solve another problem?

____ + ____ = ____

____ − ____ = ____

10. **Higher Order Thinking** Complete the subtraction equation with 11. Then write a related addition fact you could use to solve it.

____ + ____ = ____

11 − ____ = ____

11. **Assessment** Write an addition fact that will help you solve this subtraction fact.

$13 - 7 = ?$

____ + ____ = ____

Name ______________________

Homework & Practice 4-5

Use Addition to Subtract

Another Look! You can use an addition fact to help you solve a related subtraction fact.

$18 - 8 = ?$

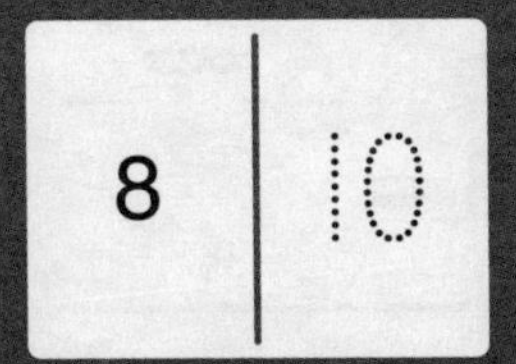

$8 + 10 = 18$

$18 - 8 = 10$

$15 - 6 = ?$

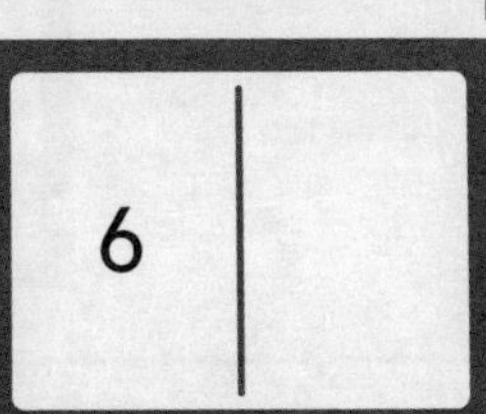

$6 +$ 9 $= 15$

$15 - 6 =$ 9

HOME ACTIVITY Write a subtraction problem for your child to solve. Have him or her say a related addition fact to help solve the subtraction problem. Provide pennies or other small objects to be used as counters, if necessary. Repeat using different subtraction problems.

Complete each model.
Then complete the equations.

1. $11 - 6 = ?$

11

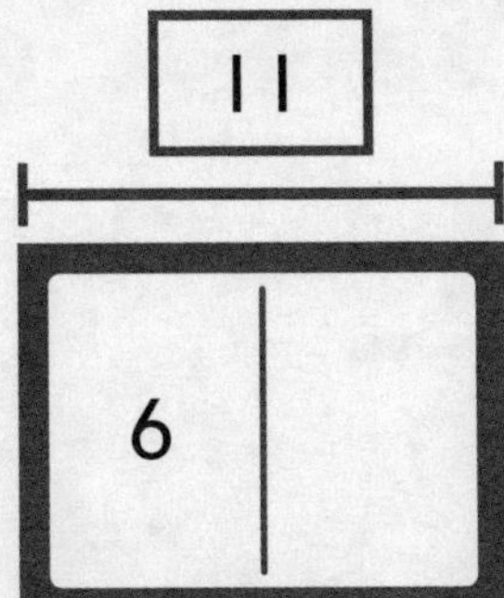

$6 +$ ____ $= 11$

$11 - 6 =$ ____

2. $12 - 9 = ?$

12

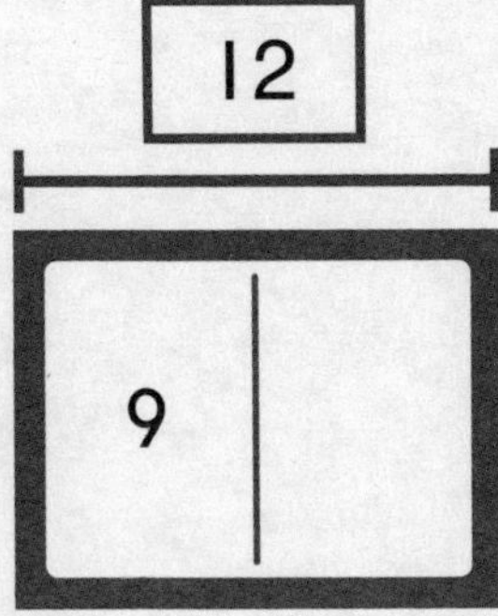

$9 +$ ____ $= 12$

$12 - 9 =$ ____

Complete each model. Then complete the equations.

3. What addition fact can Amy use to find 10 − 6?

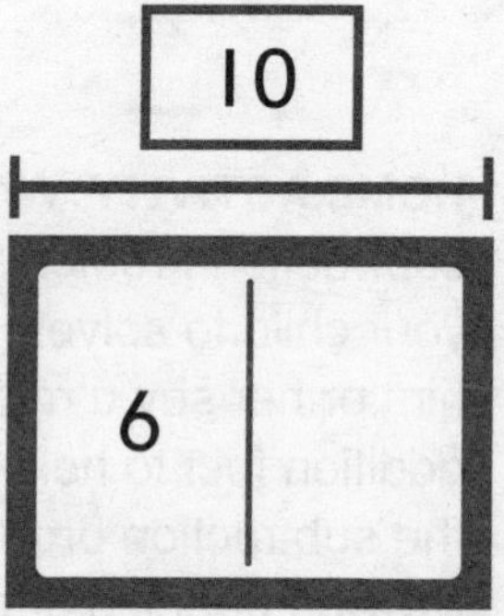

6 + ____ = 10

10 − 6 = ____

4. What addition fact can Dan use to find 16 − 8?

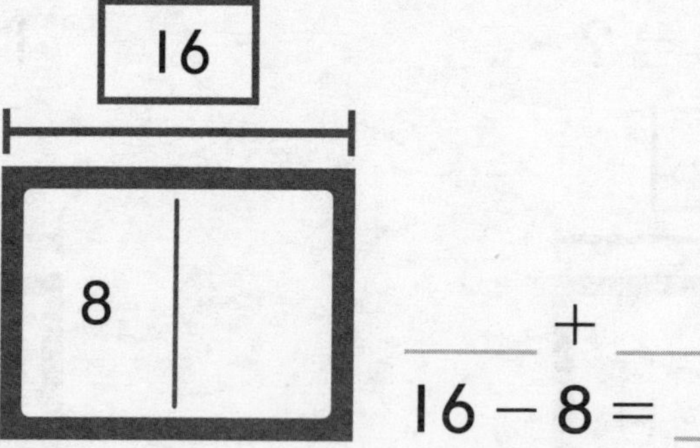

____ + ____ = ____

16 − 8 = ____

5. **Higher Order Thinking** Draw the missing shape. Then explain how you know your answer is correct.

If ⏢ + ◯ = △,

then △ − ⏢ = ____.

6. **Assessment** Write an addition fact that will help you solve 14 − 9.

____ + ____ = ____

7. **Assessment** Which addition fact will help you solve 18 − 10?

____ + ____ = ____

Name ______________________________

Solve

Lesson 4-6
Continue to Use Addition to Subtract

I can ...
use addition facts to find subtraction facts.

I can also look for things that repeat.

Solve & Share

Complete the subtraction facts.
Use the addition facts on the right to help you.

How are the subtraction facts and the completed addition facts the same? What parts are alike?

$18 - 9 = ___$	$9 + 9 = 18$
$17 - 9 = ___$	$9 + 8 = 17$
$16 - 9 = ___$	$9 + 7 = 16$

Learn Glossary

For every subtraction fact there is a related addition fact.

$$\begin{array}{r} 15 \\ -\ 7 \\ \hline ? \end{array}$$

You can think addition to help you subtract.

$$\begin{array}{r} 15 \\ -\ 7 \\ \hline ? \end{array} \qquad \begin{array}{r} 7 \\ +\ ? \\ \hline 15 \end{array}$$

I add 8 to 7 to make 15.

$$\begin{array}{r} 7 \\ +\ 8 \\ \hline 15 \end{array}$$

If 7 + 8 = 15, then 15 – 7 = 8.

$$\begin{array}{r} 15 \\ -\ 7 \\ \hline 8 \end{array}$$

Do You Understand?

Show Me! How does the fact $6 + 9 = 15$ help you solve $15 - 6$?

Guided Practice

Complete the addition fact. Then solve the related subtraction fact.

1. $\begin{array}{r} 9 \\ +\ 5 \\ \hline 14 \end{array} \qquad \begin{array}{r} 14 \\ -\ 9 \\ \hline 5 \end{array}$

2. $\begin{array}{r} 10 \\ +\ \square \\ \hline 20 \end{array} \qquad \begin{array}{r} 20 \\ -\ 10 \\ \hline \square \end{array}$

3. $\begin{array}{r} 7 \\ +\ \square \\ \hline 11 \end{array} \qquad \begin{array}{r} 11 \\ -\ 7 \\ \hline \square \end{array}$

4. $\begin{array}{r} 8 \\ +\ \square \\ \hline 13 \end{array} \qquad \begin{array}{r} 13 \\ -\ 8 \\ \hline \square \end{array}$

Name ____________________

Independent Practice

Think addition to solve each subtraction fact.

5. 15 − 8 = ☐

6. 18 − 9 = ☐

7. 13 − 9 = ☐

8. 11 − 2 = ☐

9. 16 − 7 = ☐

10. 14 − 8 = ☐

11. 17 − 7 = ☐

12. 12 − 4 = ☐

Vocabulary Circle **True** or **False** to show whether or not the **related facts** are correct.

13. If 8 + 8 = 16,
then 16 − 8 = 8.
True False

14. If 7 + 6 = 13,
then 16 − 7 = 3.
True False

Problem Solving

Write a related subtraction and addition fact to help you solve each problem.

How are the numbers in the problem related?

15. **Reasoning** Sam has some crayons. He finds 6 more. Now Sam has 13 crayons. How many crayons did Sam have before he found more?

_____ + _____ = _____

_____ − _____ = _____

_____ crayons

16. **Higher Order Thinking** Solve 13 − 4 using any strategy you choose. Use pictures, numbers, or words to show how you solved it.

17. **Assessment** Susan solves a subtraction problem. She uses 8 + 6 = 14 to help her solve it.

Which related subtraction problem did she solve?

Ⓐ 16 − 8 = 8

Ⓑ 14 − 6 = 8

Ⓒ 13 − 8 = 5

Ⓓ 8 − 6 = 2

Name ______________________

Homework & Practice 4-6

Continue to Use Addition to Subtract

Another Look! You can use a related addition fact to help you subtract.

8 − 5 = ?

Think: 5 + ? = 8

You can use the cubes to add.

If 5 + 3 = 8, then 8 − 5 = 3.

9 − 7 = ?

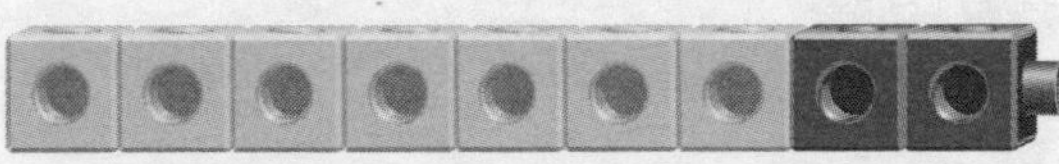

If 7 + 2 = 9,

then 9 − 7 = 2.

HOME ACTIVITY Collect 15 pennies to use as counters. Make a subtraction problem for your child to solve by removing some of the pennies. Have him or her tell you the subtraction equation. Then have your child say the related addition equation that helped him or her subtract.

Complete each addition fact.
Then solve each subtraction fact.

1. 16 − 7 = ?

If 7 + ____ = 16,

then 16 − 7 = ____.

2. 14 − 6 = ?

If 6 + ____ = 14,

then 14 − 6 = ____.

3. 17 − 8 = ?

If 8 + ____ = 17,

then 17 − 8 = ____.

4. 13 − 7 = ?

If 7 + ____ = 13,

then 13 − 7 = ____.

Write a related subtraction and addition fact to help you solve each problem.

5. **Reasoning** Josh has 12 pencils. He gives some of them to his friends. Now he has 7 pencils left. How many pencils did Josh give to his friends?

How does the word problem help me understand what the numbers mean?

____ + ____ = ____

____ − ____ = ____ ____ pencils

6. **Higher Order Thinking** Your friend says he can use the related fact $4 + 7 = 11$ to help find $11 - 3$. Is your friend correct?

Explain your answer.

7. **Assessment** Which related addition fact helps you solve $12 - 3 = ?$

Ⓐ $10 + 3 = 13$

Ⓑ $3 + 6 = 9$

Ⓒ $2 + 10 = 12$

Ⓓ $3 + 9 = 12$

8. **Assessment** Which related addition fact helps you solve $17 - 7 = ?$

Ⓐ $6 + 7 = 13$

Ⓑ $7 + 8 = 15$

Ⓒ $10 + 7 = 17$

Ⓓ $10 + 4 = 14$

Name ______________________

Lesson 4-7
Explain Subtraction Strategies

I can ...
explain the strategies I use to solve subtraction problems.

I can also make math arguments.

Solve & Share

Choose a strategy to solve the problem.

Jeff has 12 apples. He gives away 6 apples. How many apples are left? Use words, objects, or pictures to explain your work.

____ − ____ = ____

You can count on or back to solve subtraction facts.

$10 - 3 = ?$

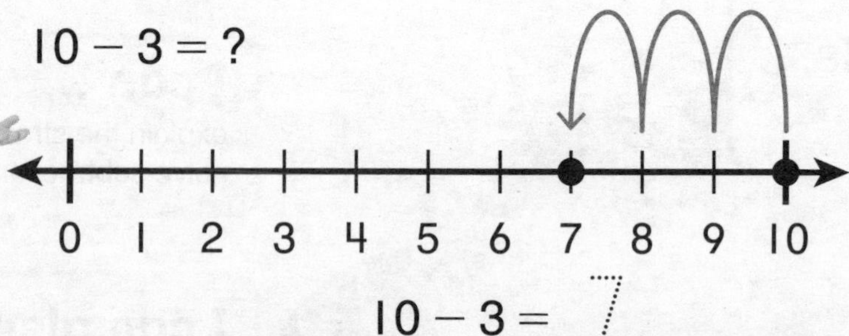

$10 - 3 =$ 7

You can make a 10 to subtract 12 − 8.

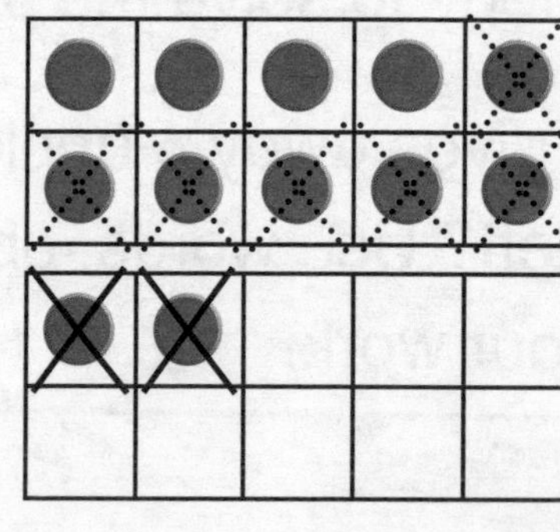

$12 - 8 =$ 4

You can think addition to subtract 14 − 6.

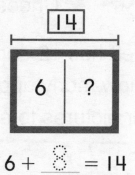

$6 +$ 8 $= 14$

$14 - 6 =$ 8

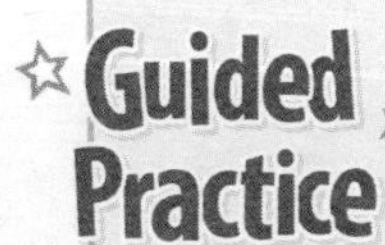

Do You Understand?

Show Me! What is one strategy you can use to solve 13 − 4?

Guided Practice

Find each difference. Circle the strategy that you used.

1. 15 − 9 = 6
   Count
   Make 10
   Think Addition
   My Way

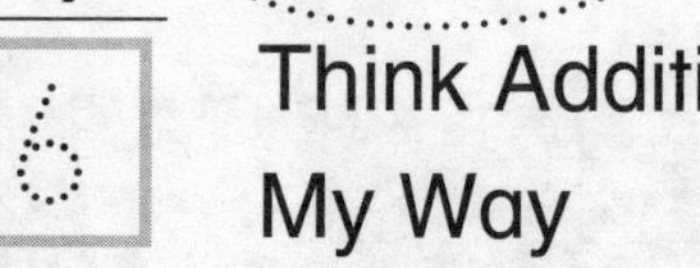

2. 9 − 7 = ☐
   Count
   Make 10
   Think Addition
   My Way

3. 13 − 3 = ☐
   Count
   Make 10
   Think Addition
   My Way

4. 17 − 8 = ☐
   Count
   Make 10
   Think Addition
   My Way

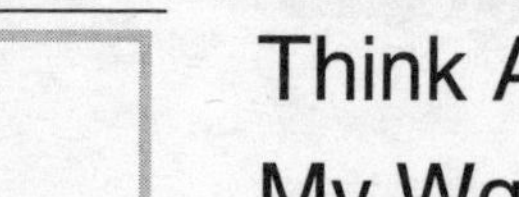

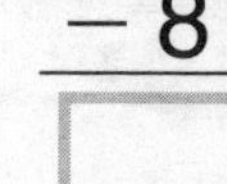

Name ______________________

Independent Practice

Choose a strategy to find each difference.

5. $15 - 5 = \square$

6. $8 - 4 = \square$

7. $9 - 3 = \square$

8. $18 - 10 = \square$

9. $14 - 9 = \square$

10. $11 - 2 = \square$

11. $12 - 4 = \square$

12. $16 - 8 = \square$

13. $7 - 7 = \square$

14. $20 - 10 = \square$

15. $13 - 5 = \square$

16. $10 - 7 = \square$

Write a subtraction equation to solve the problem. Explain which strategy you used.

17. **Higher Order Thinking** Maya has a box of 16 crayons. 7 crayons are broken. The rest are **NOT** broken. How many crayons are **NOT** broken?

____ – ____ = ____

____ crayons

____

____

____

____

Problem Solving Solve each problem below.

18. Make Sense Holly has 11 books. She has 4 more books than Jack. How many books does Jack have?

Jack has _____ books.

Circle the strategy you used to find the difference.

Count Think Addition
Make 10 My Way

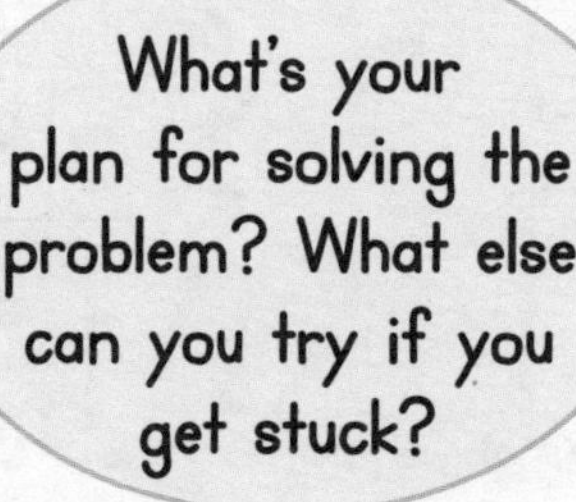

What's your plan for solving the problem? What else can you try if you get stuck?

19. Higher Order Thinking What strategy would you use to solve $10 - 6$?

20. Assessment Which addition facts will help you solve $16 - 9 = ?$ Choose all that apply.

- ☐ $9 + 7 = 16$
- ☐ $7 + 10 = 17$
- ☐ $7 + 9 = 16$
- ☐ $10 + 7 = 17$

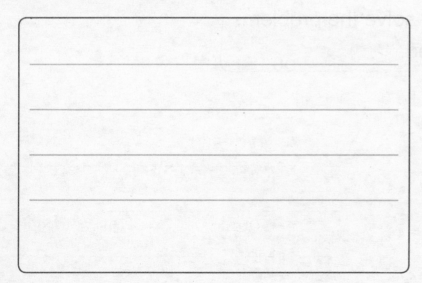

Name ____________________

Help Tools Games

Homework & Practice 4-7

Explain Subtraction Strategies

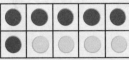

Another Look! You can use different strategies to solve problems.

Use an addition fact to solve a related subtraction problem.

$18 - 9 = ?$

$9 + 9 = 18$

$18 - 9 = 9$

Count on to make 10.

$14 - 6 = ?$

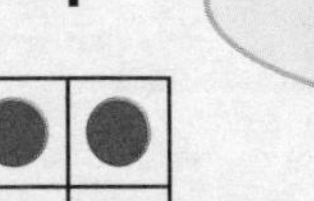
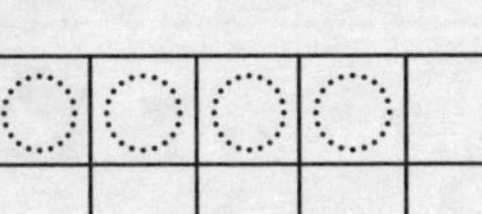
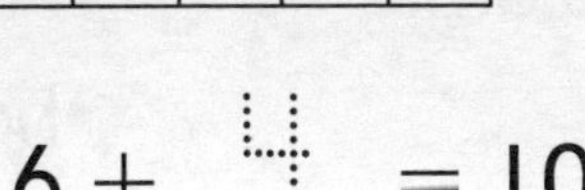

$6 + \underline{4} = 10$

$10 + \underline{4} = 14$

$14 - 6 = \underline{8}$

Choose the strategy that works best.

HOME ACTIVITY Write a subtraction equation like $19 - 9 = ?$ Ask your child to solve the problem. Ask what strategy he or she used to solve the problem, for example, making 10, using a related addition fact, counting, or another strategy.

Find each difference. Circle the strategy that you used.

1. $11 - 5 = \square$

Think: 11 is close to 10.

Count Think Addition
Make 10 My Way

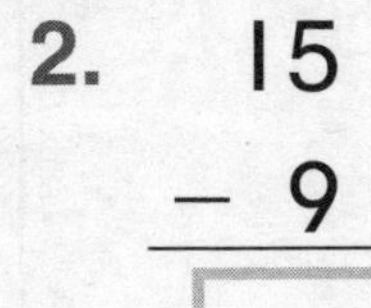

2. $15 - 9 = \square$

Think: Can an addition fact I know help me?

Count Think Addition
Make 10 My Way

Find each difference. Circle the strategy that you used.

3. $\begin{array}{r} 15 \\ -\ 7 \\ \hline \square \end{array}$ Count / Make 10 / Think Addition / My Way

4. $\begin{array}{r} 14 \\ -\ 5 \\ \hline \square \end{array}$ Count / Make 10 / Think Addition / My Way

5. $\begin{array}{r} 14 \\ -\ 9 \\ \hline \square \end{array}$ Count / Make 10 / Think Addition / My Way

6. **Higher Order Thinking** Use pictures, numbers, or words to solve the problem.

Beth finds 13 dolls in her room.
4 of the dolls have curly hair.
How many dolls do **NOT** have curly hair?

____ − ____ = ____ dolls

7. **Assessment** Ben has 10 baseballs. Andy has 2 fewer than Ben. How many baseballs does Andy have?

Which addition facts could help you solve the problem? Choose all that apply.

- ☐ $10 + 0 = 10$
- ☐ $8 + 2 = 10$
- ☐ $9 + 1 = 10$
- ☐ $2 + 8 = 10$

Name ____________________

Lesson 4-8

Solve Word Problems with Facts to 20

Solve & Share

Some books are on a shelf. Aiden puts 4 more books on the shelf. Now there are 12 books. How many books were on the shelf to start? Use objects, drawings, or equations to show your thinking.

I can ...
solve different kinds of addition and subtraction problems.

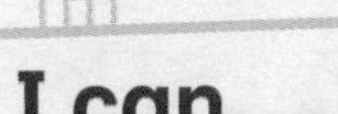

I can also make sense of problems.

There were ____ books to start.

Hunter has some pencils.

He gives 6 of them to Margo.

Now Hunter has 5 pencils.

How many pencils did Hunter start with?

Write an equation to show the problem.

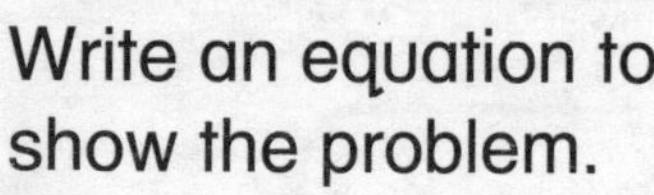

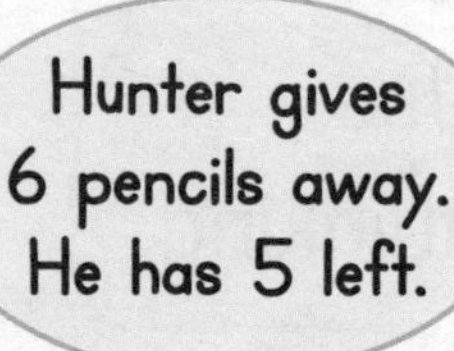

Hunter gives
6 pencils away.
He has 5 left.

? − 6 = 5

You can think addition to subtract.

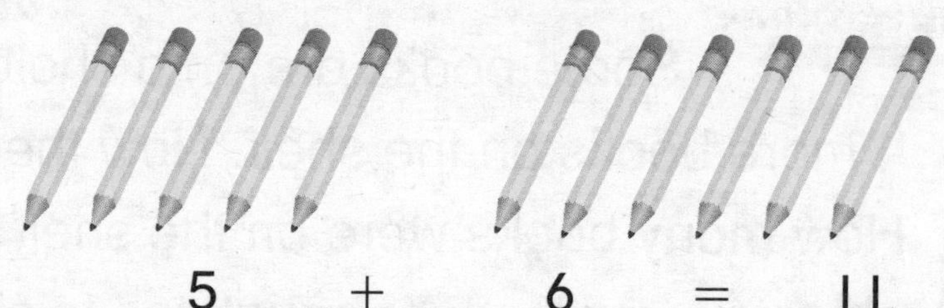

5 + 6 = 11

So, 11 − 6 = 5.

Hunter starts with 11 pencils.

Do You Understand?

Show Me! Sue has 8 crayons. She gets 8 more crayons. How many crayons does she have now? Would you add or subtract to solve the problem? Explain.

Guided Practice

Write an equation to match the story and solve. Draw a picture to help.

1. Cal rides his bike on Monday. He rides 8 miles on Tuesday. He rides 14 miles in all. How many miles did Cal ride on Monday?

___ (+) 8 = 14

miles on Monday | miles on Tuesday | miles in all

Name ______________________

Tools Assessment

Independent Practice

Write an equation to match the story. Then solve. Draw a picture to help.

2. Maggie wrote 9 pages of a story yesterday. She writes some more pages today. She writes 12 pages in all. How many pages did Maggie write today?

____ ◯ ____ = ____

____ pages

3. Gemma has 6 games. Chris has 13 games. How many fewer games does Gemma have than Chris?

____ ◯ ____ = ____

____ fewer games

4. Lily has 4 fewer ribbons than Dora. Lily has 7 ribbons. How many ribbons does Dora have?

____ ◯ ____ = ____

____ ribbons

Problem Solving Solve the problems below.

5. **Reasoning** Will has 11 toy cars. How many can he put in his red case and how many in his blue case? Draw a picture and write an equation to solve.

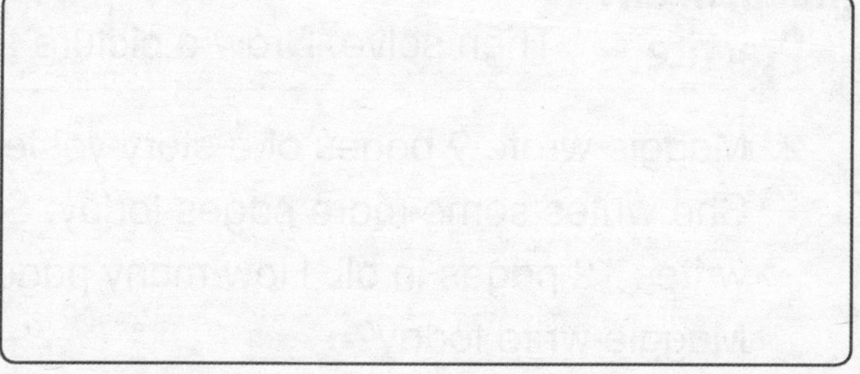

11 = ___ ◯ ___

6. **Higher Order Thinking** Write an addition and subtraction equation to match the problem. Then solve.

Jon has 5 oranges. Tiana has 12 oranges. How many more oranges does Tiana have than Jon?

___ ◯ ___ = ___

Tiana has ___ more oranges than Jon.

7. **Assessment** Mackenzie picks some apples. She eats 3 apples. Now she has 9 apples. How many apples did Mackenzie pick to start?

Ⓐ 3 Ⓑ 6 Ⓒ 9 Ⓓ 12

Name ___________________________

Homework & Practice 4-8

Solve Word Problems with Facts to 20

Another Look! You can solve word problems even when you do not know the starting number.

Carrie works on Monday and Tuesday.
She works 10 hours on Tuesday.
She works 20 hours in all.
How many hours did Carrie work on Monday?

I start with 10 and count on until I get to 20.

Write an equation to show the problem.

10 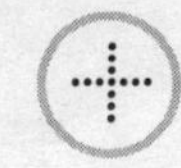 10 = 20

Hours on Monday + Hours on Tuesday = Hours in All

Carrie worked 10 hours on Monday.

HOME ACTIVITY Give your child the following problem: I have some pennies in my hand. I put 3 in a piggy bank. Now I have 8 pennies in my hand. How many pennies did I have to start with? Think of other word problems or ask your child to come up with a problem that involves adding to or subtracting from an unknown amount.

Write an equation to match the story. Then solve. Draw a picture to help.

1. Jim picks some red flowers. He also picks 7 yellow flowers. He picks 15 flowers in all. How many red flowers did Jim pick?

____ ◯ ____ = ____

____ red flowers

Add or subtract to solve each problem.

2. **Reasoning** Sloane has 13 dollars. She spends 5 dollars at the store. How many dollars did Sloane have left? Draw a picture and write an equation to solve.

___ ◯ ___ = ___

___ dollars

3. **Higher Order Thinking** Write an addition and a subtraction equation to match the problem. Then solve.

Li has 14 crackers. Joe has 8 crackers. How many more crackers does Li have than Joe?

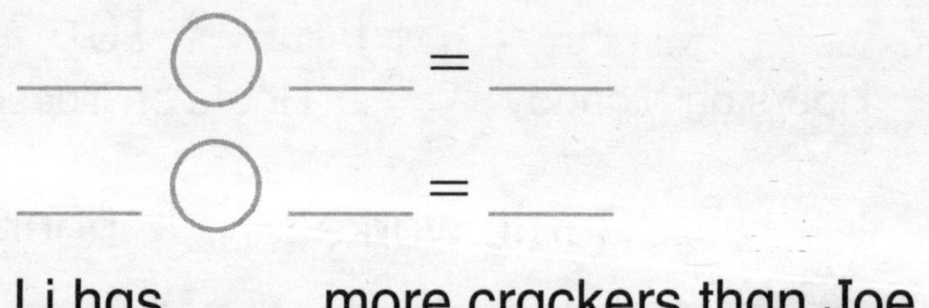

___ ◯ ___ = ___

___ ◯ ___ = ___

Li has ___ more crackers than Joe.

4. **Assessment** Charlie makes some muffins for a bake sale. Then he makes 8 more muffins. Now he has 11 muffins. How many muffins did Charlie make at first?

Ⓐ 19 Ⓑ 11 Ⓒ 8 Ⓓ 3

Name ______________________

Problem Solving

Lesson 4-9
Reasoning

Solve & Share

Write a number story for 14 − 8. Then write an equation to match your story.

I can ...
use reasoning to write and solve number stories.

I can also add and subtract within 20.

____

____

____

____

____

____

Thinking Habits
What do the numbers stand for?
How can I use a word problem to show what an equation means?

___ − ___ = ___

Write a number story for 5 + 7. Then write an equation to match your story.

How can I show what the numbers and symbols mean?

I think about what 5, 7, and the + sign mean in the problem. I can use that to write a story.

Lee sees 5 bugs in her garden.
Then 7 more bugs fly in.
How many bugs does Lee see in all?
12 bugs in all

There were 5 bugs and 7 more bugs came. So, you add.

Do You Understand?

Show Me! How would a story about 12 − 7 be alike and different than a story about 5 + 7?

Guided Practice

Complete the number story. Then complete the equation to match the story. Draw a picture to help, if needed.

1. 17 − 9 = ____

Carlos has  17 dog treats.
Tom has 9 dog treats.
How many more treats does Carlos have?

____ dog treats

Name ______________________

Tools Assessment

Independent Practice Write a number story to show the problem. Complete the equation to match your story.

2. $9 + 4 =$ ____

3. $12 - 4 =$ ____

4. $19 - 10 =$ ____

Think about how your stories match the equations and how the equations match your stories!

Performance Assessment

School Books Jon takes 2 books home. He leaves 4 books at school. How can Jon write an addition story about his school books?

5. **Reasoning** Write an addition question about Jon's books.

6. **Model** Draw a picture and write an equation to solve your addition question.

____ + ____ = ____

7. **Explain** Is 6 − 4 = 2 in the same fact family as your addition equation? Circle **Yes** or **No.** Use words, pictures, or equations to explain.

Yes **No**

Name ______________________________

Homework & Practice 4-9

Reasoning

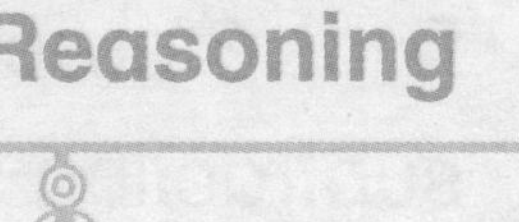

Another Look! You can write a number story for each problem. Then you can complete the equation to match.

12 − 5 = 7

Cindy picks 12 lemons.
She gives 5 away.
How many lemons does Cindy have now?
Now Cindy has 7 lemons.

9 + 5 = 14

Sarah picks 9 flowers.
Then she picks 5 more.
How many flowers does Sarah pick in all?
Sarah picks 14 flowers in all.

HOME ACTIVITY Write problems such as 15 − 9 = ___ and 7 + 9 = ___. Ask your child to write or say a number story about the problem. Then have him or her complete the equation to match the story.

Write a number story to show the problem.
Complete the equation to match your story.

1. 14 − 8 = ___

____

____

____

____

2. 8 + 8 = ___

____

____

____

____

Socks Melissa finds 5 blue socks. Then she finds 3 purple socks. She writes addition and subtraction stories about the socks.

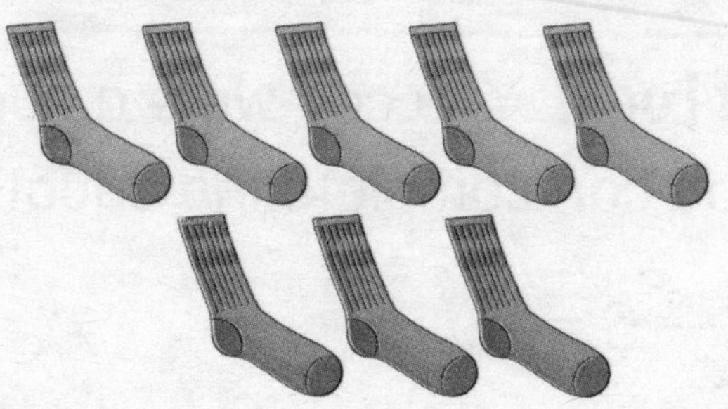

3. **Reasoning** Melissa writes this question about the socks:
How many socks did I find in all?

Write an equation to solve Melissa's question.

____ ◯ ____ = ____ ____ socks

4. **Reasoning** Melissa writes another question about the socks:
How many more blue socks than purple socks did I find?

Write an equation to solve Melissa's question.

____ ◯ ____ = ____ ____ more blue socks

5. **Explain** Melissa says the addition and subtraction equations for her problems are related facts. Is Melissa correct? Circle **Yes** or **No.** Use words, pictures, or equations to explain.

Yes **No**

Name ______________________________

Show the Word

TOPIC 4

Fluency Practice Activity

I can ...
add and subtract within 10.

Color these sums and differences. Leave the rest white.

6	7	4

9 − 5	8 − 4	1 + 3	10 − 3	4 + 3	1 + 6	7 − 1	9 − 3	5 + 1
2 + 1	6 − 2	7 − 4	5 + 2	9 − 7	7 − 0	6 − 0	6 + 2	2 + 4
8 + 2	10 − 6	2 + 6	7 + 0	6 + 3	10 − 3	4 + 2	6 + 0	10 − 4
4 + 4	3 + 1	4 − 3	8 − 1	4 + 5	6 + 1	8 − 2	2 + 1	9 + 1
8 − 7	4 + 0	6 + 4	9 − 2	3 + 4	2 + 5	3 + 3	6 − 1	6 + 3

The word is

__________ __________ __________

Word List

- difference
- doubles fact
- fact family
- related facts

Understand Vocabulary

1. Cross out the numbers below that do **NOT** show the difference for $18 - 8$.

   16 14

   11 10

2. Cross out the problems below that do **NOT** show a doubles fact.

   $4 + 5$ $6 + 4$

   $4 + 4$ $5 + 4$

3. Write the related fact.

   $12 - 7 = 5$

   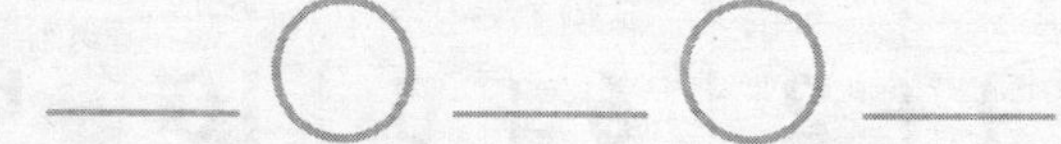

4. Write the related fact.

   $10 + 9 = 19$

   ___ ◯ ___ ◯ ___

5. Write the related fact.

   $6 = 14 - 8$

Use Vocabulary in Writing

6. Write equations using the numbers shown in the model. Then explain what the equations are called using a word from the Word List.

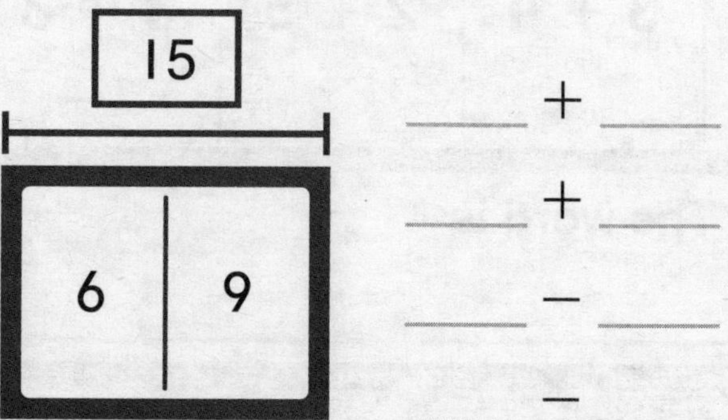

___ + ___ = ___

___ + ___ = ___

___ − ___ = ___

___ − ___ = ___

Name ______________________________

Set A ______________________________

Reteaching

You can count back on a number line to subtract.

Find 10 − 6.

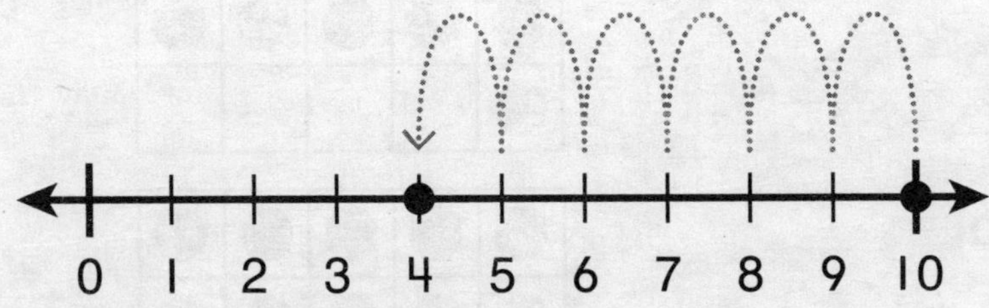

Start at 10 and count back 6 to get to 4.

10 − 6 = 4

You can also count on to subtract.

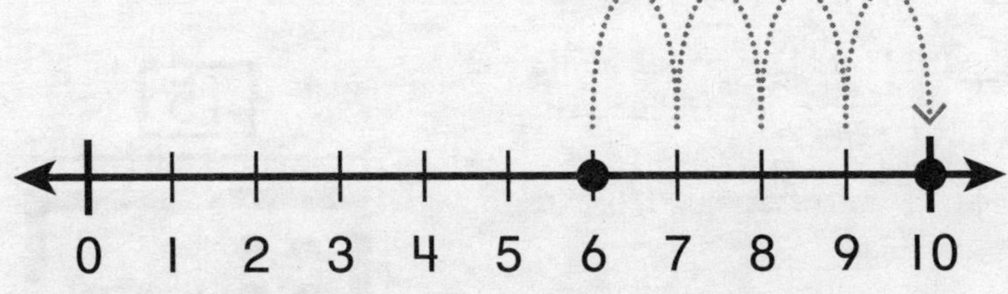

Start at 6 and count on 4 to get to 10.
6 + 4 = 10, so 10 − 6 = 4.

10 − 6 = 4

Use the number line to count back or count on and find the difference.

1. Find 9 − 6.

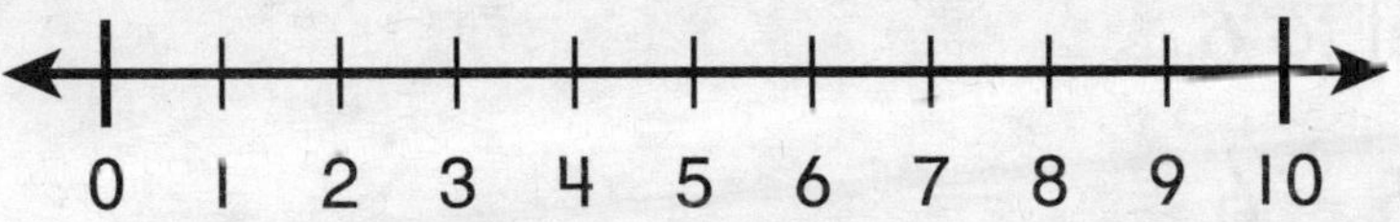

9 − 6 = ____

2. Find 10 − 5.

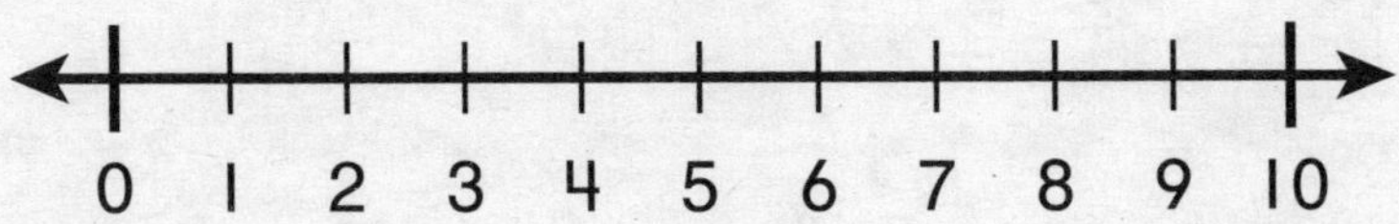

10 − 5 = ____

Set B

You can make 10 to subtract.

$15 - 6 = ?$

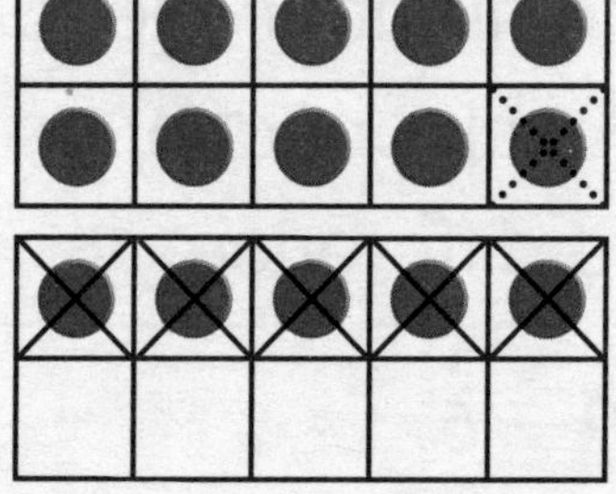

First subtract 5 from 15 to get to 10.

$15 - 5 = 10$

Then take away 1 more to get to 6.

$15 - 6 =$ 9

Make 10 to subtract. Then complete the subtraction fact.

3. $16 - 7 =$ ____

$16 -$ ____ $= 10$

$10 -$ ____ $=$ ____

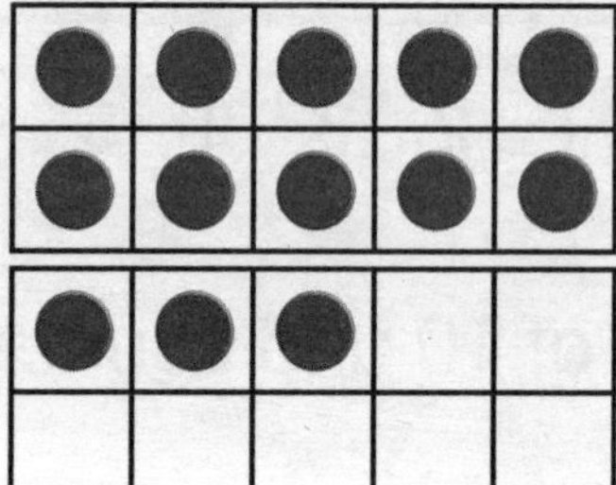

4. $13 - 6 =$ ____

$13 -$ ____ $= 10$

$10 -$ ____ $=$ ____

Set C

You can write a fact family to match the model.

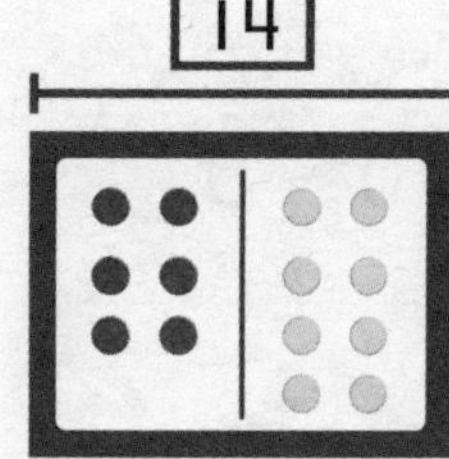

$14 = 6 + 8$

14 = 8 + 6

$6 = 14 - 8$

8 = 14 − 6

Write a fact family to match the model.

5. ____ + ____ = ____

____ + ____ = ____

____ − ____ = ____

____ − ____ = ____

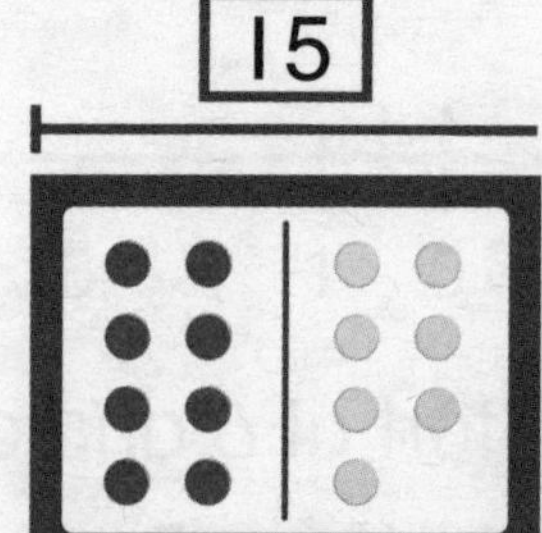

Name ______________________________

Set D

You can use addition to help you subtract.

15 − 7 = ?

Think:

7 + 8 = 15

The missing part is 8.

So, 15 − 7 = 8.

Use addition to subtract. Complete the equations.

6. 13 − 8 = ?

Think:

8 + ____ = 13

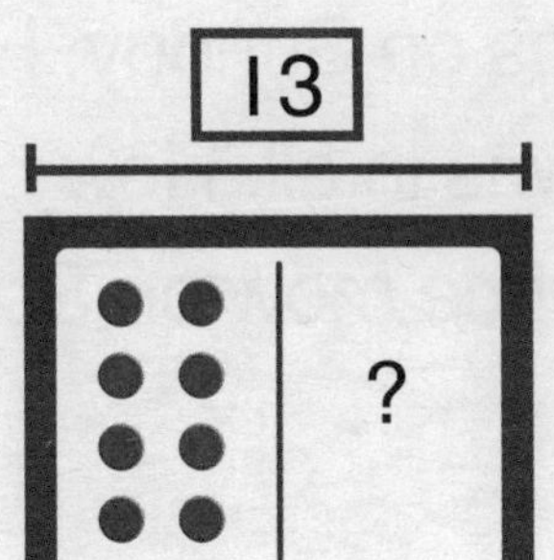

So, 13 − 8 = ____.

Set E

You can use different strategies to subtract 14 − 6.

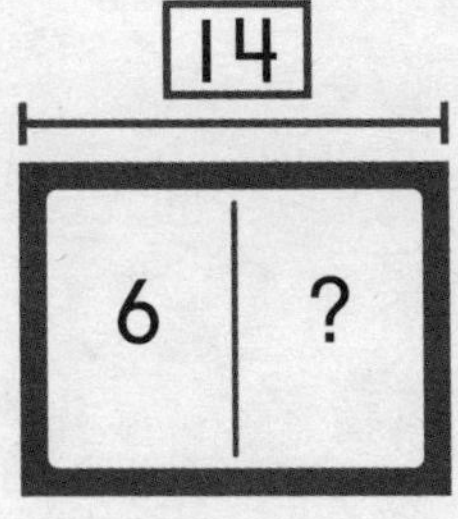

Think Addition

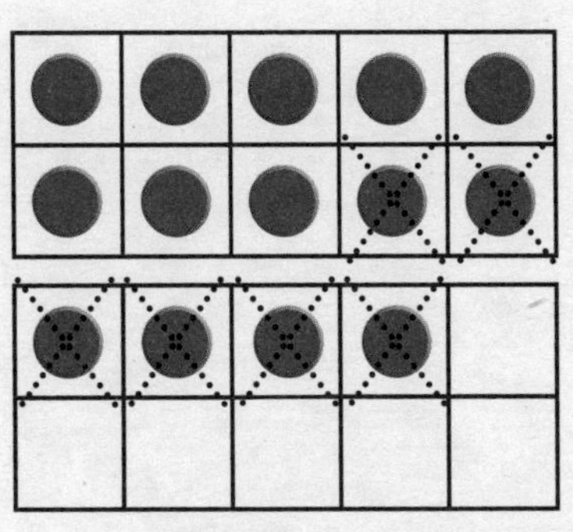

Make 10

Find each difference. Circle the strategy that you used.

7. 12 − 4 = ☐

Count

Think Addition

Make 10

My Way

8. 17 − 8 = ☐

Count

Think Addition

Make 10

My Way

Set F

You can write an equation to show a word problem.

Jaime mows some lawns on Saturday and Sunday. He mows 8 lawns on Sunday. He mows 13 lawns in all. How many lawns did Jaime mow on Saturday?

5 (+) 8 = 13

5 lawns

9. Davis has some pens. He gives 4 to Glenn. Now he has 7 pens. How many pens did Davis start with? Write an equation to solve. Draw a picture to help.

___ ◯ ___ = ___

___ pens

Set G

Thinking Habits

Reasoning

What do the numbers stand for?

How can I use a word problem to show what an equation means?

Write a number story for the problem. Then complete the equation.

10. $9 + 4 =$ ___

____

____

____

____

Name ______________________

Assessment

1. Frank has 15 books to read.
He reads 9 of them.
How many books does Frank have left to read?

____ books

2. Mark has some red marbles.
He has 8 blue marbles.
Mark has 13 marbles in all.
How many red marbles does he have?

Ⓐ 4 Ⓑ 5

Ⓒ 6 Ⓓ 7

3. Which fact family matches the picture of the big ducks and small ducks?

Ⓐ	Ⓑ	Ⓒ	Ⓓ
$8 + 0 = 8$	$5 + 9 = 14$	$5 + 8 = 13$	$8 + 9 = 17$
$0 + 8 = 8$	$9 + 5 = 14$	$8 + 5 = 13$	$9 + 8 = 17$
$8 - 0 = 8$	$14 - 5 = 9$	$13 - 5 = 8$	$17 - 9 = 8$
$8 - 8 = 0$	$14 - 9 = 5$	$13 - 8 = 5$	$17 - 8 = 9$

4. Which related subtraction fact can be solved using $7 + 8 = 15$?

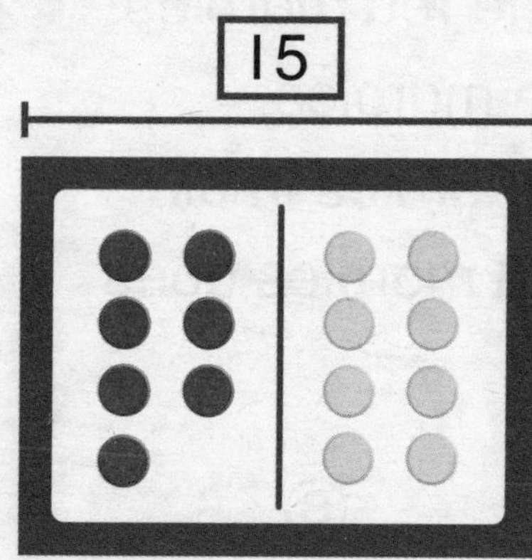

Ⓐ $15 - 8 = 7$

Ⓑ $14 - 7 = 7$

Ⓒ $8 - 7 = 1$

Ⓓ $8 - 8 = 0$

5. There are 13 birds in a tree. Then 6 birds fly away. How many birds are still in the tree?

Make 10 to solve. Use the counters and ten-frame.

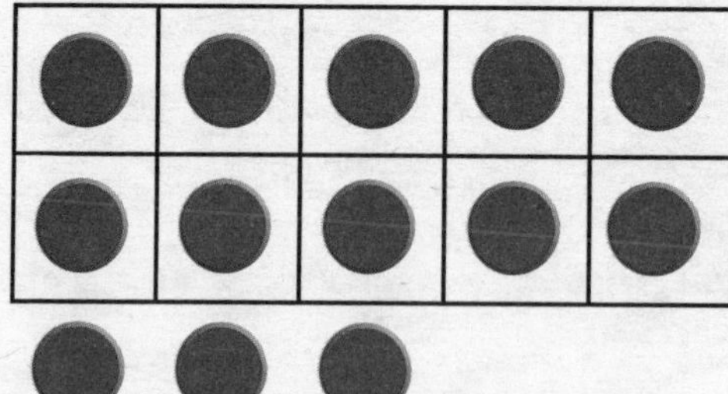

$13 - \_\_\_ = 10$

$10 - \_\_\_ = \_\_\_$

$13 - 6 = \_\_\_$

6. Gloria has 7 yellow pencils. She has 9 red pencils. Which strategy would **NOT** help you find $9 - 7$?

Ⓐ Make 10

Ⓑ Think Addition

Ⓒ Count to Subtract

Ⓓ My Way

Name ______________________

7. Nina bakes 14 corn muffins. She gives away 8 corn muffins. There are 6 left.

Which equation matches the story?

Ⓐ 15 − 8 = 7

Ⓑ 7 + 8 = 15

Ⓒ 14 − 8 = 6

Ⓓ 8 + 6 = 14

8. Which related addition fact can help you solve the subtraction fact? Choose all that apply.

16 − 7 = ?

☐ 7 + 9 = 16

☐ 7 + 8 = 15

☐ 6 + 7 = 13

☐ 9 + 7 = 16

9. Use the number line to count on or count back to find the difference. Show your work.

12 − 4 = ____

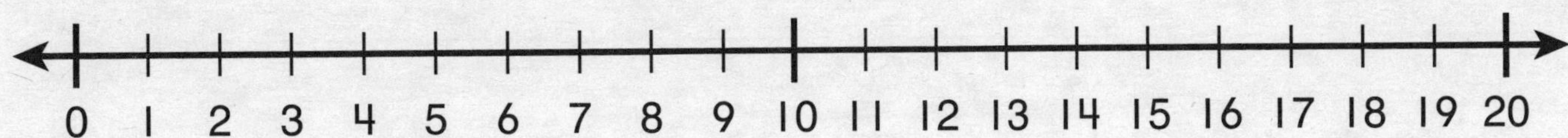

10. Ming has 14 books. She sells 8 books. How many books does she have left?

Make 10 to solve. Use counters and the ten-frame.

_____ books

---

11. A box has 16 skateboard parts. Maria used some of the parts. Now there are 7 parts left. Write a subtraction equation to show how many parts Maria used.

_____ − _____ = _____ Maria used _____ parts.

---

12. Write a number story for 19 − 10.

Then write an equation to match your story and solve the problem.

____

____

____

____

____

Name ___

Maria's Stickers

Maria collects stickers.

The chart shows the different stickers she has.

Maria's Stickers	
Type of Sticker	**Number of Stickers**
moon	15
cloud	7
sun	9
rainbow	8
star	12

1. How many more moon stickers than sun stickers does Maria have?

Count, make 10, or think addition to solve.

___ more moon stickers

2. Maria gives some cloud stickers to Tom. Now she has 5 cloud stickers. How many cloud stickers did Maria give away?

Write an equation to solve the problem.

___ ◯ ___ = ___

___ cloud stickers

3. Complete the fact family using the number of cloud and rainbow stickers.

$7 + 8 = 15$

____ + ____ = ____

____ − ____ = ____

____ − ____ = ____

4. Wendy gives Maria 3 more rainbow stickers. How many rainbow stickers does Maria have now? Complete the equation to solve.

8 ◯ ____ = ____

____ rainbow stickers

5. Write a story to show and solve $12 - 8$. Make your problem about star stickers. Draw a picture and write an equation to match your story.

____

____

____

____

____

____ ◯ ____ = ____

TOPIC 5 Work with Addition and Subtraction Equations

Essential Question: How can adding and subtracting help you solve or complete equations?

Animals cannot speak like we do. They communicate in other ways.

Some animals that live underwater communicate using sonar.

Wow! Let's do this project and learn more.

Math and Science Project: Underwater Communication

Find Out Talk to friends and relatives about how animals such as dolphins use sonar. Ask them to help you learn more about sonar in a book or on a computer.

Journal: Make a Book Show what you found out. In your book, also:

- Draw a picture of one way that sonar is used.
- Make up and solve addition and subtraction problems about the animals that use sonar to communicate.

Name ___________________________

Review What You Know

Vocabulary

1. Circle the **addends** in the equation.

$4 + 5 = 9$

2. Circle the equation that is a **related fact** for $10 - 8 = 2$.

$8 - 6 = 2$

$8 + 2 = 10$

3. Circle the number that will complete the **fact family**.

$3 + \underline{\ ?\ } = 10$

$\underline{\ ?\ } + 3 = 10$

$10 - 3 = \underline{\ ?\ }$

$10 - \underline{\ ?\ } = 3$

8

14

7

5

Subtraction Stories

Use cubes to solve. Write the subtraction equation.

4. 8 squirrels are on the ground. 5 are eating acorns. How many squirrels are **NOT** eating acorns?

___ − ___ = ___

5. Brett has 5 markers. Pablo has 3 markers. How many more markers does Brett have than Pablo?

___ − ___ = ___

Related Facts

6. Write the related subtraction facts.

9 = 4 + 5

___ = ___ − ___

___ = ___ − ___

Name ____________________

Lesson 5-1

Find the Unknown Numbers

I can ...
find the unknown number in an equation.

I can also make math arguments.

Solve & Share

Find the missing number in this equation:

$$7 + \_\_\_ = 13$$

Explain how you found the missing number.

Look at this problem:

12 − ____ = 3

This means that 12 take away some number is the same as 3.

You can use counters to find the missing number.

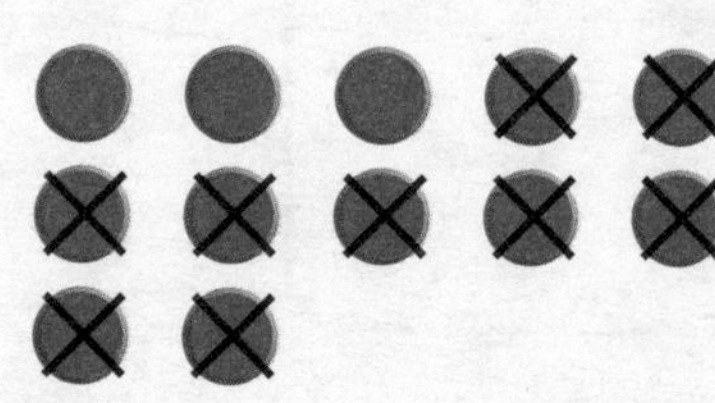

12 − 9 = 3

You can also use addition to find the missing number.

3 + 9 = 12,

so 12 − 9 = 3.

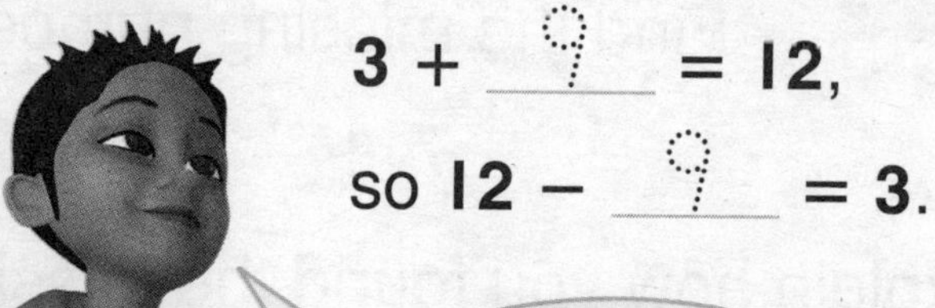

9 is the missing number. 9 makes the equation true.

Do You Understand?

Show Me! What is the missing number in the equation ____ + 4 = 9? How do you know?

Guided Practice

Write the missing numbers. Then draw or cross out counters to show your work.

1. 14 − 7 = 7

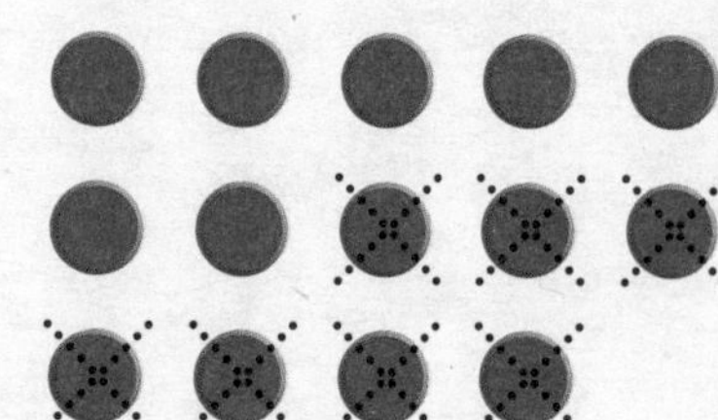

2. 4 + ____ = 12

Name ______

Independent Practice

Write the missing numbers. Draw counters to show your work.

3. ____ − 9 = 8

4. ____ = 8 + 3

5. ____ + 6 = 12

6. 8 + ____ = 15

7. 14 − ____ = 6

8. ____ = 11 − 8

9. **Number Sense** Write the missing number to make each equation true.

9 + ____ = 19

20 = ____ + 10

____ − 10 = 9

____ − 10 = 10

How does solving one problem help you with the next?

Problem Solving

Solve each number story. Write the missing numbers. Use counters if needed.

10. Reasoning Adam wants to visit 13 states on a road trip. He has visited 7 states so far.
How many states does Adam have left to visit?

13 ◯ ____ = ____

____ states

11. Reasoning Chelsea makes costumes for her dance class. She needs to make 11 costumes in all. She has 4 costumes left to make. How many costumes did Chelsea already make?

11 = ____ ◯ ____

____ costumes

12. Higher Order Thinking Find the missing number in the equation 5 + ____ = 14. Then write a story that matches the problem.

13. Assessment Match each number with the equation it is missing from.

17 − ____ = 7	6
____ + 6 = 12	3
4 + ____ = 13	10
____ − 1 = 2	9

Name ______________________

Help Tools Games

Homework & Practice 5-1

Find the Unknown Numbers

Another Look! You can find the missing number in an addition or subtraction equation. Add counters to the empty side of the mat until there are 17 in all.

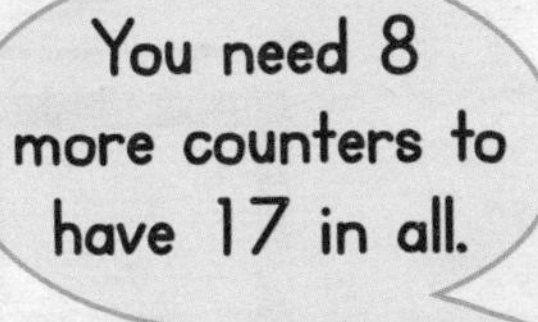

You need 8 more counters to have 17 in all.

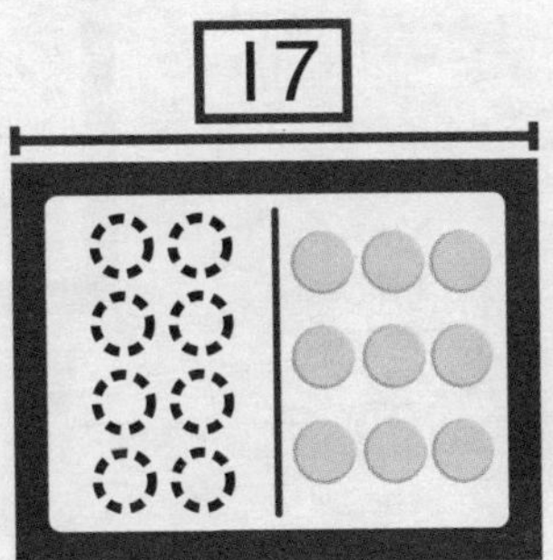

8 + 9 = 17   17 − 8 = 9

HOME ACTIVITY On a piece of paper, write an equation with a missing number, such as 7 + ______ = 16. Give your child a pile of small objects and ask her or him to place the correct amount of objects down for the missing number. Repeat with another equation with a different operation, such as 18 − ______ = 8.

Draw the missing counters. Then complete the equation.

1.

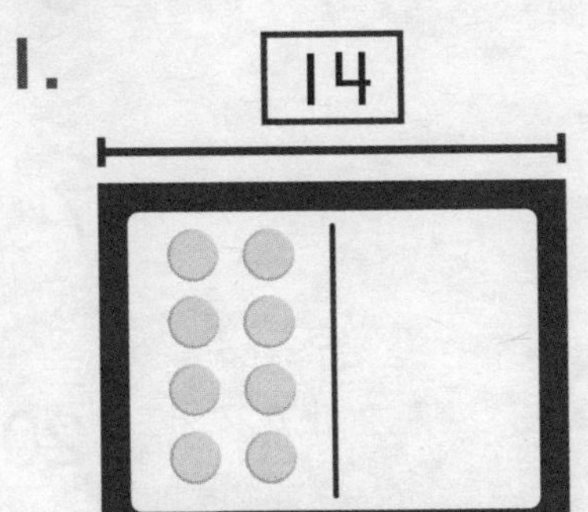

8 + ______ = 14

2.

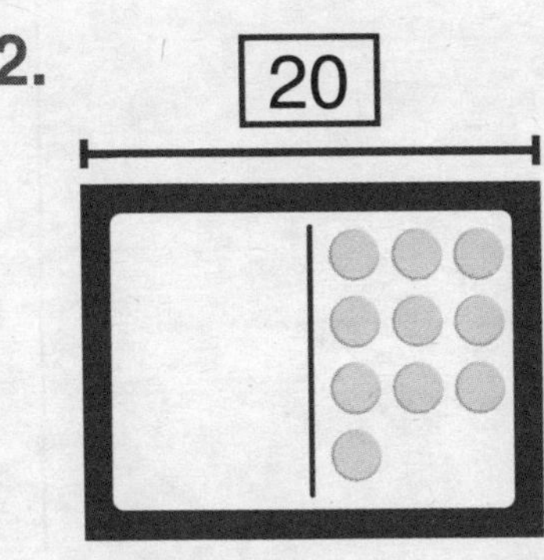

20 − 10 = ______

Complete the mat to help you find the missing numbers.

3. ____ = 8 + 5

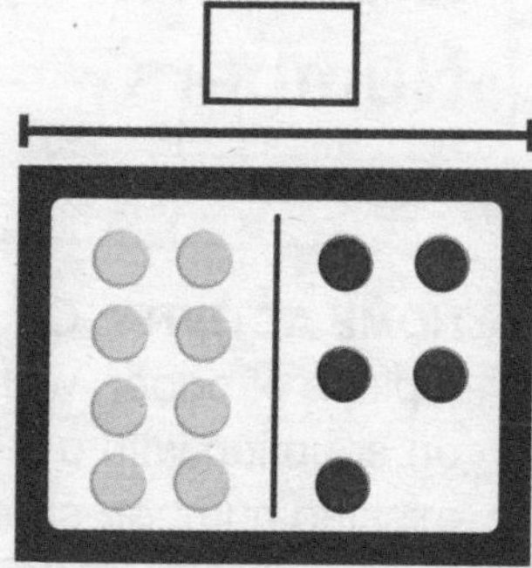

4. 16 − ____ = 9

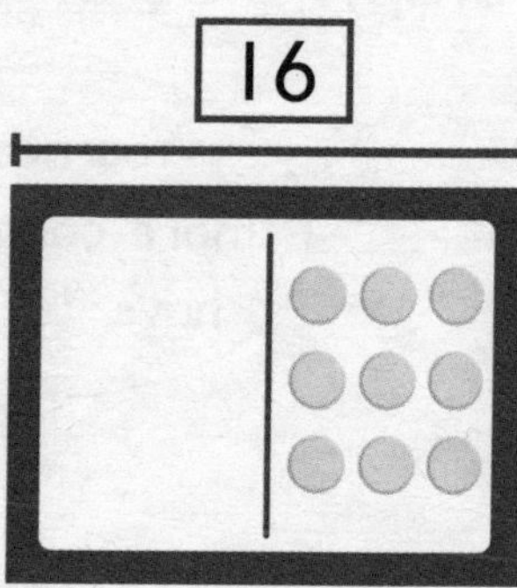

5. 9 + ____ = 18

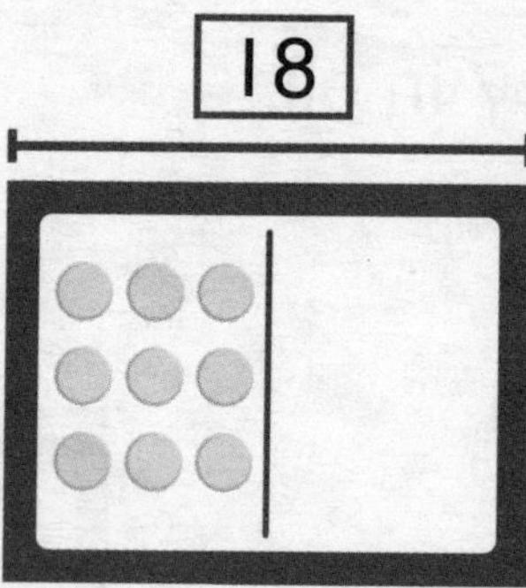

6. **Higher Order Thinking** Find the missing number in the equation 18 = 10 + ____. Then write a story that matches the problem.

7. **Assessment** Match each number with the equation it is missing from.

17 − ____ = 10	8
____ + 6 = 14	5
4 + ____ = 9	7
____ − 10 = 10	20

Name ________________________________

Lesson 5-2
True or False Equations

I can ...
understand that the equal sign means "has the same value as."

I can also reason about math.

Solve & Share

This equation looks different to me. Do you think it's a true equation?

Explain how you know.

$5 = 11 - 6$

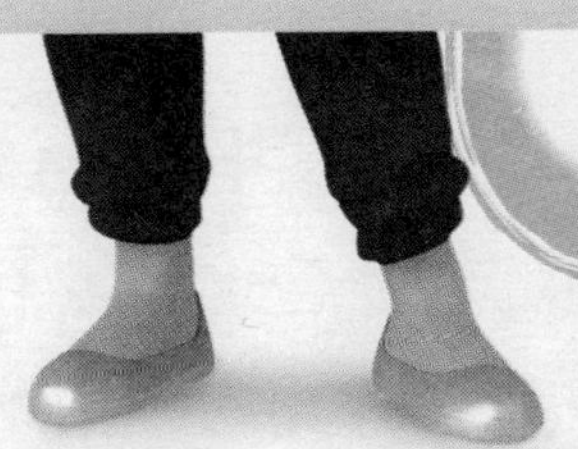

A-Z
Learn
Glossary

Is this equation true?

$3 + 6 = 4 + 5$

To find out, solve each side of the equation.

$3 + 6$

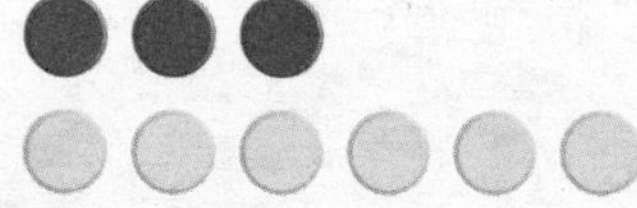

$4 + 5$

This equation is true. Both sides equal 9.

$3 + 6 = 4 + 5$

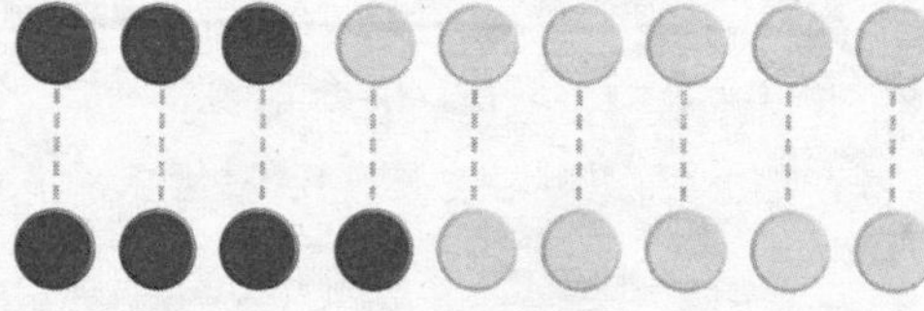

$9 = 9$

Even equations with no operation symbols can be true.

8 = 8 is a true statement.

Do You Understand?

Show Me! Is the equation $4 = 11 - 6$ true? Explain.

Guided Practice

Tell if each equation is **True** or **False**. Use the counters to help you.

1. $5 + 2 = 9 - 3$

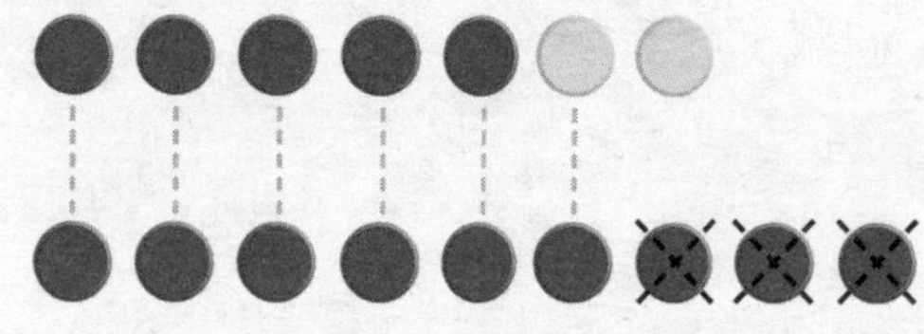

True False

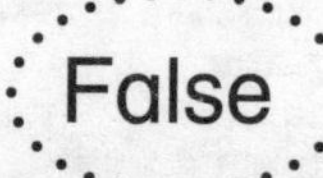

2. $7 = 8 - 1$

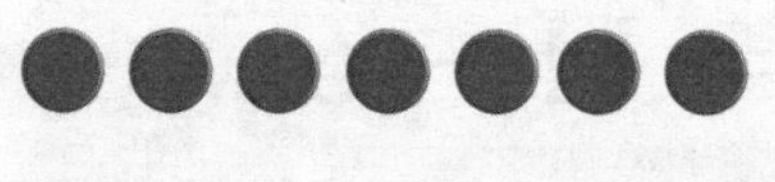

True False

Name ______________________

Independent Practice

Tell if each equation is **True** or **False**.
You can draw counters to help.

3. $5 + 5 = 6 + 4$

True False

4. $9 = 9 - 1$

True False

5. $3 + 3 = 11 - 8$

True False

6. $13 - 4 = 15 - 6$

True False

7. $7 + 7 = 12 - 5$

True False

8. $10 + 8 = 9 + 9$

True False

9. $7 + 3 = 10 + 2$

True False

10. $6 + 8 = 8 + 6$

True False

11. $4 + 2 = 6 + 1$

True False

Problem Solving

Write an equation to show the problem. Fill in the missing numbers. Then tell if the equation is **True** or **False**.

12. **Be Precise** Shawna has 8 paper airplanes. She gives away 1 plane. Frank has 5 paper airplanes and gets 2 more.

Make sure you
use numbers, units,
and symbols correctly.
Does the equation
match the story?

____ − ____ = ____ + ____

True   False

Shawna has ____ planes. Frank has ____ planes.

13. **Higher Order Thinking** Can you prove that $4 + 2 = 5 + 1$ is true without solving both sides of the equation? Explain.

____

____

____

____

____

____

14. **Assessment** Which equations shown below are **false**? Choose all that apply.

- ☐ $10 - 3 = 14 - 7$
- ☐ $4 + 3 = 7 + 1$
- ☐ $6 + 6 = 8 + 3$
- ☐ $17 - 8 = 9$

Name ____________________

Homework & Practice 5-2

True or False Equations

Another Look! Use connecting cubes to model true or false equations of different types.

Draw lines to match the cubes.

If both sides are not equal, then the equation is false.

$4 = 4$

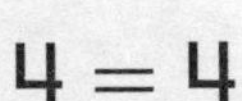

This equation is **true**.

$5 = 2 + 7$

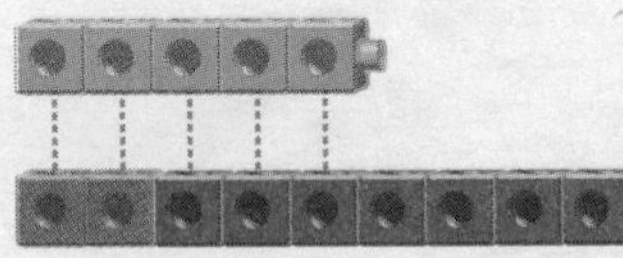

This equation is **false**.

$2 + 8 = 9 - 4$

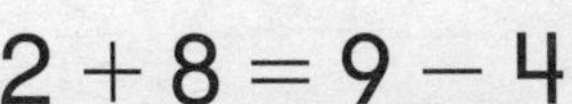

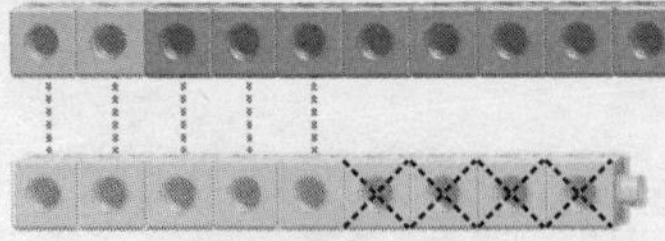

This equation is **false**.

HOME ACTIVITY Write a plus sign, minus sign, and equal sign, each on three notecards or pieces of paper. Gather 20 small objects, such as buttons or pennies. Set up the notecards and objects to show true or false equations, such as $3 + 5 = 9 - 1$ or $6 - 2 = 3 + 3$. Ask your child to tell if each equation is **true** or **false**.

Draw lines to match the cubes. Tell if each equation is **True** or **False**.

1. $9 = 7 + 2$

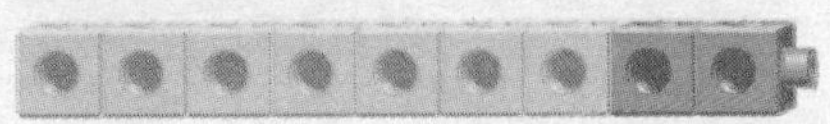

True False

2. $7 + 3 = 9 - 3$

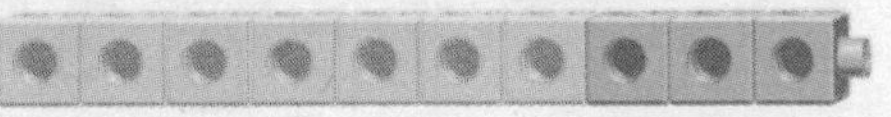

True False

3. $10 - 2 = 1 + 7$

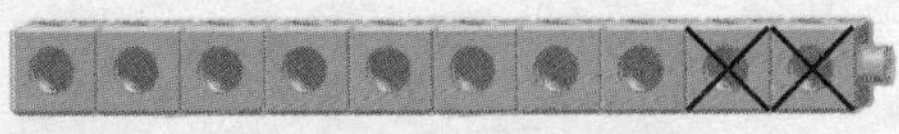

True False

Model Draw pictures to show each equation. Then circle **True** or **False**.

4. $10 - 2 = 7 + 4$

True False

5. $6 = 9 - 5$

True False

6. $8 + 5 = 10 + 3$

True False

7. Higher Order Thinking Jamie says that $19 - 10$ is equal to $20 - 10$ because both sides use subtraction. Is Jamie correct? Explain why or why not.

____

____

____

____

____

____

8. **Assessment** Which equations below are **true**? Choose all that apply.

- ☐ $8 - 7 = 11 - 10$
- ☐ $12 - 4 = 6 + 3$
- ☐ $10 - 1 = 9 + 2$
- ☐ $9 + 2 = 10 + 1$

Name ______________________________

Lesson 5-3
Make True Equations

Solve & Share

What number goes in the blank to make the equation true? How do you know?

I can ... fill in the missing number in equations to make them true.

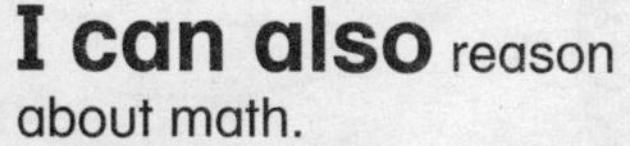

I can also reason about math.

$2 + 5 = \_\_\_ + 6$

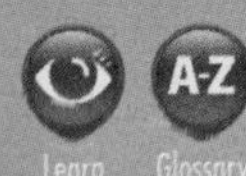

Fill in the missing number to make this equation true.

$10 - \_\_\_ = 3 + 4$

I can solve one side of the equation first. I know that 3 + 4 = 7.

You can use counters to find the missing number.

$10 - \_\_\_ = 7$

The equal sign means "the same value as," so I need to subtract something from 10 to get 7.

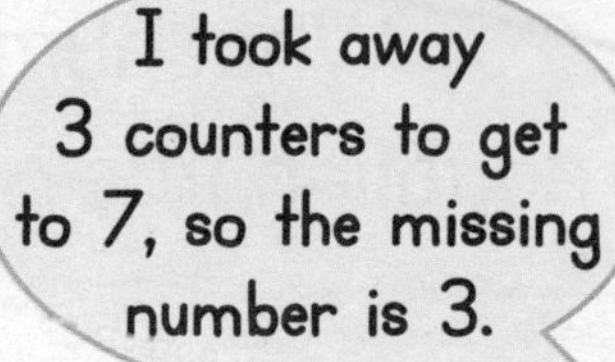

I took away 3 counters to get to 7, so the missing number is 3.

$10 - \underline{3} = 3 + 4$

Do You Understand?

Show Me! What number can you write in the blank to make this equation true? Use pictures or words to show how you know.

$8 + \_\_\_ = 6 + 6$

Guided Practice

Write the missing numbers to make the equations true. Draw counters to help.

1. $10 + \underline{?} = 5 + 7$

   $10 + \underline{?} = \underline{12}$

   $10 + \underline{2} = \underline{12}$

2. $4 + 5 = 6 + \underline{?}$

   $\_\_\_ = 6 + \underline{?}$

   $\_\_\_ = 6 + \_\_\_$

Name ______________________________

Independent Practice

Write the missing number that makes each equation true.

3. ____ + 6 = 4 + 9

4. 14 − 7 = ____ − 3

5. 8 + ____ = 9 + 4

6. 10 − ____ = 7 − 3

7. 15 − 10 = 10 − ____

8. 7 + 4 = 8 + ____

9. 10 + 2 = ____ + 4

10. 13 − 10 = ____ − 7

11. ____ + 7 = 9 + 1

12. **Math and Science** Kari and Chris make "telephones" with paper cups and string. They take a piece of string that is 13 feet long and cut it into two pieces. One piece is 8 feet long. How long is the other piece of string? Write the missing number in the addition and subtraction equations.

____ = 13 − 8

13 = ____ + 8

____ feet

You can think about subtraction as a missing addend problem.

Problem Solving Solve each problem below.

13. **Reasoning** Kim has 14 tennis balls. Danny has 4 tennis balls. How many more tennis balls does Kim have than Danny?

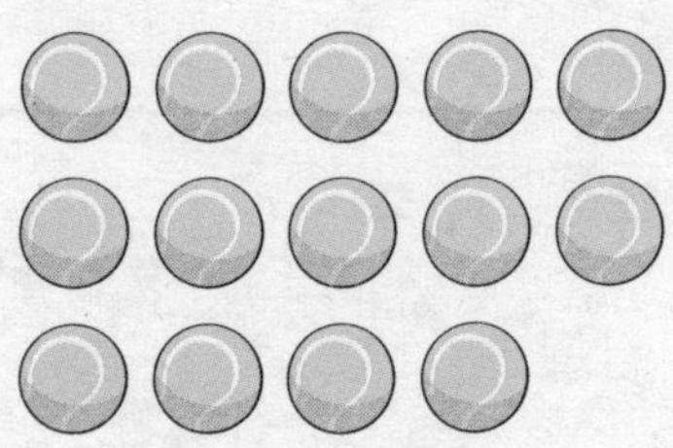

14 − ____ = ____ ____ more

14. **Reasoning** Ron finds 10 rocks but drops 1 rock. Anson finds 3 rocks. How many more rocks would Anson have to find to have the same number of rocks as Ron?

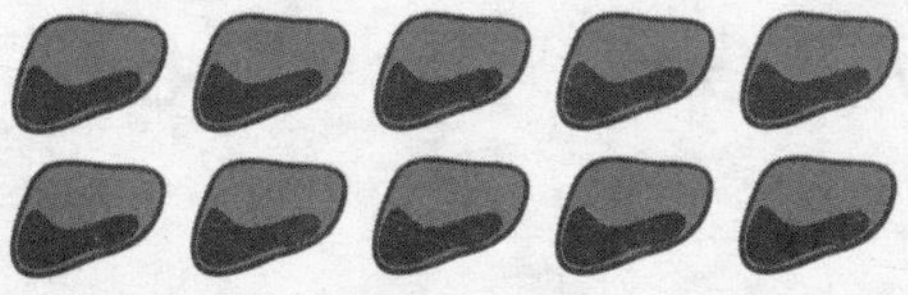

10 − 1 = 3 + ____ ____ rocks

15. **Higher Order Thinking** Jose has 5 red crayons and 8 blue crayons. Tasha has 10 red crayons and some blue crayons. If Tasha has the same number of crayons as Jose, how many blue crayons does she have? Tell how you know.

16. **Assessment** Draw an arrow to show which number will make the equation true.

1 2 3 4 5 6 7 8

4 + 7 = 5 + ____

Name ___________________________

Homework & Practice 5-3
Make True Equations

Another Look! Solving one side of a true equation can help you determine the value of the other side.

$9 + \_\_\_ = 7 + 8$

You could also use counters to model the equation.

Both sides of a true equation must have the same value.

First, solve 7 + 8. $7 + 8 = 15$

Next, solve 9 + ? = 15 $9 + 6 = 15$

So, $9 + 6 = 7 + 8$.

HOME ACTIVITY Write down a number between 0 and 20. Ask your child to write down an addition or subtraction fact that would equal the number. Repeat with other numbers. Have your child give you a number and then you give an addition or subtraction fact. Ask him or her to tell you if you made a true or false equation.

Write the missing numbers to make the equations true. Draw counters to help.

1.

$7 + \_\_\_ = 8 + 6$

$8 + 6 = \_\_\_$

$7 + \_\_\_ = \_\_\_$

2.

$2 + 4 = 16 - \_\_\_$

$2 + 4 = \_\_\_$

$\_\_\_ = 16 - \_\_\_$

Solve each problem below.

3. **Reasoning** Greg has 15 hats. Tamara has 10 hats. She wants to have the same number of hats as Greg. How many more hats does Tamara need?

$15 = 10 + \_\_\_$

___ more

4. **Reasoning** Laila uses the same number of counters as Frank. What number would make this equation true?

$8 + 1 = 16 - \_\_\_$

5. **Higher Order Thinking** Write the missing number that makes the equation true. Use pictures or words to explain how you know.

$3 + 4 = 8 - \_\_\_$

6. **Assessment** Draw an arrow to show which number will make the equation true.

1 2 3 4 5 6 7 8

$4 + \_\_\_ = 1 + 8$

Name ______________________

Lesson 5-4

Word Problems with Three Addends

I can ... use different strategies to solve word problems with 3 addends.

I can also model with math.

Solve & Share

I have 6 oranges, Alex has 2 pears, and Jada has 4 apples. How many pieces of fruit do we have in all?

Write 2 different addition equations to solve the problem.

___ + ___ + ___ = ___

___ + ___ + ___ = ___

Vince collects red rocks. He separates them into 3 baskets. How many red rocks does he have in all?

I can add 5 + 4 first and then add 6.

5 + 4 = 9
9 + 6 = 15

I can add 4 + 6 to make 10 and then add 5.

4 + 6 = 10
10 + 5 = 15

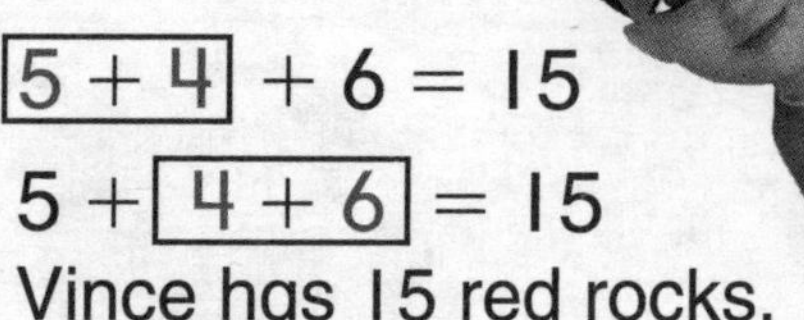

I can group the numbers either way. The sum is the same.

[5 + 4] + 6 = 15
5 + [4 + 6] = 15
Vince has 15 red rocks.

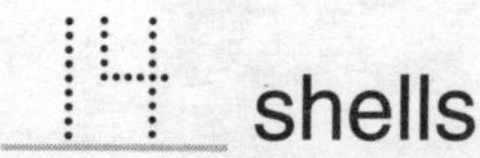

Do You Understand?

Show Me! How can grouping numbers in a different way help you to solve a problem?

Guided Practice Write an equation to solve each problem. Choose a way to group the addends.

1. Tess finds some shells at the beach. She finds 7 pink shells, 3 black shells, and 4 white shells. How many shells does Tess find in all?

7 + 3 + 4 = 14   14 shells

2. Tom sees some birds. He sees 4 red birds, 2 blue birds, and 6 black birds. How many birds does Tom see in all?

____ + ____ + ____ = ____   ____ birds

Name ______________________

Tools Assessment

Independent Practice Write an equation to solve each problem. Choose a way to group the addends.

3. Pat has cards of his favorite athletes. He has 8 baseball cards, 2 football cards, and 3 basketball cards. How many cards does Pat have in all?

____ + ____ + ____ = ____

____ cards

4. Bob plants seeds. He plants 2 brown seeds, 6 white seeds, and 8 black seeds. How many seeds does Bob plant in all?

____ + ____ + ____ = ____

____ seeds

Write the missing numbers for each problem.

5. Algebra 16 = 7 + ____ + 6

6. Algebra 11 = 2 + 2 + ____

7. A-Z **Vocabulary** Julio finds 3 ladybugs and some ants. Then he finds 5 beetles. Julio finds 14 bugs in all. How many ants did Julio find? Write the missing **addend**.

14 = 3 + ____ + 5

Julio finds ____ ants.

8. Higher Order Thinking Rosa picks 12 flowers from her garden. She picks some purple flowers. Then she picks 4 pink flowers and 3 yellow flowers. How many purple flowers did Rosa pick?

12 = ? + 4 + 3

She picks ____ purple flowers.

Problem Solving Solve each problem below.

9. Generalize Dan throws 3 beanbags at the target. The numbers on the target show the score for each beanbag.

Write an addition equation to find Dan's score.

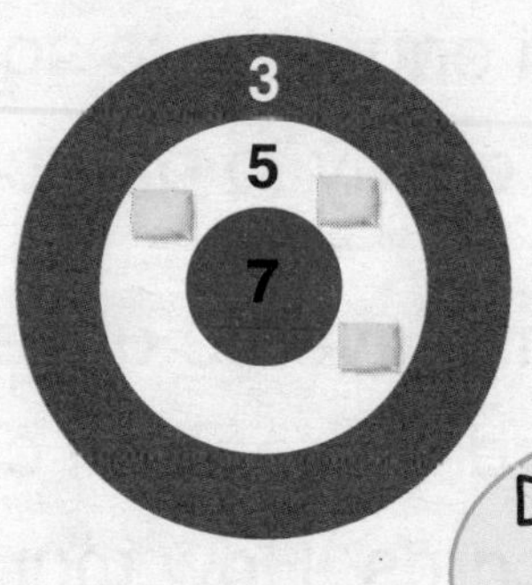

____ + ____ + ____ = ____

10. Higher Order Thinking Write a story problem about toys. The story should match the addition equation below.

$4 + 1 + 9 = 14$

____

____

____

____

11. Assessment Joy throws 3 beanbags at the target. She scores 17 points. Which picture shows her target?

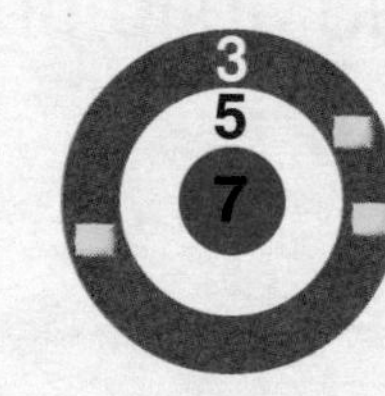

Name ____________________

Another Look! You can group addends in different ways. Then you can write an equation.

 +  + 

Sally has some fruit. She has 3 apples, 5 bananas, and 5 pears. How many pieces of fruit does she have in all?

First, add the bananas and pears.

5 + 5 = 10

Then add the apples.

10 + 3 = 13

Sally has 13 pieces of fruit in all.

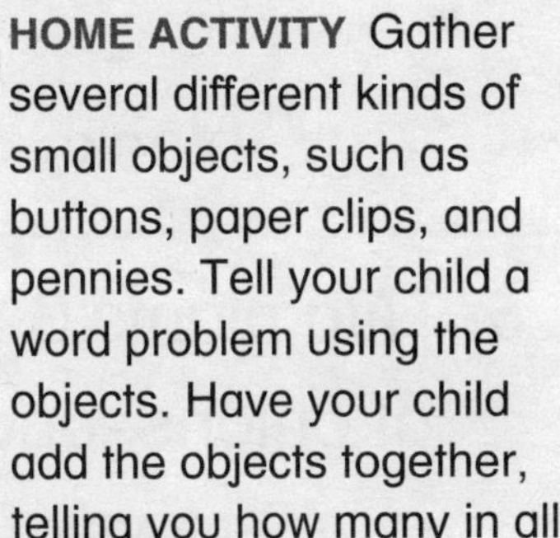

HOME ACTIVITY Gather several different kinds of small objects, such as buttons, paper clips, and pennies. Tell your child a word problem using the objects. Have your child add the objects together, telling you how many in all.

Find each sum. Choose a way to group the addends.

1.   

___ + ___ + ___ = ___

2.   

___ + ___ + ___ = ___

Write an equation to solve each problem.

3. Todd plays with some blocks. He has 3 red blocks, 3 yellow blocks, and 6 blue blocks. How many blocks is Todd playing with in all?

___ + ___ + ___ = ___

___ blocks

4. Emma has 7 green beads, some purple beads, and 6 yellow beads. She has 17 beads in all. How many purple beads does Emma have?

___ + ___ + ___ = ___

___ purple beads

5. Rita plants 3 rows of carrots, 4 rows of onions, and 7 rows of lettuce. How many rows of vegetables did Rita plant in all?

___ + ___ + ___ = ___

___ rows

6. Julien builds 8 tables, 3 chairs, and 4 desks. How many pieces of furniture did Julien build?

___ + ___ + ___ = ___

___ pieces

7. Higher Order Thinking Write a story problem about the lunchroom that matches the equation $5 + 8 + 2 = 15$.

___

___

___

___

8. Assessment At the animal shelter, Kim feeds 2 rabbits, 6 dogs, and 4 cats. How many animals does Kim feed in all?

18	16	15	12
Ⓐ			Ⓓ

Name ______________________

Lesson 5-5
Add Three Numbers

I can ...
find different strategies to add three numbers.

I can also model with math.

Solve & Share

Carlos made stacks of 6 books, 4 books, and 6 books. How can you use addition to find the number of books in all three stacks?

Write two different equations to show how many books in all.

____ + ____ + ____ = ____

____ + ____ + ____ = ____

You can add three numbers.

8 + 6 + 2

You can make 10.

(8) + 6 + (2) = 16

You can make a double.

8 + (6) + (2) = 16

8

6 + 2 = 8
8 + 8 = 16

You can add any two numbers first.

Do You Understand?

Show Me! Why can you pick any two numbers to add first when you add three numbers?

Guided Practice

Add the circled numbers first. Write their sum in the box. Then write the sum of all three numbers.

1. (2) + (9) + 1 = 12 [11]

2 + (9) + (1) = 12 [10]

2. (6) + (3) + 2 = ____ [ ]

6 + (3) + (2) = ____ [ ]

Name ____________________

Independent Practice

Circle two numbers to add first. Write their sum in the box at the right. Then write the sum of all three numbers.

3.
6
6
+ 1
☐ ☐

4.
3
7
+ 8
☐ ☐

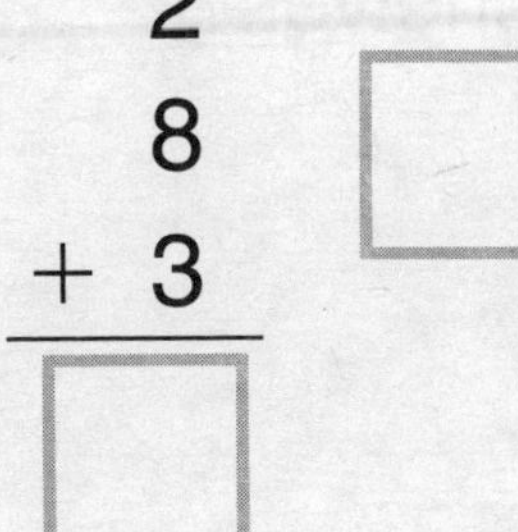

5.
2
8
+ 3
☐ ☐

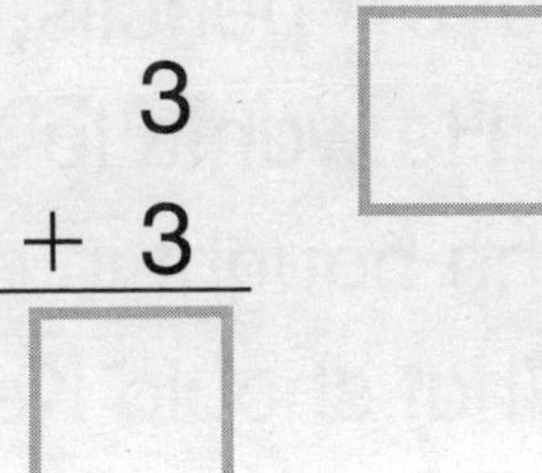

6.
7
3
+ 3
☐ ☐

7.
2
2
+ 8
☐ ☐

8.
5
0
+ 9
☐ ☐

9. Number Sense Find the missing numbers. The numbers on each branch add up to 15.

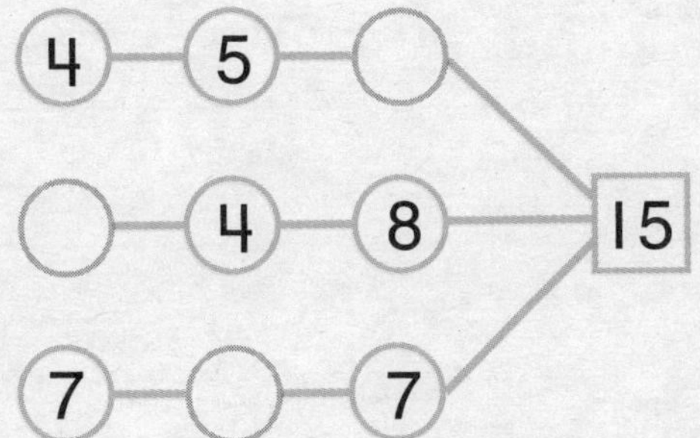

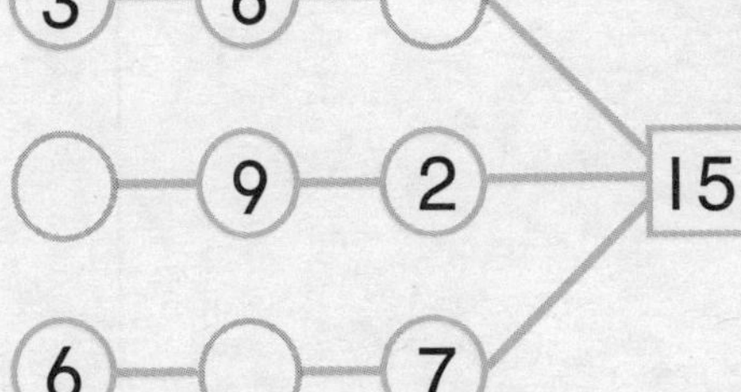

Problem Solving Write an equation to solve each problem below.

10. **Look for Patterns** Maya puts 7 books on a shelf and 3 books on another shelf. Then she puts 5 books on the last shelf. How many books did Maya put on all three shelves?

Can you break the problem into simpler parts?

____ + ____ + ____ = ____

____ books

11. **Higher Order Thinking** Explain how to add $7 + 2 + 3$. Use pictures, numbers, or words.

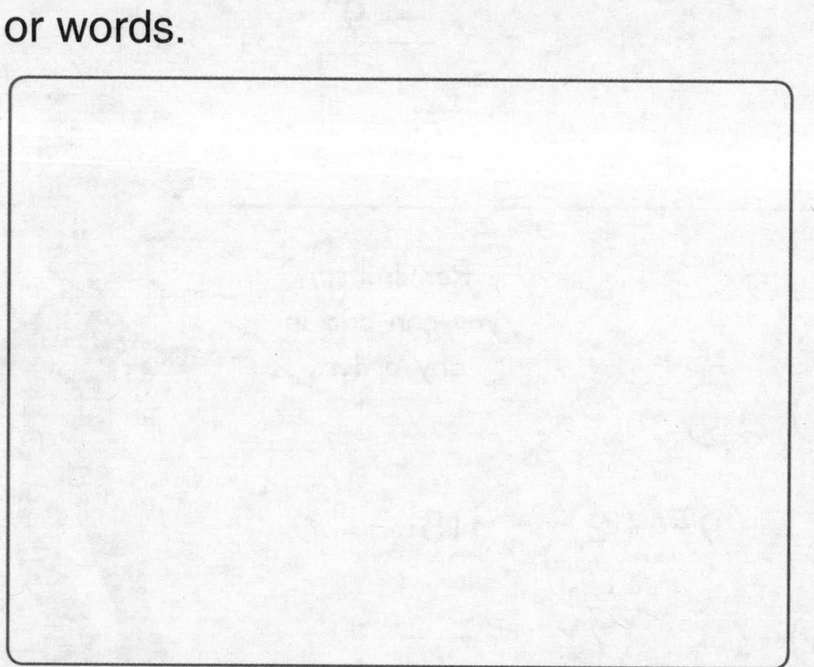

12. **Assessment** Ken buys 4 pencils, 6 markers, and 7 pens. He wants to know how many items he bought in all. He added $4 + 6$ first. What should Ken add next? Explain.

____

____

____

Name ______________________

Help Tools Games

Homework & Practice 5-5

Add Three Numbers

Another Look! When you add three numbers, look for facts you know. Then add the third number.

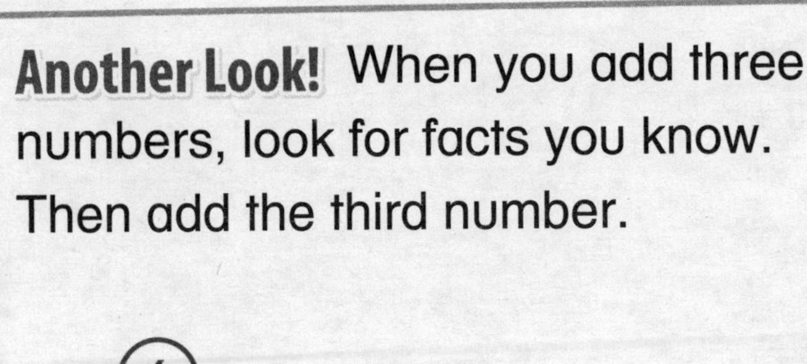

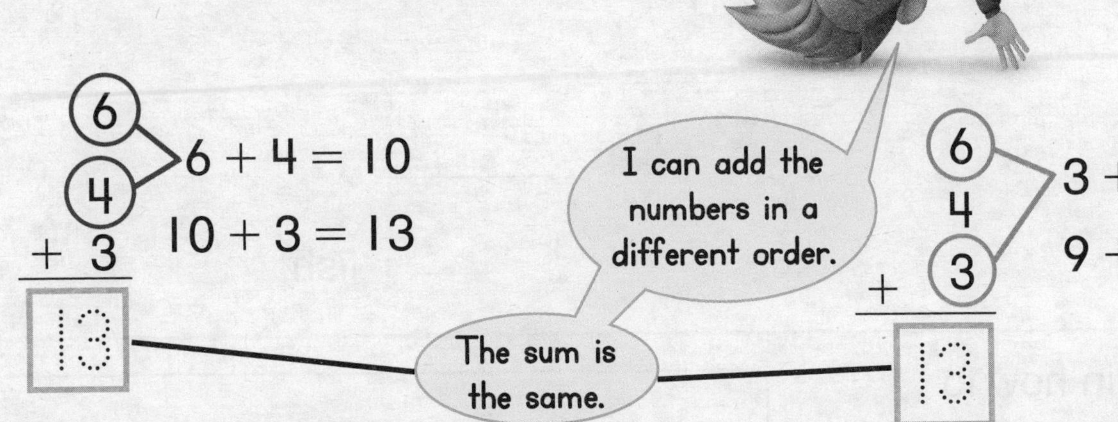

I can add the numbers in a different order.
The sum is the same.

6 + 4 + 3 = 13: $6 + 4 = 10$, $10 + 3 = 13$

6 + 4 + 3 = 13: $3 + 6 = 9$, $9 + 4 = 13$

HOME ACTIVITY Tell your child three numbers that have a sum less than or equal to 20. Have him or her add the three numbers to find the sum. Ask your child to think aloud as he or she adds the first two numbers, and then the third number to that sum. Repeat with several sets of numbers.

Find each sum using different ways. Add the circled numbers first. Then add the third number.

1. 5 + 2 + 5 = ___

$5 + 5 =$ ___

___ $+ 2 =$ ___

5 + 2 + 5 = ___

$2 + 5 =$ ___

___ $+ 5 =$ ___

Add the numbers shown. Circle the numbers you add first.

2. 

+

turtles

3. 

+

fish

4. **Higher Order Thinking** Explain how to add 3 + 3 + 4. Use pictures, numbers, or words.

5. **Assessment** Matt buys pieces to make a model car. He buys 1 block of wood, 4 tires, and 2 cans of paint. Matt wants to know how many items he bought in all. If he adds 1 + 2 first, what should Matt add next? Explain.

Name ______________________________

Solve

Lesson 5-6

Solve Addition and Subtraction Word Problems

I can ...
solve word problems involving comparisons.

I can also make sense of problems.

Solve & Share

Jose has 5 more erasers than Lois. Jose has 7 erasers. How many erasers does Lois have? Write your answers below.

Jose's erasers

Lois' erasers

Steve has 13 books. Claire has 4 fewer books than Steve. How many books does Claire have?

You can use a bar model to show the problem.

Steve's books

13	
?	4
Claire's books	**4 fewer books**

You can write an addition or subtraction equation to see how many books Claire has.

$13 - 4 = \underline{9}$

$4 + \underline{9} = 13$

13	
9	4

So, Claire has 9 books.

Do You Understand?

Show Me! Tom made 8 fewer sandcastles than Tina. Tina made 10 sandcastles. How many sandcastles did Tom make?

☆ Guided Practice ☆

Use the models to solve the problems.

1. Sal has 8 more magazines than Gemma. Sal has 15 magazines. How many magazines does Gemma have?

Sal's magazines

15	
7	8
Gemma's magazines	8 more magazines

$\underline{8} + \underline{7} = \underline{15}$

Gemma has ____ magazines.

Name ______________________

Tools Assessment

Independent Practice

Use the models to complete the problems.

2. Alan picks up 3 toys. Then he picks up 8 more. How many toys did Alan pick up in all?

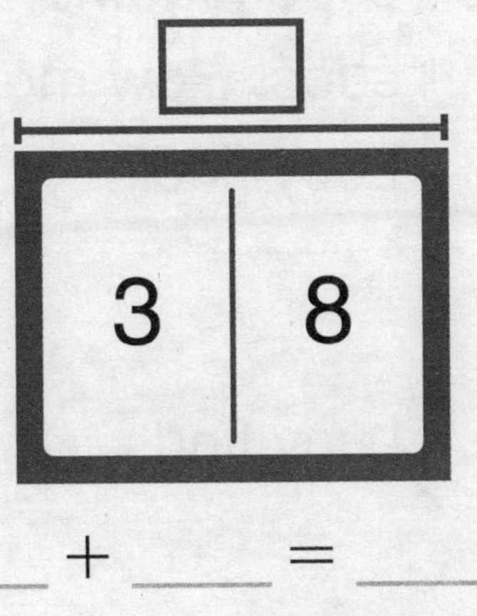

___ + ___ = ___

Alan picked up ___ toys in all.

3. Jack makes 5 fewer fruit cups than Sandi. Sandi makes 11 fruit cups. How many fruit cups did Jack make?

11	
___	5

___ − ___ = ___

Jack makes ___ fruit cups.

Fill in the missing number for the model or the equation. Choose addition or subtraction to solve.

4. Harry has 5 fewer buttons than Tina. Harry has 7 buttons. How many buttons does Tina have?

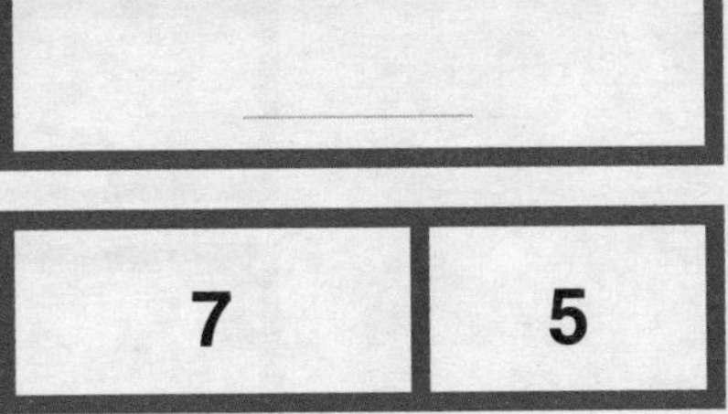

___ ◯ ___ = ___ ___ buttons

5. Mark calls some people. Jane calls 8 people. They called 17 people in all. How many people did Mark call?

___ ◯ ___ = ___ ___ people

Problem Solving Solve the problems below.

6. **Make Sense** Ashlyn had some stuffed animals. She gives 5 to Anna. Now Ashlyn has 7 stuffed animals. How many stuffed animals did Ashlyn have before?

____ ◯ ____ = ____

Ashlyn had ____ stuffed animals before.

7. **Make Sense** Lucy and Tim find 15 bottle caps together. Tim finds 7 of the bottle caps. How many of the bottle caps does Lucy find?

____ ◯ ____ = ____

Lucy finds ____ bottle caps.

8. **Higher Order Thinking** Draw a model to show the equation. Then write and solve the equation.

16 − 10 = ___?___

____ − ____ = ____

9. **Assessment** Tanner's family has 3 more pets than Ava's family. Tanner's family has 7 pets. How many pets does Ava's family have?
Complete the bar diagram and write an equation to match the story.

7	
____	3

____ ◯ ____ = ____

Name ____________________

Help Tools Games

Homework & Practice 5-6

Solve Addition and Subtraction Word Problems

Another Look! You can use addition or subtraction to solve word problems.

Bill has 10 more berries than Ken.
Bill has 14 berries.
How many berries does Ken have?

I will start with 10 red counters. Then I will add yellow counters to make 14. How many yellow counters are there?

Bill has 10 more than Ken. I will subtract.

14 − 10 = ____

10 + ____ = 14

14 − 10 = 4

10 + 4 = 14

Ken has 4 berries.

HOME ACTIVITY Model a comparison situation, such as, Tom has 3 more cards than Julie. Tom has 10 cards. How many cards does Julie have? Have your child use small objects to model the story. Then ask him or her to write an equation that matches the story. Repeat with other similar comparison problems.

Draw counters to show the problem. Then solve.

1. Shelly has 10 pumpkins. She gives some to Nola. Now Shelly has 6 pumpkins. How many pumpkins did Shelly give Nola?

____ ◯ ____ = ____

Shelly gives Nola ____ pumpkins.

Draw counters to solve.

2. Victor writes 10 more poems than Ann. Ann writes 10 poems. How many poems does Victor write?

___ ◯ ___ = ___

Victor writes ___ poems.

3. Barb has 13 crayons. She gives 6 crayons to Javier. How many crayons does Barb have left?

Barb has ___ crayons left.

4. **Higher Order Thinking** Write a story that uses the word **more**. Then solve.

___ ◯ ___ = ___

5. **Assessment** Sam draws 6 fewer pictures than Tina. Tina draws 15 pictures. How many pictures does Sam draw? Draw or cross out counters and write an equation to match the story.

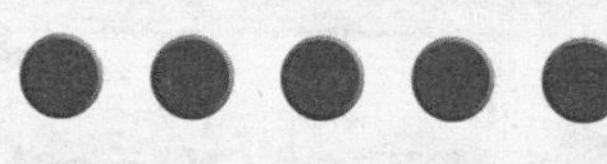

___ ◯ ___ = ___

Sam draws ___ pictures.

Name ______________________________

Problem Solving

Lesson 5-7
Precision

Solve & Share Discuss the equation below with a partner. Decide whether it is true or false. Explain your thinking.

I can ...
understand that the equal sign means "the same value as" and I will use precise language when talking about it.

I can also add and subtract within 20.

$9 = 5 + 2 + 2$

Thinking Habits
Am I using numbers and symbols correctly?
Is my answer clear?

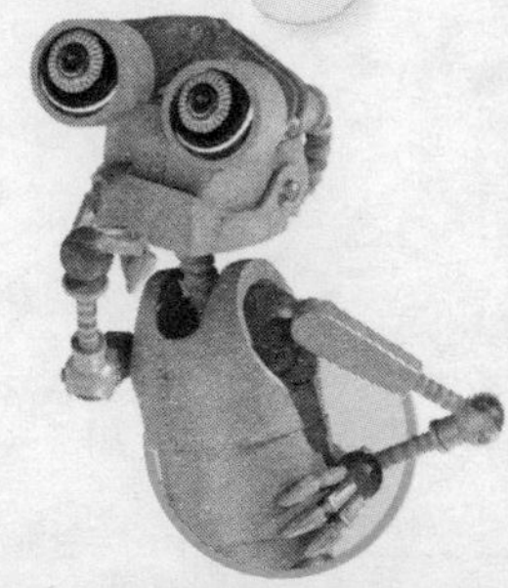

A-Z
Learn
Glossary

What missing number can you write to make the equation true?

14 = 5 + ___ + 8

How can I be precise as I solve this problem?

I can use words, numbers, and symbols correctly.

The equal sign means "the same value as." 14 has the same value as 5 plus some number plus 8.

5 + 8 = 13,
so 14 = 13 + ___.

13 + 1 = 14,
so 1 is the missing number.

14 = 5 + 1 + 8.

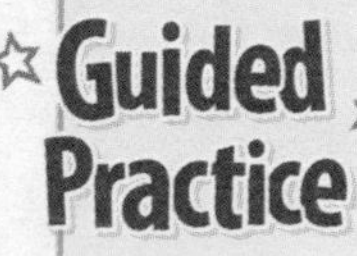

Do You Understand?

Show Me! Is the equation below true or false? How do you know?

10 + 5 = 9 + 3 + 3

Guided Practice

Write the symbol (+, −, or =) or number to make the equation true. Then tell how you know you found the correct symbol or number.

1. 3 + 8 = 4 + [7]

2. 4 + 3 + [ ] = 13

Name ______________________________

Tools
Assessment

Independent Practice Write the symbol (+, −, or =) or number to make the equation true. Then tell how you know you found the correct symbol or number.

3. 19 ◯ 10 = 9

____

____

____

4. 20 = ☐ + 5 + 5

____

____

____

5. 10 + 1 ◯ 6 + 5

____

____

____

6. 9 − 2 = 10 ◯ 3

____

____

____

7. **Algebra** Write the missing number in the equation below. Explain how you know.

42 + 55 = 55 + ☐

____

____

Think about the meanings of the symbols.

Problem Solving

Performance Assessment

Balloon Party Dani has 7 green and 4 yellow balloons. Gene has 15 blue balloons.

8. Explain If Gene gives 4 of his balloons away, then he and Dani will have the same number. Fill in the blanks to make the equation true. Use +, −, or =.

7 ◯ 4 ◯ 15 ◯ 4

Explain how you chose the symbols.

____

____

____

____

____

How do you know the equation is true?

____

____

____

9. Be Precise If Gene keeps all 15 blue balloons, how many balloons would Dani need to buy to have the same number as Gene? Complete the equation to find the answer.

7 ◯ 4 ◯ ___ ◯ 15

Did you use numbers and symbols correctly? Explain how you know.

____

____

____

____

Name ____________________

Homework & Practice 5-7

Precision

Another Look! You can write a missing number to make an equation true.

$3 + 9 = \_\_\_ + 6$

First, solve the side you know.

$3 + 9 = 12$

I know the meaning of the = symbol is "the same as".

Then, use what you know to solve the other side.

$12 = 6 + 6$

12 is a double: 6 + 6. The missing number is 6!

$3 + 9 = 6 + 6$ is the same as $12 = 12$.

HOME ACTIVITY Place 2 small groups of objects (less than or equal to 10) on the table. Ask your child to tell you the addition problem that is represented (for example, $5 + 7 = 12$). Then have him or her rearrange the objects into a different 2 groups. Ask your child again to tell you the addition fact that is represented (for example, $9 + 3 = 12$). Help your child write an equation that shows that his or her addition fact is equal to yours (for example, $5 + 7 = 9 + 3$).

Write the missing number to make the equation true. Then, write the number that makes both sides equal.

1. $\square - 0 = 7 + 8$

___ = ___

2. $6 + 4 = \square + 9$

___ = ___

3. $8 - 5 = 13 - \square$

___ = ___

Performance Assessment

Checkers James and Amy played 12 games of checkers last week. This week they played 7 games on Monday and 2 games on Wednesday.

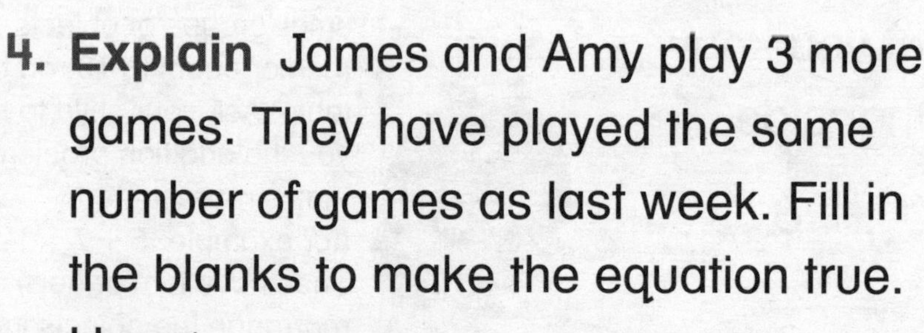

4. **Explain** James and Amy play 3 more games. They have played the same number of games as last week. Fill in the blanks to make the equation true. Use +, −, or =.

12 ◯ 7 ◯ 2 ◯ 3

Explain how you chose the symbols.

____

____

____

____

____

How do you know the equation is true?

____

____

5. **Be Precise** Amy lost 4 of the games she played last week. How many games did she win?

Write an equation to find your answer.

____ ◯ ____ ◯ ____

Amy won ____ games.

Use precise math language to explain how you know your equation and answer are correct.

____

____

____

____

____

Name ______________________________

Fluency Practice Activity

I can ...
add and subtract within 10.

Point & Tally

Find a partner. Get paper and a pencil.

Each partner chooses a different color: light blue or dark blue.

Partner 1 and Partner 2 each point to a black number at the same time. Subtract Partner 1's number from Partner 2's number.

If the answer is on your color, you get a tally mark.

Work until one partner gets twelve tally marks.

Partner 1
5
0
3
1
4
2

6	4	1	8	9	5
2	10	0	3	1	7

Partner 2
8
6
5
10
7
9

Tally Marks for Partner 1	Tally Marks for Partner 2

TOPIC 5

Vocabulary Review

Glossary

Word List

- add
- equation
- more
- subtract

Understand Vocabulary

1. Circle **True** or **False** for the addition equation below.

   $4 + 6 = 5 + 2 + 3$

   True False

2. Circle **True** or **False** for the subtraction equation below.

   $10 = 11 - 2$

   True False

3. Write the number you need to add to make the equation true.

   $7 - 3 = 2 +$ ____

4. Write the number you need to add to make the equation true.

   ____ $+ 4 + 2 = 10$

5. Write the number you need to subtract to make the equation true.

   $9 = 10 -$ ____

Use Vocabulary in Writing

6. Write a story problem with a true equation using at least two words from the Word List.

Name ____________________

TOPIC 5

Set A

Reteaching

Solve to find out if the equation is **True** or **False**.

$6 + 5 = 3 + 8$

Solve one side first. $6 + 5 = 11$

Solve the other side. $3 + 8 = 11$

$11 = 11$

This equation is **True**.

Tell whether each equation is **True** or **False**.

1. $8 - 5 = 4 + 1$

   True **False**

2. $3 + 1 = 12 - 8$

   True **False**

Set B

Write the missing numbers to make the equations true.

$4 + 7 = 6 + \_\_\_$

Both sides should be equal.

$4 + 7 = 11$

So, $6 + \underline{5} = 11$.

The missing number is 5.

$4 + 7 = 6 + \underline{5}$

Find and write the missing numbers to make the equations true.

3. $11 = \_\_\_ + 4$

4. $\_\_\_ - 4 = 5$

5. $10 + 5 = 6 + \_\_\_$

6. $9 - \_\_\_ = 13 - 10$

7. $14 - \_\_\_ = 2 + 2$

Set C

You can add three numbers in any order. 2 + 8 + 2 = ?

Make a 10. Then add 2.

(2) + (8) + 2 = 12

Make a double. Then add 8.

(2) + 8 + (2) = 12

Find the sum. Solve in any order.

8. 5 + 5 + 4 = ____

9. 9 + 5 + 1 = ____

10. 6 + 4 + 4 = ____

11. 3 + 3 + 5 = ____

Set D

Thinking Habits

Precision

Am I using numbers and symbols correctly?

Am I adding and subtracting accurately?

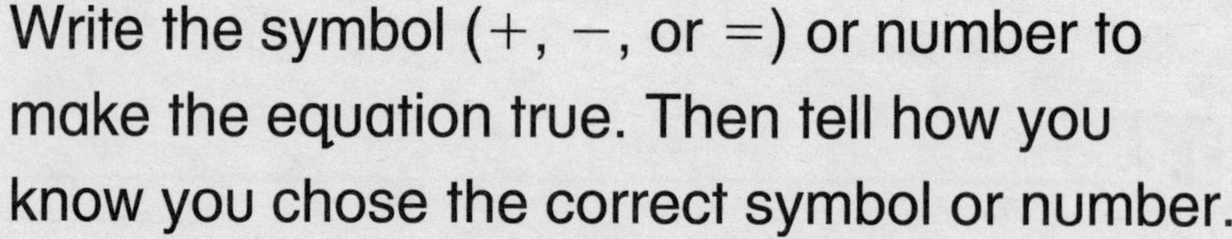

Write the symbol (+, −, or =) or number to make the equation true. Then tell how you know you chose the correct symbol or number.

12. 10 − 5 = 2 ◯ 3

____

____

____

13. 4 + 5 = 10 ◯ 1

____

____

____

Name ______________________________

1. Complete the model. Then write the missing number in the equation.

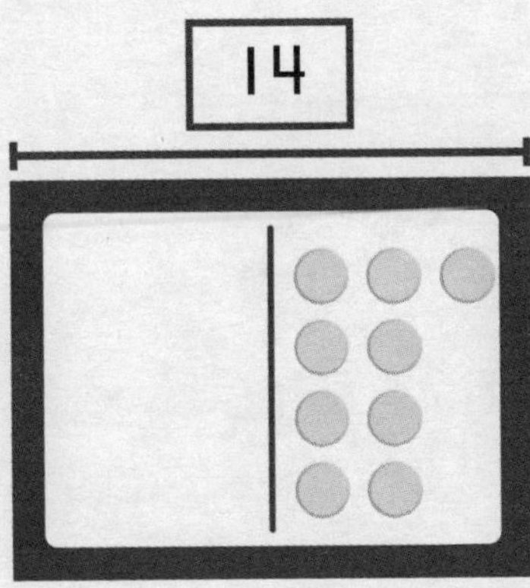

14 = ____ + 9

2. Tell if the equation is **True** or **False**.

4 + 7 = 13 − 3

True **False**

3. Which number is missing?

16 − __?__ = 2 + 6

Ⓐ 10

Ⓑ 9

Ⓒ 8

Ⓓ 7

4. Tasha has 2 dogs and 3 cats. She also has 7 goldfish. How many pets does Tasha have in all?

2 + 3 + 7 = ____

5. Bill has 10 apples. He uses 8 of them to make muffins. Josh has 6 apples. How many should he use so he has the same number as Bill?

$10 - 8 = 6 - \_\_\_$

___ apples

6. Kerry, Tom, and Nicole want to play tennis. Kerry has 5 tennis balls. Tom has 5 tennis balls. Nicole has 3 tennis balls. How many tennis balls do they have in all?

Ⓐ 13

Ⓑ 14

Ⓒ 15

Ⓓ 16

7. In a soccer game, Andrew scores 3 fewer goals than Elsie. Elsie scores 9 goals. How many goals did Andrew score? Complete the bar diagram and write an equation to match the story.

9	
___	3

___ ◯ ___ = ___

___ goals

8. Write the missing symbol (+, −, or =) to make the equation true. Use precise math language to explain how you chose the symbol.

$16 = 4 + 8$ ◯ 4

____

____

____

Name ____________________

TOPIC 5

Performance Assessment

A Vase of Flowers

Terry and his brother, Dave, put flowers in a vase for their mother.

5 Roses

5 Daisies

2 Carnations

8 Lilies

1. Complete the equation below to show the number of lilies and roses. Use numbers and symbols (+, −, =).

____ + 5 ◯ ____

2. How many roses, daisies, and carnations are in the vase?

Write an equation to solve.

____ + ____ + ____ = ____

Explain how you added. Use pictures, numbers, or words.

3. Terry puts the roses and the daisies in the vase. Dave puts the carnations and the lilies in the vase. Did they put an equal number of flowers in the vase?

Complete the equation.

____ + ____ = ____ + ____

Fill in the missing numbers.

Terry puts ____ flowers in the vase.

Dave puts ____ flowers in the vase.

Did Terry and Dave each put an equal number of flowers in the vase? Circle **Yes** or **No**.

Yes **No**

4. Dave says there are 3 more daisies than carnations. What equation can he use to find out if he is right?

5 ◯ ____ ◯ ____

5. Terry says that if there were 2 fewer lilies, then the number of lilies would be equal to the number of daisies. He writes the equation below. Is this equation true or false? Explain how you know.

$8 - 2 = 5$

____

____

6. Terry and Dave buy more carnations. Now they have 10 in all. How many carnations did they buy? Complete the equation using +, −, or =.

10 ◯ 2 ◯ 8 ____ more carnations

Use precise math language to explain how you chose the symbols.

____

____

____

TOPIC 6

Represent and Interpret Data

Essential Question: What are some ways you can collect, show, and understand data?

There are many different types of telephones.

The first telephone was invented over 100 years ago.

Wow! Let's do this project and learn more.

Math and Science Project: Different Types of Phones

Find Out Talk to friends and relatives about the types of phones they use. Ask how phones have changed in their lifetimes.

Journal: Make a Book Show what you found out. In your book, also:

- Draw pictures of more than one type of phone. Which phone do you think is better for making calls?
- Collect data about the types of phones people use.

Name ______________________________

Review What You Know

Vocabulary

1. Circle the cubes that make the **equation** true.

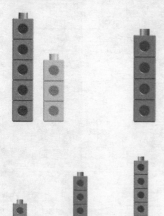

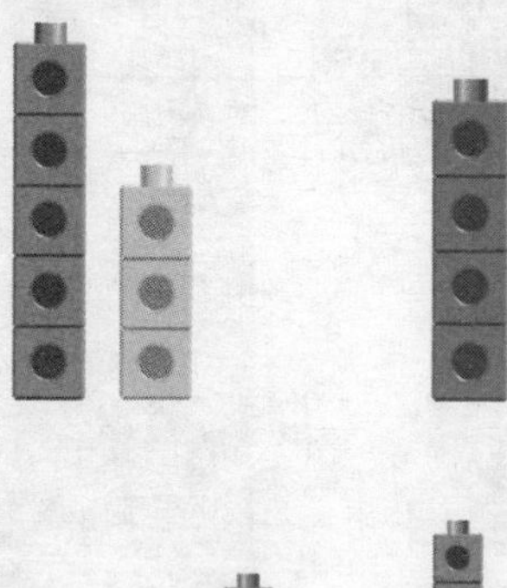

5 + 3 = 4 + ?

2. Write the numbers that tell how many pieces of fruit. Then circle the group with **fewer**.

3. Write the numbers that tell how many balls. Then circle the group with **more**.

Find the Missing Part

4. Write the number that will make the equation true.

15 − 8 = ____ + 1

5. Write each missing number.

5 + 3 + 2 = ____

9 + ____ + 7 = 17

Near Doubles Facts

6. Write the missing number to solve this near doubles fact.

7 + ____ = 15

My Word Cards

Study the words on the front of the card. Complete the activity on the back.

A-Z Glossary

tally marks

marks that are used to record data

Cats	III
Dogs	II

data

information you collect

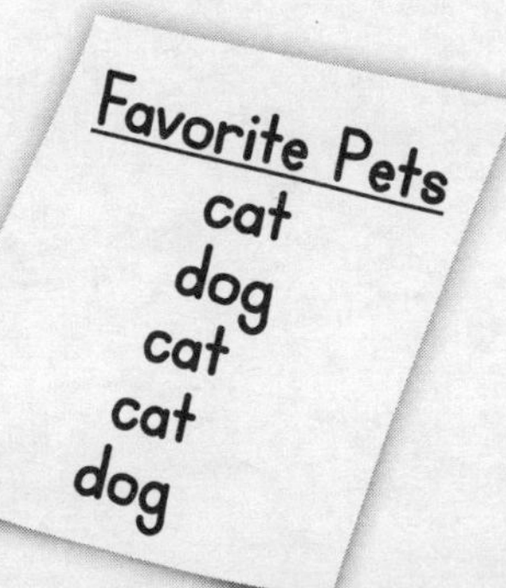

tally chart

a chart that uses tally marks to show data

Broccoli	Carrots
卌 I	卌 IIII

survey

to gather information

Cats III
Dogs II

picture graph

a graph that uses pictures to show data

Favorite Pets			
Cat	🐱	🐱	🐱
Dog	🐶	🐶	

My Word Cards

Use what you know to complete the sentences.
Extend learning by writing your own sentence using each word.

A chart that uses tally marks to show data is a

____

____________________.

____

are information that you collect.

You can use

____

____

to show data.

A ____________________

____

is a graph that uses pictures to show data.

You can ask

____

questions to collect information.

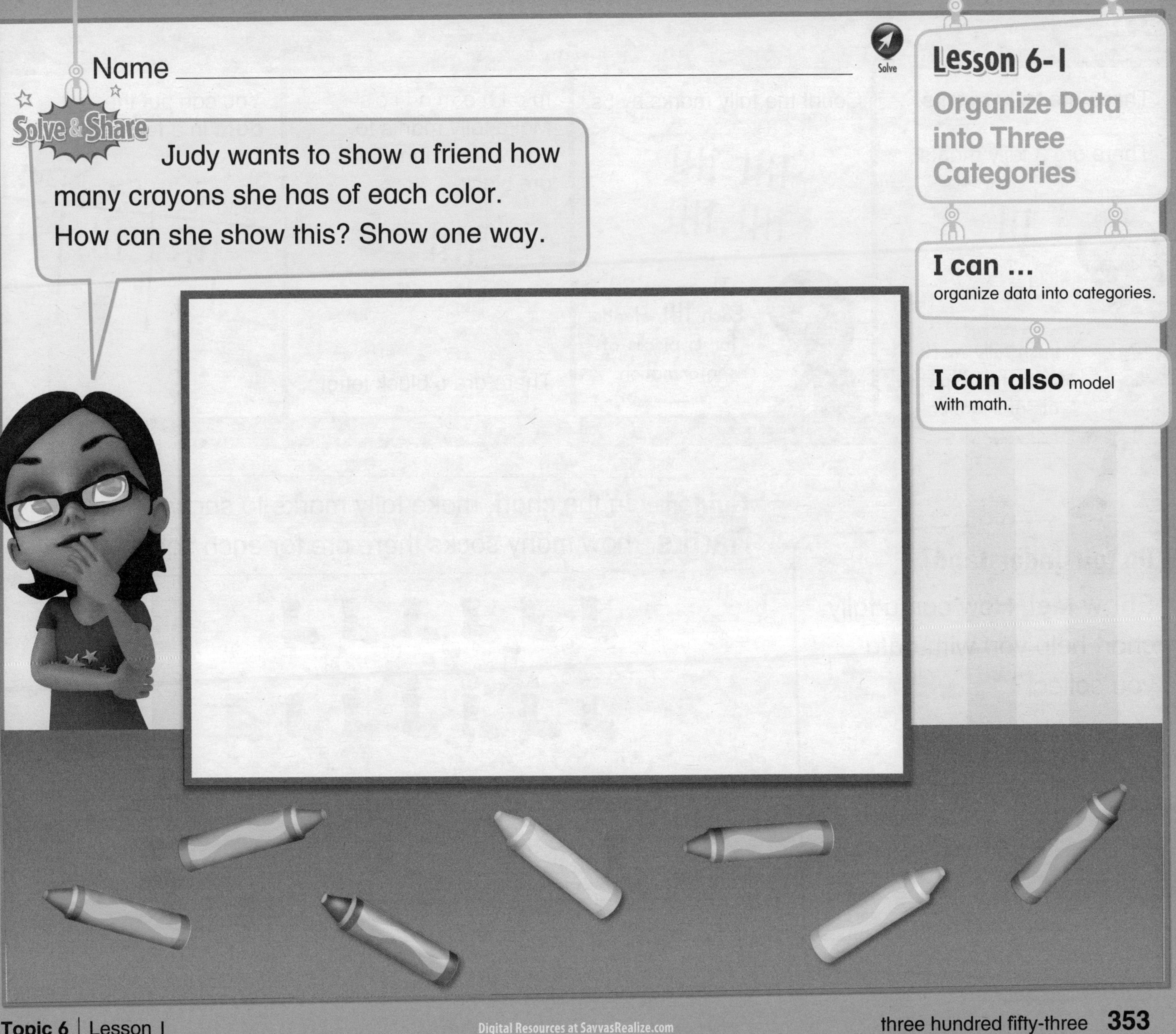

Name ______________________________

Solve & Share

Judy wants to show a friend how many crayons she has of each color. How can she show this? Show one way.

Solve

Lesson 6-1

Organize Data into Three Categories

I can ...
organize data into categories.

I can also model with math.

These are **tally marks**.

There are 3 tally marks.

Count the tally marks by 5s.

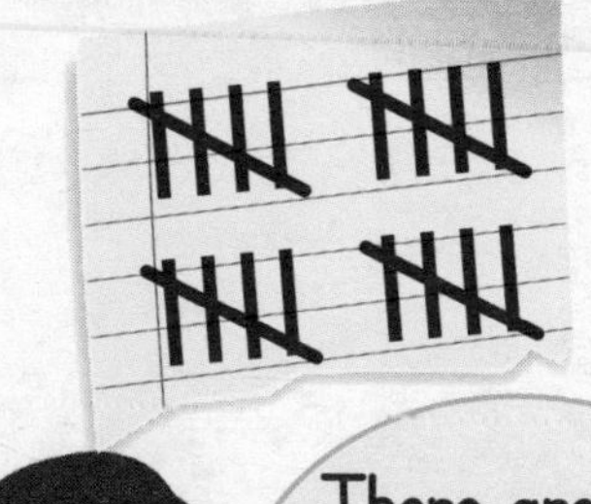

There are 20. Each 𝍸 stands for 5 pieces of information.

mathematics
Make tally marks to show how many letters are black.

There are 6 black letters.

You can put the **data** in a **tally chart**.

Black	Red	Blue
𝍸 I	III	II

Do You Understand?

Show Me! How can a tally chart help you with data you collect?

Guided Practice

In the chart, make tally marks to show how many socks there are for each color.

1.

Green	Orange 	Blue 
𝍸 I		

Name ______________________

Independent Practice

Use the tally chart from Guided Practice to answer each question.

2. Which color sock has the most tally marks?

______

3. How many blue socks are there?

______

4. How many socks are there in all?

______

Use the tally chart below to answer each question.

Saul's Closet

Shirts	Shorts	Shoes
𝍸 II	IIII	II

5. How many shorts does Saul have?

______

6. Which item in his closet does Saul have the most of?

______

7. Math and Science Rita recorded data about different types of shoes. She made a tally mark each month for each shoe until that type of shoe wore out. Which type of shoe lasted the longest? How many months before it wore out?

Rita's Shoes

Sneakers	Sandals	Loafers
IIII	II	𝍸

______

Problem Solving Use the picture to solve each problem below.

8. Model Draw tally marks to show how many hats there are of each color.

Blue	Green	Purple

9. Be Precise How do you know that purple caps are shown the least?

Think about the definition of *least*.

10. Higher Order Thinking Write and answer your own question about the tally chart used in Items 8 and 9.

11. Assessment Which sentences are true? Choose all that apply.

- ☐ There are 12 blue caps.
- ☐ There are 7 green caps.
- ☐ There are 3 purple caps.
- ☐ There are 12 caps in all.

Name ______________________________

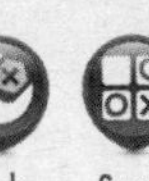

Homework & Practice 6-1

Organize Data into Three Categories

Another Look! You can make tally marks to show information.
The tally chart shows the ways students get to school.

Getting to School

Walk	School Bus
卌 II	卌 卌

I equals 1 and 卌 equals 5.

To count the students that walk, count 5, 6, 7.
7 students walk to school.

__7__ students walk.

To count the students that ride the bus, count 5, 10.
10 students ride the bus.

__10__ students ride the bus.

__17__ students in all go to school.

HOME ACTIVITY Have your child explain the chart at the left in his or her own words. Be sure your child understands that each single tally represents 1 and that 4 single tally marks with 1 diagonal tally mark on top represents 5.

Use the tally chart to answer each question.

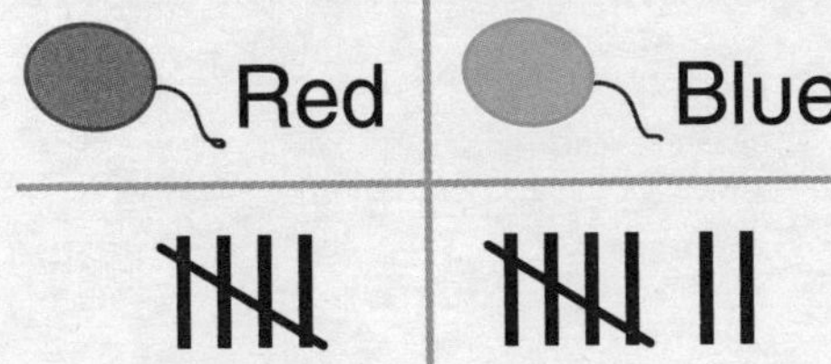

Balloons

Red	Blue
卌	卌 II

1. Which color balloon has the most tally marks?

____

2. How many balloons are there in all?

______

A first grade class voted on their favorite colors. Answer each question about the tally chart.

Favorite Colors

Blue	Red	Green
𝍸 II	III	𝍸 I

3. How many students like red?

_____

4. How many students like green?

_____

5. How many students voted in all?

_____

6. **Higher Order Thinking** Write and answer another question about the tally chart shown above.

7. **Assessment** Which sentences are true? Choose all that apply.

- ☐ 3 students like green.
- ☐ 7 students like blue.
- ☐ The colors blue and green have the same number of votes.
- ☐ Red has the least votes.

Name ____________________

Lesson 6-2
Collect and Represent Data

I can ...
collect information and organize it using a picture graph.

Content Standards 1.DA.1, 1.CA.2, 1.CA.4
Process Standards PS.2, PS.3, PS.4, PS.6

Solve & Share

What is your favorite activity to do outside?

Ask several classmates to choose Jump Rope, Basketball, or Ride a Bike. Complete the tally chart to show your data. Then answer the questions.

Favorite Outside Activity	
Jump Rope	
Basketball	
Ride a Bike	

1. Which activity has the least votes? ____________

2. Which activity has the most votes? ____________

Joey asks 9 friends a survey question.

Which is your favorite sport to play? Basketball, soccer, or baseball?

Joey makes 1 tally mark to show what each friend says.

Favorite Sport	
Basketball	III
Soccer	𝍸
Baseball	I

Joey uses the data in the tally chart to make a **picture graph**.

Favorite Sport						
Basketball						
Soccer						
Baseball						

Look at the pictures! Students like Soccer the most.

Do You Understand?

Show Me! Look at the **Favorite Sport** picture graph above. What sport do Joey's friends like least? How do you know?

☆ Guided Practice ☆

Kurt asks his friends a survey question. Use the data he collected to make a picture graph.

1.

Favorite Fruit		
Pear	Banana	Apple
𝍸 III	III	𝍸

Favorite Fruit									
Pear									
Banana									
Apple									

Name ________________________________

Independent Practice Use the data in the tally chart to make a picture graph. Then answer each question.

2. **Favorite Rainy Day Activity**

Games	Paint	Read
𝍸 II	III	𝍸 I

Favorite Rainy Day Activity						
Games						
Paint						
Read						

3. Which activity is the favorite?

____

4. How many students chose Read?

____

5. **Higher Order Thinking** Look at the picture graph you made for Item 2. Write two sentences that are true about the data.

____

____

____

Problem Solving Use the data in the tally chart to solve each problem below.

6. **Model** Gina asks her friends a survey question. Then she makes a tally chart to show their favorite music instrument. Use her data to make a picture graph.

Favorite Music Instrument

Guitar	Drum	Flute
𝍸	|||	||||

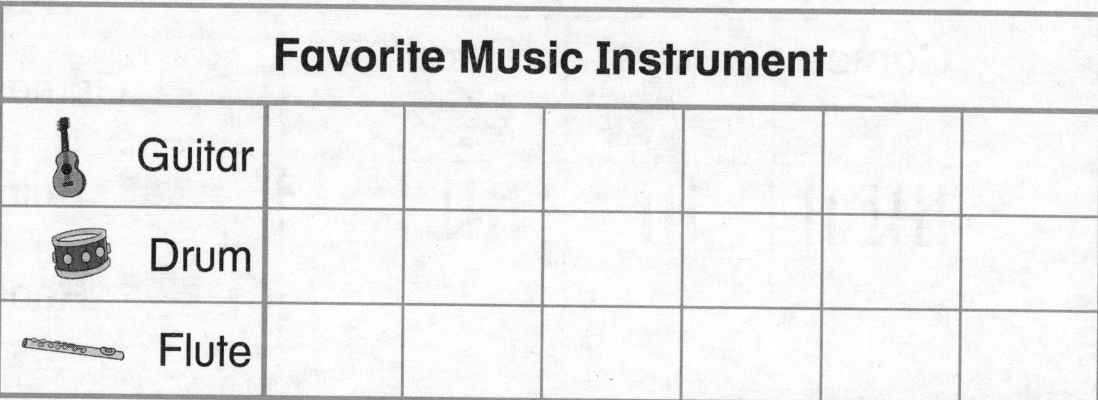

7. **Higher Order Thinking** How many students voted in all? ____

Write an equation to show your answer.

____ = ____ + ____ + ____

8. **Assessment** Which musical instrument has the most votes?

Ⓐ Guitar

Ⓑ Piano

Ⓒ Flute

Ⓓ Drum

9. **Assessment** How many students like the flute?

5	4	3	2
Ⓐ	Ⓑ	Ⓒ	Ⓓ

Name ________________________

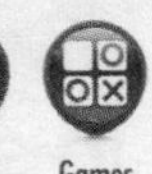

Homework & Practice 6-2

Collect and Represent Data

Another Look! The data in a tally chart can be used to complete the picture graph.

Favorite Items to Collect

Shells	Stamps	Coins
III	~~IIII~~ I	IIII

Favorite Items to Collect

Shells	🐚	🐚	🐚			
 Stamps	☐	☐	☐	☐	☐	☐
Coins	○	○	○	○		

The graph shows that most students like to collect stamps.

How many students like to collect coins? 4

HOME ACTIVITY Make a tally chart titled Favorite Fruit. Show 4 tally marks next to Apples, 6 tally marks next to Bananas, and 3 tally marks next to Cherries. Have your child make a picture graph to illustrate the data. Then ask him or her questions about the information in the picture graph such as, "Which fruit is the least favorite?"

1. Write the items in order from the favorite item to the least favorite item.

________ ________ ________

favorite   least favorite

2. The graph shows that ____ students in all like to collect shells, stamps, or coins.

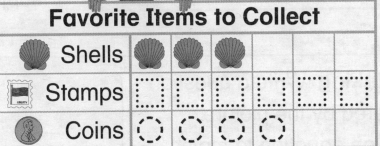

Use the picture graph to solve each problem below.

3. How many students voted for reading as their favorite subject? _____

4. Which is the favorite school subject? _____

5. **Higher Order Thinking** Write a question that can be answered by the picture graph. Then write an equation to match your question.

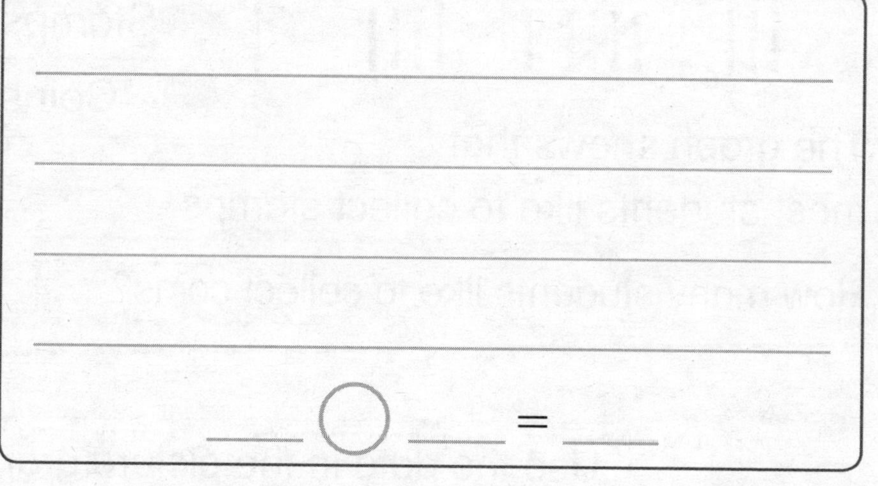

6. **Assessment** How many students voted for Science?

Ⓐ 5 Ⓑ 6 Ⓒ 7 Ⓓ 13

7. **Assessment** How many students voted in all?

Ⓐ 18 Ⓑ 17 Ⓒ 12 Ⓓ 11

Name ______________________________

Solve & Share

Solve

Lesson 6-3
Interpret Data

I can ...
interpret organized data.

I can also make sense of problems.

12 students were asked, "Which vegetable do you like most at lunch, corn or peas?"
This list shows their answers.
Complete the tally chart and picture graph to show the data. What do these data tell you about what students like?

Favorite Lunchtime Vegetable	
Corn	
Peas	

Favorite Lunchtime Vegetable									
Corn									
Peas									

The picture graph shows how many students like milk, water, or juice with lunch.

What does the graph tell you about what students like to drink at lunch?

Lunch Drinks						
Milk	milk	milk	milk	milk	milk	milk
Water	water					
Juice	juice	juice	juice			

I can count and compare what drinks students like.

6 students like milk.
3 students like juice.
Only 1 student likes water.

So, the graph tells me that students like milk better than juice or water with lunch.

Do You Understand?

Show Me! What other information do you know about what students like to drink at lunch?

☆ **Guided Practice** ☆ Use the picture graph above to answer the questions.

1. How many more students like milk than juice?

3 more students

2. How many fewer students like water than milk?

____ fewer students

3. How many more students like juice than water?

____ more students

Name ____

Tools Assessment

Independent Practice

Use the data in the tally chart to answer each question.

4. Use the data in the tally to make a picture graph.

Our Favorite Colors

Red	Blue	Purple
IIII	卌 II	卌 III

Our Favorite Colors

5. How many more students like purple than red?

_____ more students

6. Which color is the favorite?

_____

7. Algebra Use this equation to determine how many fewer students like blue than purple.

_____ + 7 = 8

_____ fewer

8. Higher Order Thinking Write and answer a question about the data in the picture graph.

____

____

Problem Solving Solve each problem below.

9. Look at the tally chart.

Our Pets

Dogs	Cats	Fish
卌 I	III	II

How many friends have dogs for pets? _____

How many friends have fish for pets? _____

10. Be Precise Look at the picture graph.

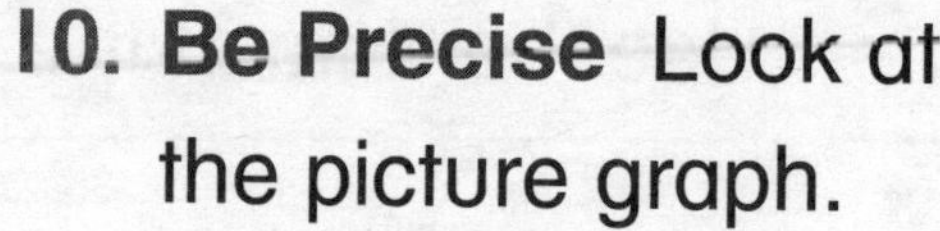

How many more friends have dogs than fish? _____

How many fewer friends have cats than dogs? _____

Think about the meaning of *more* and *fewer*.

Our Pets

Dogs	Cats	Fish

11. Higher Order Thinking Look at the tally chart in Item 9. How many friends have pets? Write an equation to show your work.

____

____

____

12. Assessment Which question **CANNOT** be answered by looking at the graph in Item 10?

Ⓐ How many friends have cats?

Ⓑ How many friends have hamsters?

Ⓒ How many fewer friends have fish than dogs?

Ⓓ How many more friends have dogs than cats?

Name ____________________

Help
Tools
Games

Homework & Practice 6-3
Interpret Data

HOME ACTIVITY Draw a 2-column picture graph. Label one column "Heads" and the other column "Tails." Then have your child flip a penny. Have him or her record 10 flips in the picture graph. Talk about the results.

Another Look! Ms. Olson asked her students a survey question. She put tally marks in the tally chart to show the data.

Use the data in the tally chart to complete the picture graph.

Stickers We Like

Moon	Flower	Star
II	~~IIII~~ II	~~IIII~~ I

Stickers We Like

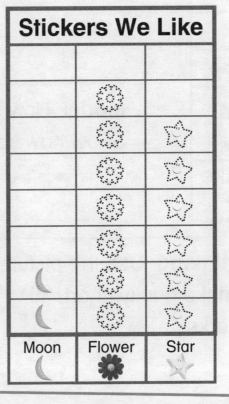

Moon	Flower	Star
	✿	
	✿	☆
	✿	☆
	✿	☆
	✿	☆
☾	✿	☆
☾	✿	☆

Picture graphs can show the data in a different way.

Use the data in the picture graph to answer each question.

1. Which sticker is the least favorite?

____

2. Write the stickers in order from favorite to least favorite.

__________ __________ __________
favorite least favorite

3. How many more students like the star than the moon?

____

Use the picture graph to answer each question.

What We Like to Do on a Trip		
Swim	Hike	Bike

4. **Model** How many fewer people like to ride a bike than swim? Show how you added or subtracted to find the answer.

5. **Model** How many more people like to swim than hike? Show how you added or subtracted to find the answer.

____ ◯ ____ = ____

6. **Higher Order Thinking** Use the picture graph above to make a tally chart. Show the tally marks.

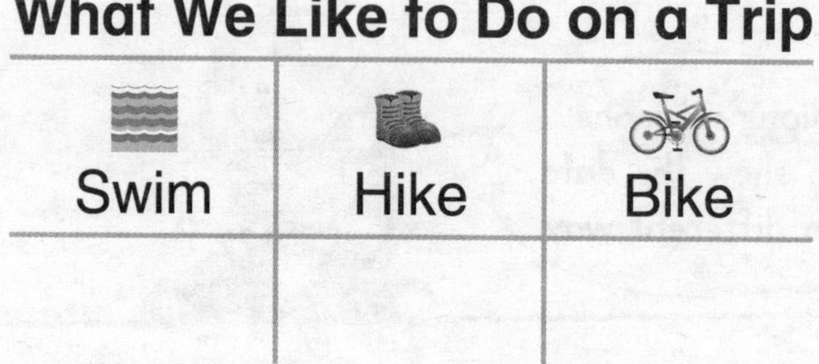

What We Like to Do on a Trip		
Swim	Hike	Bike

7. **Assessment** Which question **CANNOT** be answered by looking at the picture graph from Items 4 and 5?

Ⓐ How many more people like to swim than ride a bike?

Ⓑ How many people like to dance?

Ⓒ How many fewer people like to hike than ride a bike?

Ⓓ How many people voted?

Name ____________________

Solve

Lesson 6-4
Continue to Interpret Data

I can ...
use a picture graph to interpret data.

Content Standards 1.DA.1, 1.CA.2
Process Standards PS.2, PS.5, PS.7

Solve & Share

At the park, Susan sees 13 animals in all. 9 are birds. The rest are rabbits. How can Susan complete the table to show this? Show your work.

Birds	Rabbits

Abby asks 15 students if they like broccoli or carrots better. 6 choose broccoli. The rest choose carrots. How many chose carrots?

Use a tally chart to find the missing data.

Broccoli	Carrots
𝍸 |	𝍸 ||||

6 choose broccoli. I can count up to 15 to find how many chose carrots.

You can also write an equation to show the problem.

$15 - 6 = \underline{9}$

How many more students chose carrots than broccoli? Write an equation to compare.

$9 - 6 = \underline{3}$

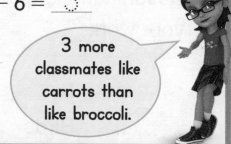

3 more classmates like carrots than like broccoli.

Do You Understand?

Show Me! How did Abby know to count up from 6 to 15 in the problem above?

Guided Practice

Draw the missing symbols in the picture graph. Then use the graph to solve the problem.

1.

Favorite Fruit							
Apple	🍎	🍎	🍎				
Orange	🍊	🍊	🍊	🍊	🍊	🍊	

Jim asks 9 members of his family for their favorite fruit.

6 people say they like oranges. The rest say they like apples.

How many people say they like apples? ____ people

Name ______________________________

Tools Assessment

Independent Practice Use the graphs to answer the questions. Fill in the missing data.

2. A shelf at a store holds 11 stuffed animals. There are 5 stuffed bears and the rest are stuffed penguins.

How many stuffed penguins are on the shelf?

Sylvie's Stuffed Animals								
Bears	🧸	🧸	🧸	🧸	🧸			
Penguins								

____ stuffed penguins

3. Zach plays 17 games in a season. 9 of the games are soccer games and the rest are baseball.

How many baseball games does Zach play in one season?

Zach's Games									
Baseball									
Soccer	⚽	⚽	⚽	⚽	⚽	⚽	⚽	⚽	⚽

____ baseball games

4. Number Sense Jen's class makes a graph about two of their favorite kinds of movies.

How many students took the survey?

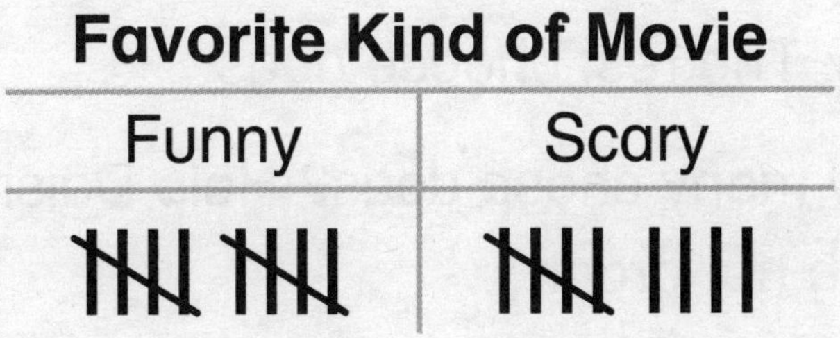

____ students

Favorite Kind of Movie

Funny	Scary
𝍸 𝍸	𝍸 IIII

Problem Solving Use the graphs and charts to answer the questions. Fill in the missing data.

5. **Reasoning** Jaime makes a weather graph. He records the weather each day. How many days has Jaime recorded the weather?

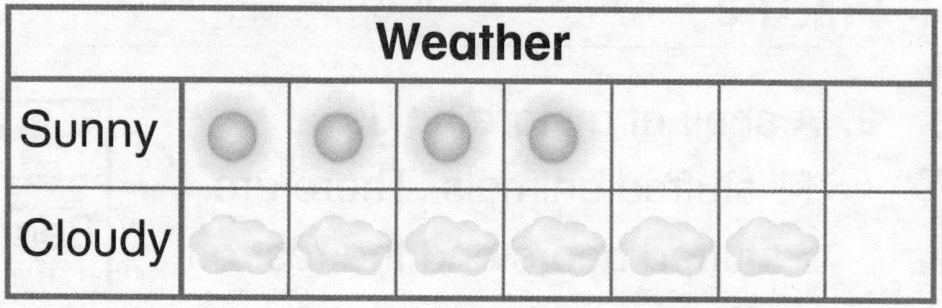

____ days

Weather							
Sunny	☀	☀	☀	☀			
Cloudy	☁	☁	☁	☁	☁	☁	

6. **Higher Order Thinking** Ryan asks 20 students which subject is their favorite. He forgot to record responses for the students that chose Science.

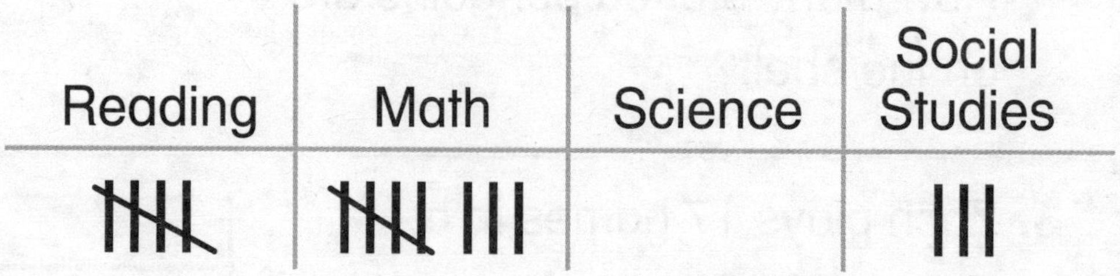

Reading	Math	Science	Social Studies
~~IIII~~	~~IIII~~ III		III

Draw the missing tally marks. Explain how you know you drew the right number.

7. **Assessment** Daisi asks 9 students if they like cats or dogs better. 4 choose cats. The rest choose dogs.

How many chose dogs? Help Daisi finish her graph.

____ students

Favorite Animal							
Cat	🐱	🐱	🐱	🐱			
Dog	🐶	🐶	🐶				

Name ______________________________

Homework & Practice 6-4
Continue to Interpret Data

Another Look! You can use a picture graph to solve problems.

Adam asks 13 friends whether they like butter or jelly on their toast.

How many students' responses does he have left to record?

How Do You Like Your Toast?							
Butter	🧈	🧈	🧈				
Jelly	🫙	🫙	🫙	🫙	🫙		

There are 8 pictures on the graph.
If I start at 8, I need to count up 5 more to get to 13.

13 − 8 = <u>5</u> responses

HOME ACTIVITY Create a tally chart to record data about some items in your home. Ask your child to make a picture graph to represent the data in your scenario. Ask your child, "Which category has the most responses? How many in all?" Then ask your child to come up with a different scenario for recording data.

Fill in the missing tally marks. Then use the chart to solve the problem.

1. Maggie asks 12 members of her family for their favorite kind of cereal. 4 people say they like Corny Cones. The rest say they like Great Granola.

   How many people said they liked Great Granola?

   _____ people

Corny Cones	Great Granola
IIII	

Use the data to solve the problems.

2. Lindsay asks her friends whether they like Recess or Gym more.

How many friends took the survey? ____ friends

Recess	Gym
卌 卌	卌 II

---

3. **Higher Order Thinking** Write a problem that can be solved using this picture graph.

____

____

Flowers in the Garden							
Roses	🌹	🌹	🌹	🌹	🌹		
Daisies	🌼	🌼	🌼	🌼	🌼	🌼	🌼

---

4. ✔ **Assessment** Miguel asks 16 friends to come to his birthday party. He makes a graph to show who is coming and who is not.

How many of Miguel's friends have not responded yet? Write an equation to solve.

____ ◯ ____ ◯ ____ ____ friends

Birthday Party													
Coming	☺	☺	☺	☺	☺	☺							
Not Coming	☹	☹	☹										

Name ____________________

Solve

Problem Solving

Lesson 6-5
Make Sense and Persevere

I can ... persevere to solve problems about sets of data.

I can also add and subtract using data.

Solve & Share

Kelly asks 12 students if they like using pens, markers, or pencils best. The tally chart shows their responses.

How many students would need to change their vote from markers to pencils to make pencils the favorite? Complete the new chart to explain.

Pens	Markers	Pencils
III	~~IIII~~ II	II

Pens	Markers	Pencils

_____ students need to change to pencils.

Thinking Habits

What do I need to find?

What do I know?

Sarah asks 15 people if they like football or baseball. 1 more person chose football than chose baseball.

How many people chose each sport? What would the tally chart look like?

What's my plan for solving this problem?

I can...
- think about what I know.
- think about what I need to find.

Think of all the addition facts you know that add to 15.

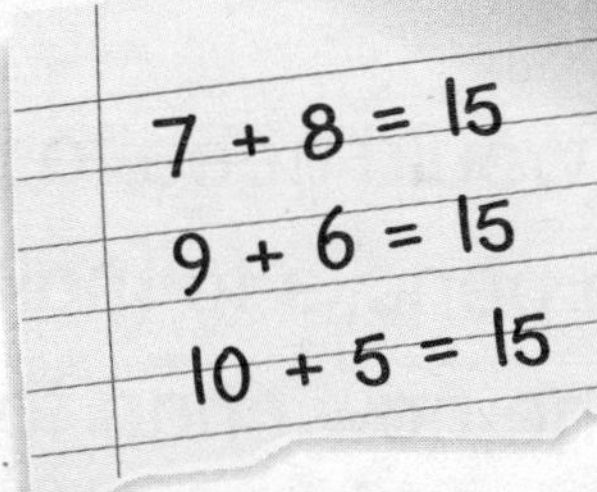

7 and 8 add to 15 and 8 is 1 more than 7.

So, 8 people chose football and 7 people chose baseball.

Favorite Sport

Baseball	Football
卌 II	卌 III

Do You Understand?

Show Me! For the survey above, why couldn't 9 choose football and 6 choose baseball?

Guided Practice

Use the tally chart to answer the questions.

1. 3 more students take the survey. Now, football and baseball have the same number of votes.

How many votes does each have? Use pictures, words, or equations to explain.

Favorite Sport

Baseball	Football

Tools
Assessment

Name ______________________________

Independent Practice

Use the chart and graph to solve the problems below.

Linzie asks 18 students if they like milk, water, or juice with lunch. 7 students like milk. 3 students like water. The rest of the students like juice.

Lunch Drinks

Milk	Water	Juice
𝍸 II	III	

2. How many students like juice? Complete Linzie's tally chart to solve.

____ students like juice.

3. What is the favorite drink?

____

4. The next day Linzie asks the same question again. 3 students change their response from juice to water. What is the favorite drink now?

____

5. **Vocabulary** Linzie records her new **survey** results in the picture graph below.

Complete the graph to show how many students like juice.

Lunch Drinks

Milk	🥛	🥛	🥛	🥛	🥛	🥛	🥛	
Water	💧	💧	💧	💧	💧	💧		
Juice								

Draw pictures to show the data!

Performance Assessment

Going to School

Ebony asks 14 classmates if they take the bus, walk, or ride in a car to school.

4 students ride in a car. The remaining students vote equally for taking the bus or walking to school.

Going to School

Bus	Walk	Ride
		IIII

6. **Make Sense** How can you find out how many students take the bus or walk to school?

____

____

____

____

7. **Model** Complete the tally chart to show how Ebony's classmates voted. Write an equation to show how many walk and take the bus.

___ ◯ ___ ◯ ___

8. **Explain** How do you know your answers are correct? Use pictures, words, or equations to explain.

____

____

____

Name ____________________

Homework & Practice 6-5

Make Sense and Persevere

Another Look! 9 students answer a survey about their favorite pet. 4 students vote for dog. 3 students vote for fish. The rest of the students vote for cat. How many students vote for cat? Complete the picture graph to show the results of the survey.

Favorite Pet						
Dog	🐕	🐕	🐕	🐕		
Fish	🐟	🐟	🐟			
Cat	🐈	🐈				

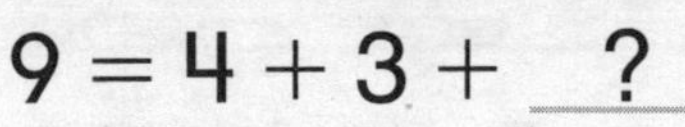

$9 = 4 + 3 + \underline{?}$

$9 = 7 + \underline{2}$

HOME ACTIVITY Along with your child, think of a survey question to ask friends or family members. For instance, "Do you prefer grapes, bananas, or pineapples?" Record the results of your survey in a tally chart. Think of some questions about the data, such as, "How many more people chose bananas than grapes?" Have your child write an equation to solve the problem.

Use the picture graph above to answer the question.

1. 4 more students take the survey. Now cat has the most votes and fish has the fewest votes. Use pictures, words, or equations to explain how the 4 students voted.

____

Performance Assessment

Snack Time

Phil asks friends to choose their favorite snack.

The tally chart at the right shows the results.

Favorite Snack

Pretzels	Yogurt
	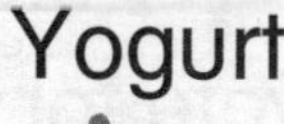 

2. **Reasoning** Which snack is the favorite? How many more friends chose that snack?

____

____

3. **Model** How many of Phil's friends answered the survey? Write an equation to show your thinking.

____

____

4. **Make Sense** Phil adds grapes as a third choice in his survey. He asks the same friends to answer the survey again. The new survey results are shown in the tally chart at the right. How did the votes change? Use pictures, words, or equations to explain.

Favorite Snack

Pretzels	Yogurt	Grapes

III	~~IIII~~ I	

____

____

Name ______________________________

Fluency Practice Activity

I can ...
add and subtract within 10.

Find a partner. Point to a clue. Read the clue. Look below the clues to find a match. Write the clue letter in the box next to the match. Find a match for every clue.

Clues

A 4 + 6	**E** 8 + 1
B 8 − 2	**F** 3 + 4
C 3 − 1	**G** 8 − 7
D 10 − 5	**H** 1 + 3

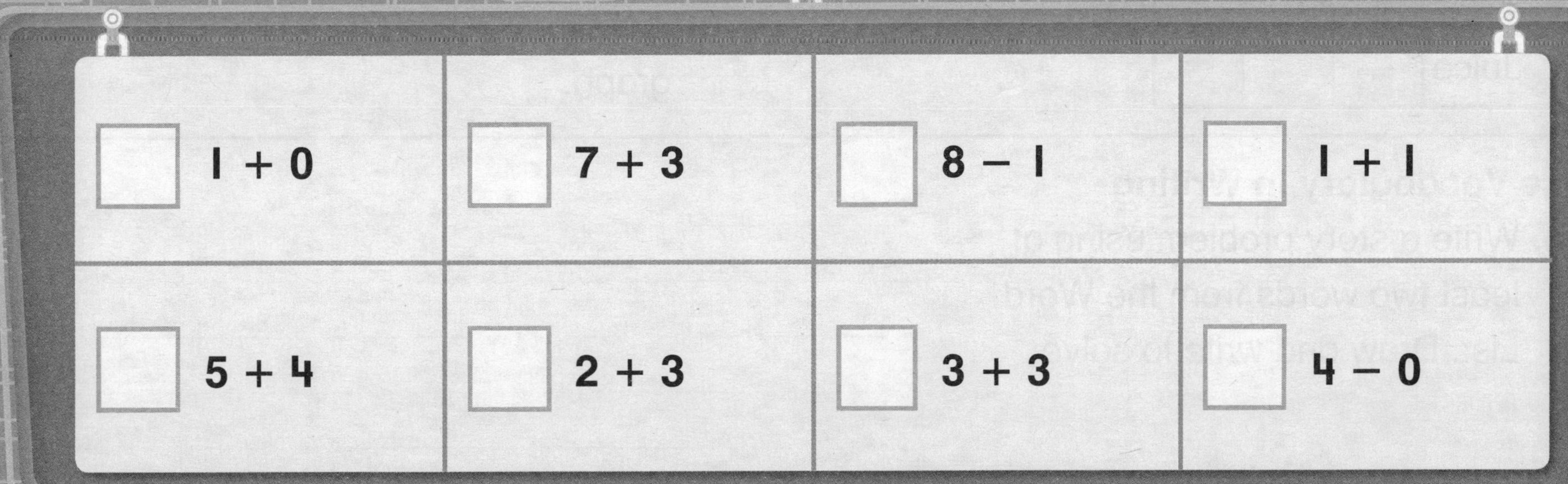

☐ 1 + 0	☐ 7 + 3	☐ 8 − 1	☐ 1 + 1
☐ 5 + 4	☐ 2 + 3	☐ 3 + 3	☐ 4 − 0

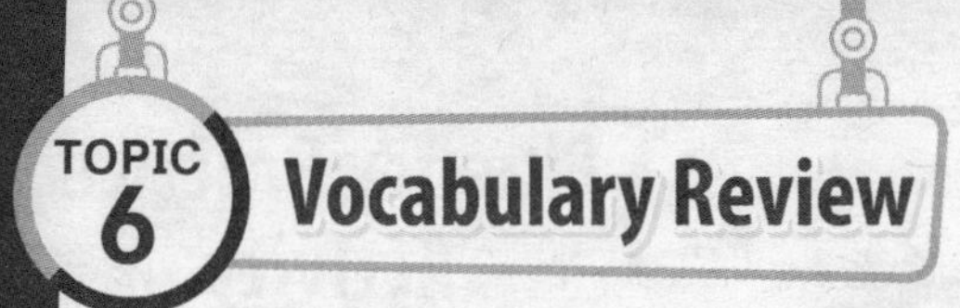

Word List
- data
- picture graph
- survey
- tally chart
- tally marks

Understand Vocabulary

Circle the correct answer for each question using the image at the left.

Blue	Red	Green
IIII	III	~~IIII~~

1. Green shows ____ tally marks.

   3 4 5 6

2. The picture is called a ________.

   picture graph tally chart survey tally mark

Fill in the blanks using words from the Word List.

Favorite Drinks			
Milk			
Juice			

3. This graph is called a ________ ________.

4. "What is your favorite drink?" could be the ________ question for this graph.

5. You can use the ________ to answer questions about the graph.

Use Vocabulary in Writing

6. Write a story problem using at least two words from the Word List. Draw and write to solve.

Name ____________________

Set A

TOPIC 6

Reteaching

You can collect and sort data into a table.

Jimmy asks 10 friends what meal takes the longest to eat.

Longest Meal

Breakfast	Lunch	Dinner
III	I	~~IIII~~ I

Each I is one friend's answer.

The graph shows Jimmy's data using objects.

Longest Meal						
Breakfast	■	■	■			
Lunch	■					
Dinner	■	■	■	■	■	■

Each ■ is one friend's answer.

6 friends said dinner was their longest meal.

Use the data from Jimmy's survey to solve each problem.

1. How many friends said dinner was their longest meal?

____ friends

2. How many friends said breakfast or dinner was their longest meal?

____ friends

Write an equation to answer each question.

3. How many more friends chose breakfast than lunch?

____ − ____ = ____ ____ more

4. How many more chose dinner than breakfast?

____ − ____ = ____ ____ more

Set B

You can use data in a picture graph to ask and answer questions.

Mari asks 16 of her friends for their favorite activity. She records their answers in a graph.

Favorite Activity							
Soccer	⚽	⚽	⚽	⚽			
Tennis	🎾	🎾	🎾	🎾	🎾	🎾	🎾
Running	👟	👟	👟	👟	👟		

Thinking Habits

Make Sense and Persevere

What are the amounts?

What am I trying to find?

Use Mari's picture graph to answer each question.

5. How many people chose soccer or running?

____ − ____ = ____ OR ____ + ____ = ____

6. Mari asks some more friends and they all chose tennis as their favorite activity.

Now the number of students who like tennis is the same as the number of students who like soccer or running.

How many more friends did Mari ask?

____ more

Explain how you know.

____

____

____

____

Name ______________________________

1. Which set of tally marks shows the number of hats in the picture graph?

Hat	🧢	🧢	🧢	🧢
Mitt	🧤	🧤		

Ⓐ ||

Ⓑ ||||

Ⓒ 𝍸

Ⓓ 𝍸 |

---

2. Look at the picture graph in Item 1. How many fewer mitts than hats are there?

Ⓐ 4

Ⓑ 3

Ⓒ 2

Ⓓ 1

---

3. Use the picture graph to answer the question.

Which of the following statements are true? Choose all that apply.

Zoo Animals					
Penguin	🐧	🐧	🐧	🐧	🐧
Bear	🐻	🐻	🐻		

☐ There are 2 more penguins than bears.

☐ There are 2 fewer bears than penguins.

☐ There are more bears than penguins.

☐ There are 8 bears and penguins.

Use the tally chart to solve each problem below.

4. **Favorite Winter Activity**

Skating	卌
Skiing	|||
Sledding	卌 ||

Kyla asks her friends a survey question. Which is their favorite winter activity?

____

5. Use the tally chart from Item 4 to complete the picture graph below.

Favorite Winter Activity							
Skating							
Skiing							
Sledding							

6. How many students took the survey? Write an equation to show your work.

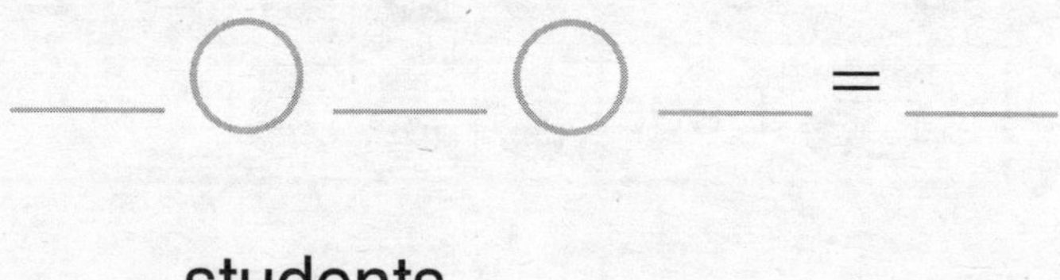

____ students

7. More students take the survey. Skiing is now the favorite activity. What is the fewest number of votes needed for this to happen? Explain.

____

____

____

Name ______________________________

Dinosaur Project Mrs. Johnson's class is doing a dinosaur project. The tally chart shows which dinosaurs the students chose.

Dinosaur Project

Triceratops	T-Rex	Apatosaurus
𝍸 ||||	𝍸 𝍸 ||	𝍸 ||

1. How many more students chose T-Rex than Triceratops? Explain how you know. Use pictures, numbers, or words.

_____ more students

2. Two students were absent when the class made the tally chart. They chose their dinosaur the next day. Mrs. Johnson said that now two dinosaurs had the same number. Which dinosaur did the 2 students choose? How do you know?

3. Mrs. Bee's class is also doing a dinosaur project. The tally chart shows which dinosaurs the students chose.

The students will draw their dinosaurs on the picture graph below when they finish their reports.

Fill in the picture graph to show what it will look like when all the reports are finished.

Dinosaur Project

Triceratops	T-Rex	Apatosaurus
~~||||~~ |||	~~||||~~ ||||	~~||||~~ |

4. How many students still need to finish a report on the T-Rex? How many need to finish a report on the Apatosaurus? Use pictures, words, or equations to explain.

TOPIC 7 Extend the Counting Sequence

Essential Question: How can you use what you already know about counting to count past 100?

All babies do different things to help themselves survive.

They might cry or make noise to let their parents know that they need something.

Wow! Let's do this project and learn more.

Math and Science Project: Parents and Babies

Find Out Talk to friends and relatives about different types of animal parents and babies. Ask for help finding information about how babies communicate with their parents.

Journal: Make a Book Show what you found out. In your book, also:

- Draw how animal parents protect babies and how animal babies communicate with parents.
- Go outside or to the zoo and count animal parents and babies. How high can you count?

Name ______________________

Review What You Know

Vocabulary

1. Circle the number that is the **sum** in the equation.

17 = 9 + 8

2. Write the **parts** shown in the model.

8

___ + ___

3. Circle the word that tells which part is missing.

7 + __?__ = 17

sum

equals

addend

Find the Sum

4. Margie finds 7 rocks. Kara finds 6 rocks. How many rocks did they find in all?

_____ rocks

5. Tom has 6 toy cars. Jane has some toy cars. They have 11 toy cars in all. How many toy cars does Jane have?

_____ toy cars

The Missing Number

6. Find the missing number to solve this addition fact.

_____ = 10 + 5

A-Z Glossary

My Word Cards

Study the words on the front of the card. Complete the activity on the back.

hundred chart

1	2	3	4	5	6	7	8	9	10
11	12	13	14	15	16	17	18	19	20
21	22	23	24	25	26	27	28	29	30
31	32	33	34	35	36	37	38	39	40
41	42	43	44	45	46	47	48	49	50
51	52	53	54	55	56	57	58	59	60
61	62	63	64	65	66	67	68	69	70
71	72	73	74	75	76	77	78	79	80
81	82	83	84	85	86	87	88	89	90
91	92	93	94	95	96	97	98	99	100

tens digit

The **tens digit** in 25 is 2.

row

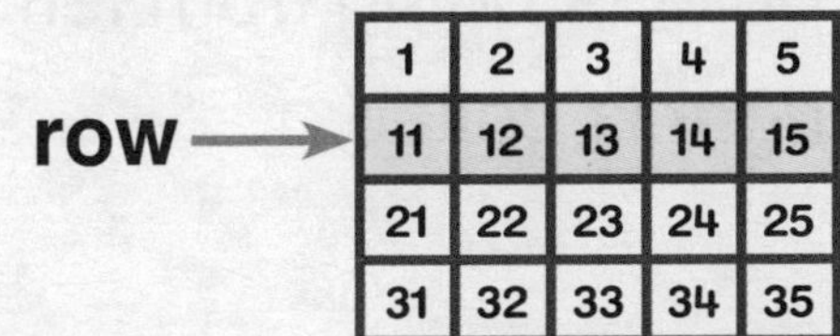

1	2	3	4	5
11	12	13	14	15
21	22	23	24	25
31	32	33	34	35

ones digit

The **ones digit** in 43 is 3.

column

1	2	3	4	5
11	12	13	14	15
21	22	23	24	25
31	32	33	34	35

column

My Word Cards

Use what you know to complete the sentences.
Extend learning by writing your own sentence using each word.

A straight line of numbers or objects going from left to right is called a

_______________.

A number that tells how many tens is called a

____

_______________.

A _______________

____

shows all of the numbers from 1 to 100.

A straight line of numbers or objects going from top to bottom is called a

_______________.

A number that tells how many ones is called a

____

_______________.

Name ______________________

Solve & Share

Lesson 7-1
Count by 10s to 120

I can …
count by 10s to 120.

Content Standards 1.NS.1, 1.NS.2
Process Standards PS.4, PS.7, PS.8

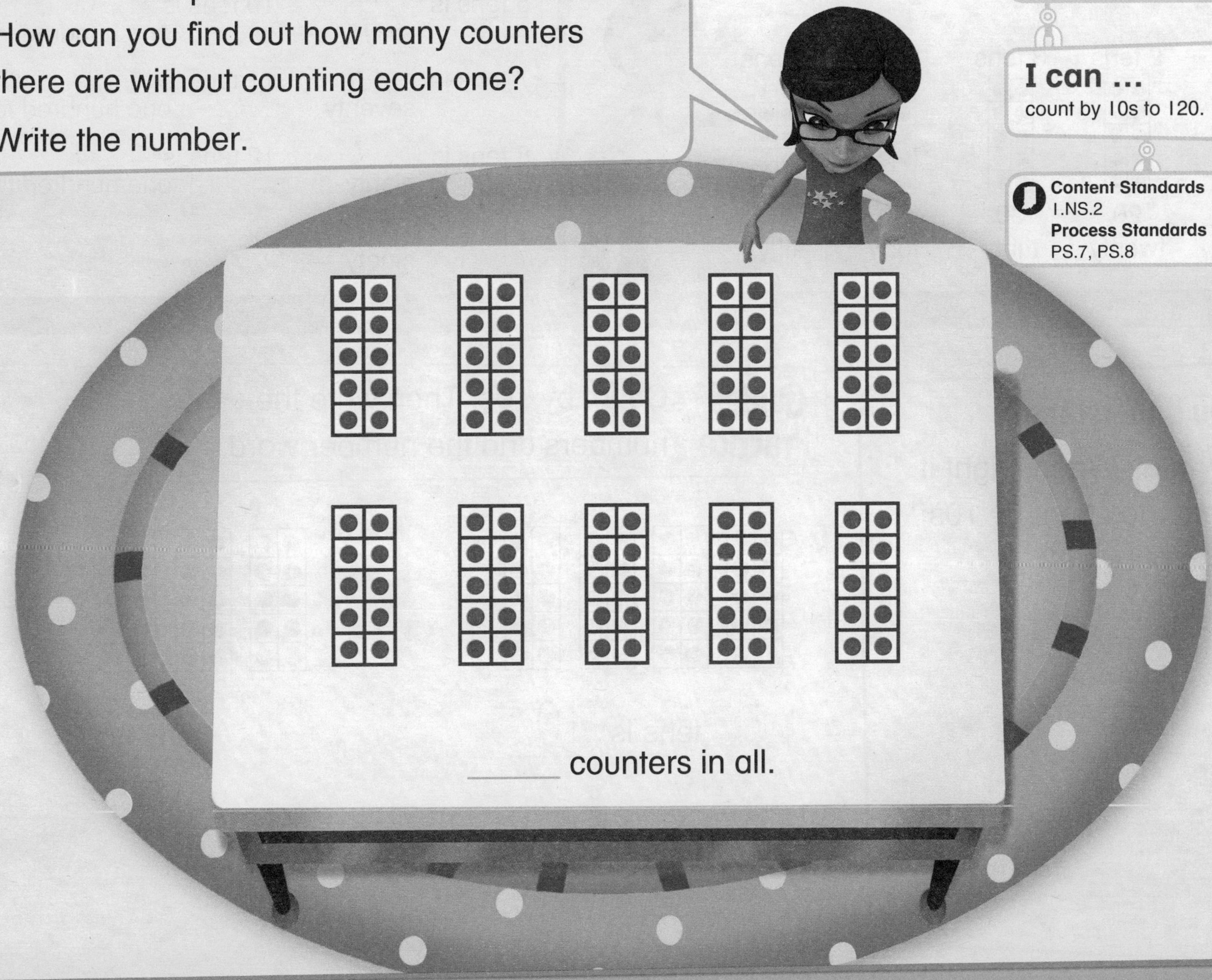

Alex put counters in some ten-frames. How can you find out how many counters there are without counting each one? Write the number.

_____ counters in all.

How can you count to 50 by tens?

I can use ten-frames to count by 10s!

1 ten	2 tens	3 tens	4 tens	5 tens
10	20	30	40	50
ten	twenty	thirty	forty	fifty

You can also follow the pattern to count by 10s.

6 tens is 60 sixty

7 tens is 70 seventy

8 tens is 80 eighty

9 tens is 90 ninety

10 tens is 100 one hundred

11 tens is 110 one hundred ten

12 tens is 120 one hundred twenty

Do You Understand?

Show Me! When might it be better to count by 10s instead of by 1s?

Guided Practice

Count by 10s. Then write the numbers and the number word.

1. 4 tens is 40

forty

2. ____ tens is ____

____

Name ______________________________

Independent Practice

Count by 10s. Write the numbers and the number word.

3. 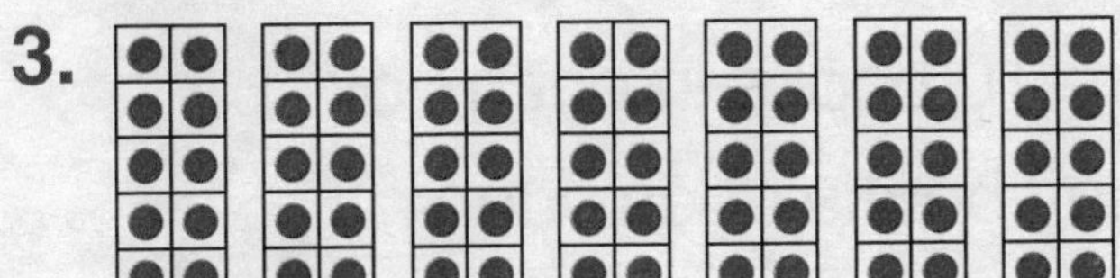

_____ tens is _____

____

4. 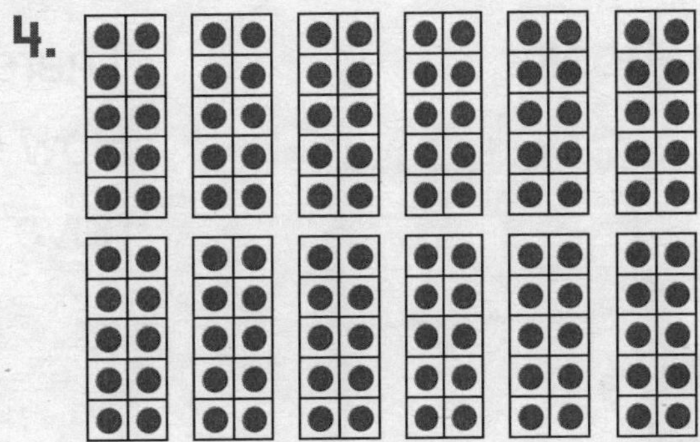

_____ tens is _____

____

5.

_____ tens is _____

____

Write the missing numbers.

6. **Number Sense** Jake wrote a pattern.
He forgot to write some numbers.

What numbers did Jake forget to write?

10, 20, 30, 40, _____, 60, _____, _____, 90, 100, _____, 120

Problem Solving

Draw counters in the ten-frames to solve each problem below. Then write the numbers and the number word.

7. **Model** José has 3 boxes. 10 books are in each box. How many books does José have in all?

_____ tens

_____

____

8. **Model** Juan has 4 boxes. There are 10 books in each box. How many books does Juan have in all?

_____ tens

_____

____

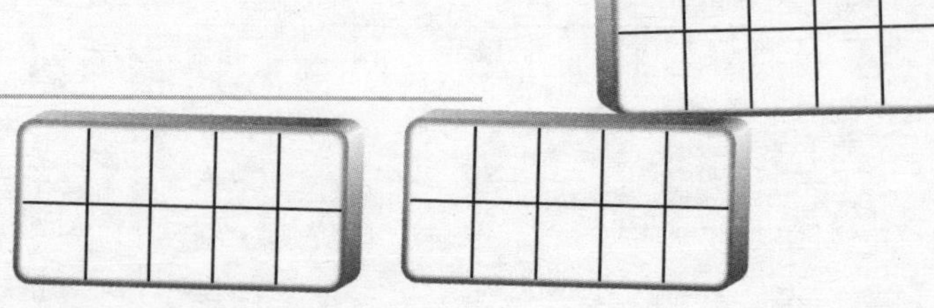

9. **Higher Order Thinking** Dan counts by 5s to 50. Ed counts by 10s to 50. Write the numbers Dan says.

5, _____, _____, _____, _____,

_____, _____, _____, _____, 50

Write the numbers Ed says.

10, _____, _____, _____, 50

What numbers do both boys say?

_____, _____, _____, _____, _____

10. **Assessment** Mary has some books. She puts them in piles of 10 without any left over. Which number does **NOT** show how many books Mary could have?

Ⓐ 50

Ⓑ 60

Ⓒ 65

Ⓓ 70

Name ______________________

Help
Tools
Games

Homework & Practice 7-1
Count by 10s to 120

Another Look! You can use ten-frames to count groups of 10.

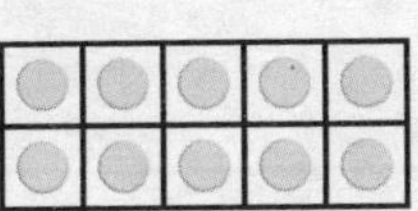

The ten-frame shows 1 group of 10.

HOME ACTIVITY Have your child practice counting by 10s to 120. Then ask questions such as, "How many 10s make 50? What number does 3 groups of 10 make?"

You can count the ten-frames by 10s.

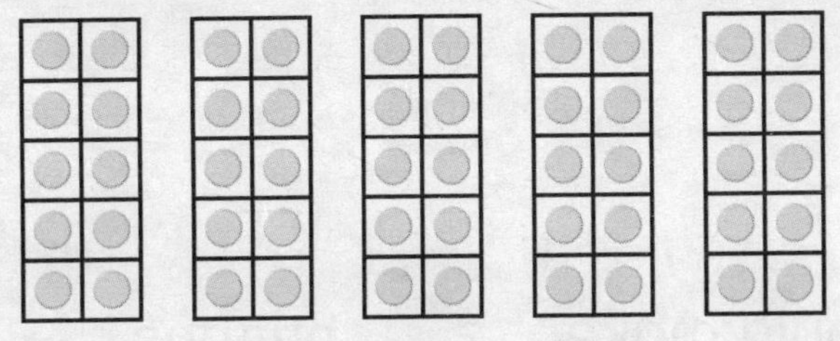

10 20 30 40 50

50 is 5 groups of 10.

50 is fifty.

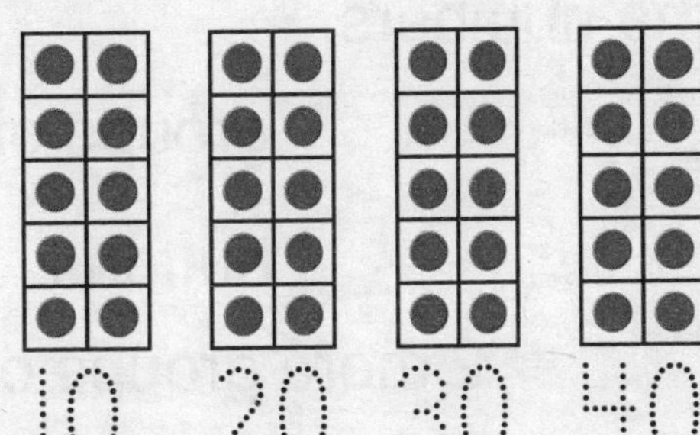

10 20 30 40

40 is 4 groups of 10.

40 is forty.

Count by 10s. Write the numbers and the number word.

1. 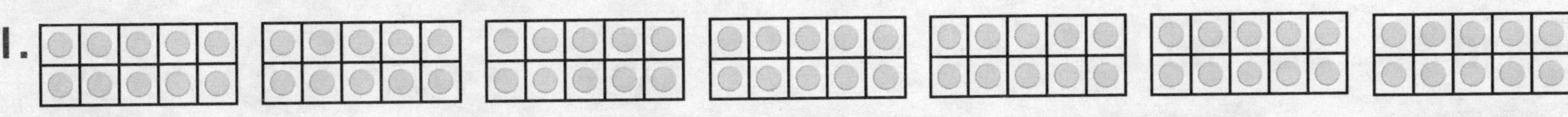

_____ _____ _____ _____ _____ _____ _____

_____ is _____ groups of 10. _____ is _____________.

Count by 10s. Write each missing number.

2. ____, 20, ____, ____, 50, ____

3. 70, ____, 90, ____, ____, ____

4. 50, ____, ____, ____, 90, ____

5. ____, ____, 50, ____, ____, 80

6. **Higher Order Thinking** Circle groups of 10. Then count by 10s and write the numbers.

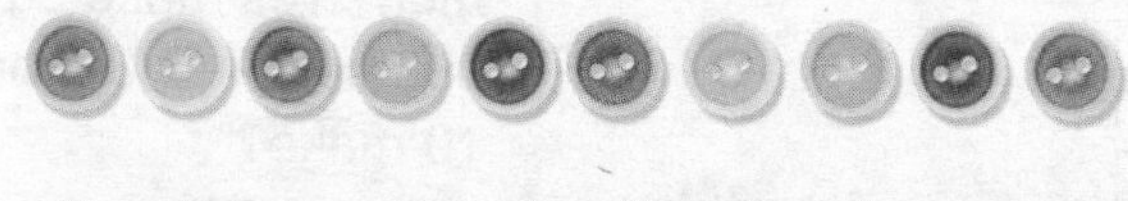

____ groups of 10

____ buttons

2 more groups of 10 would make ____ buttons.

7. **Assessment** Jen buys 2 bags of marbles. Each bag has 10 marbles. How many marbles does Jen buy?

Ⓐ 2 Ⓑ 12 Ⓒ 20 Ⓓ 22

8. **Assessment** Mike has 4 boxes of crayons. Each box has 10 crayons. How many crayons does Mike have?

Ⓐ 4 Ⓑ 10 Ⓒ 14 Ⓓ 40

Name ______________________

Solve & Share

Lesson 7-2
Count by 1s to 120

I can ...
count by 1s to 120.

I can also look for patterns.

Jada and Alex take turns counting by 1s. Jada counts on from 98 to 100. Now, it is Alex's turn to keep counting. Write the next three numbers Alex should count. Tell how you know you are right.

This block shows 100. You say one hundred for this number.

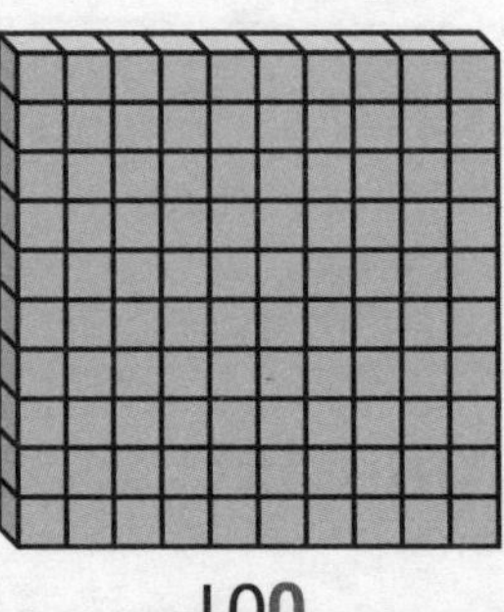

The next number you say is one hundred one because you have 1 hundred and 1 one.

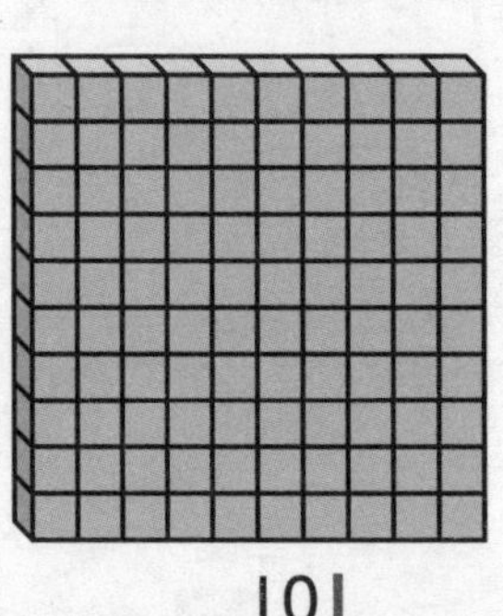

When you count forward, you keep counting by 1s.

101, 102, 103, 104, 105

105 means 1 hundred and 5 ones. You say one hundred five.

When you count higher, you start with the words one hundred.

116, 117, 118, 119, 120

116 is one hundred sixteen.

Do You Understand?

Show Me! How would you say and show 110 when you count? What number comes next?

Guided Practice

Count forward by 1s. Write the numbers.

1. 116, 117, 118, 119, 120

2. ____, 110, ____, ____, 113

3. 104, ____, ____, 107, ____

Name ____________________

Independent Practice

Count forward by 1s. Write the numbers.

4. 110, ____, ____, ____, 114

5. 52, ____, ____, 55, ____

6. ____, 94, ____, 96, ____

7. ____, 102, 103, ____, ____

8. ____, ____, 115, ____, 117

9. 67, ____, ____, ____, 71

Use the clues to find each mystery number.

10. **Number Sense** Clue 1: The number comes after 116. Clue 2: The number comes before 120.
The mystery number might be:

____, ____, ____

Clue 3: The number has 8 ones.
Circle the mystery number.

11. **Number Sense** Clue 1: The number comes before 108. Clue 2: The number comes after 102.
The mystery number might be:

____, ____, ____, ____, ____

Clue 3: The number has 5 ones.
Circle the mystery number.

Problem Solving Solve each problem below.

12. **Vocabulary** Marta is counting to 120. She says the number that is one **more** than 113. What number does she say?

_____

13. In this chart, Tom writes the numbers 102 to 108 in order. Then he spills water on it. Some numbers rub off. Help Tom fill in the missing numbers.

102		104	105			108

14. **Reasoning** Shelly counts 109 bottle caps. Then she counts 4 more. How many bottle caps has Shelley counted?

_____ bottle caps

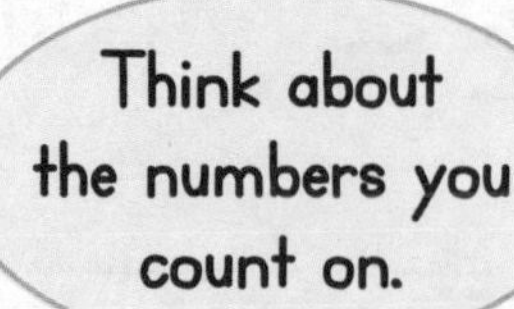
Think about
the numbers you
count on.

15. **Higher Order Thinking** Pick a number greater than 99 and less than 112. Write the number in the box.

Then write the three numbers that come before it and the number that comes after it.

_____, _____, _____, ☐, _____

16. **Assessment** Which shows the correct order for counting forward by 1s? Choose all that apply.

- ☐ 103, 104, 105, 102
- ☐ 117, 118, 119, 120
- ☐ 101, 102, 103, 104
- ☐ 114, 112, 110, 108

Name ______________________

Homework & Practice 7-2

Count by 1s to 120

Another Look! You can use place-value blocks to count forward by 1s.

1 hundred is equal to 10 tens.

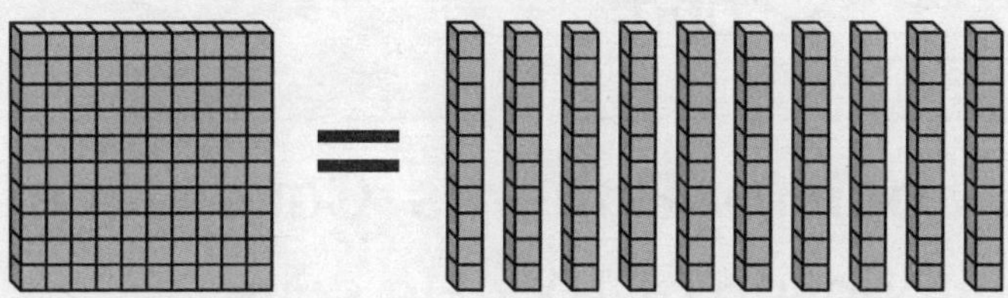
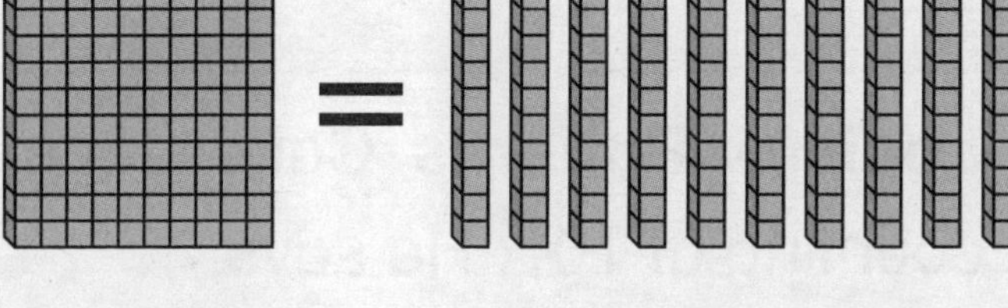

HOME ACTIVITY Say a number between 100 and 105. Have your child count forward by 1s to 120. Repeat with other numbers.

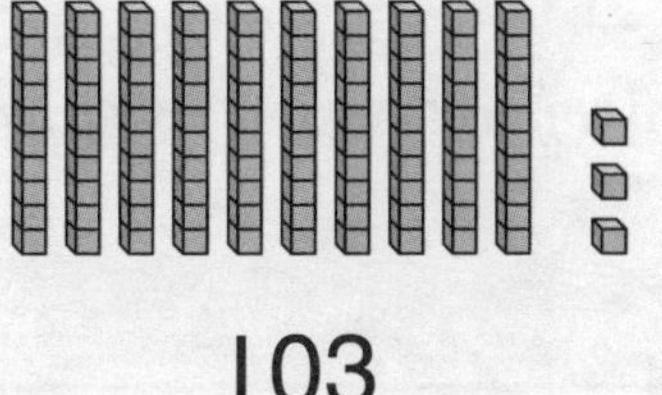
103

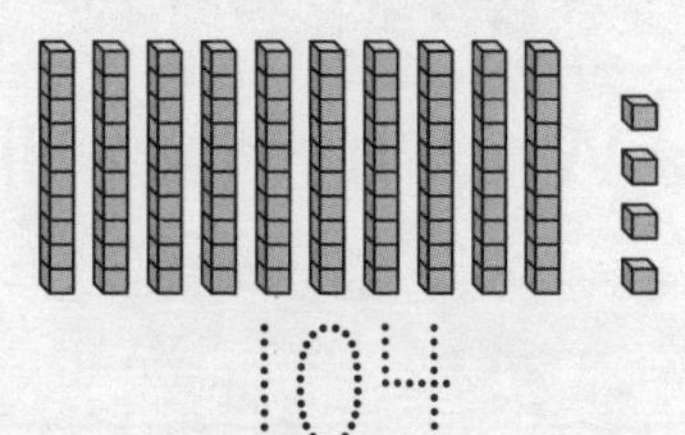
104

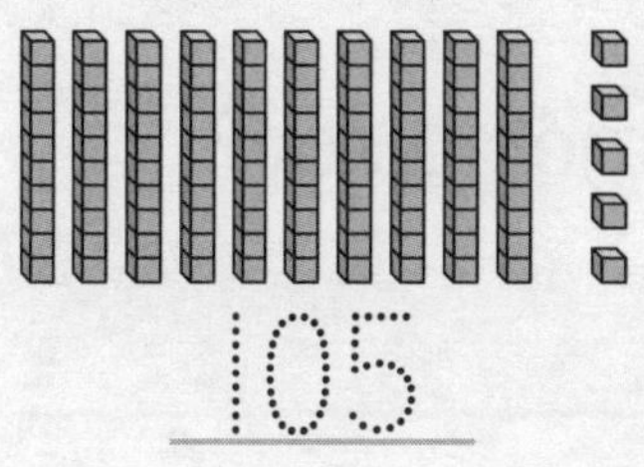
105

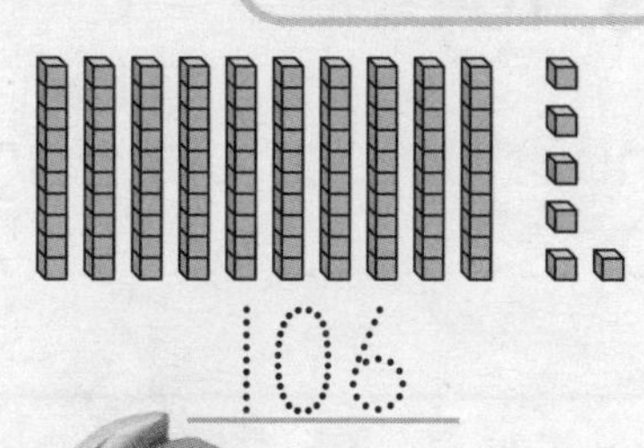
106

Start at 103. Count forward to 106.

Count forward by 1s. Write the numbers.

1. 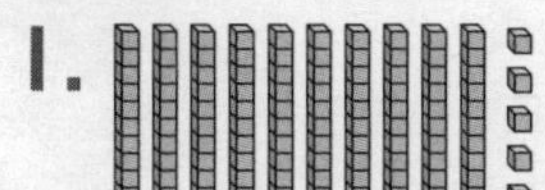 105 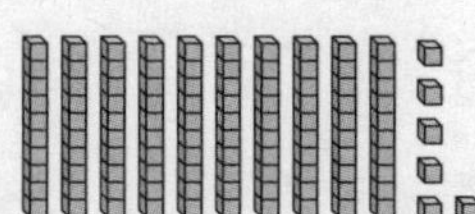 ____ 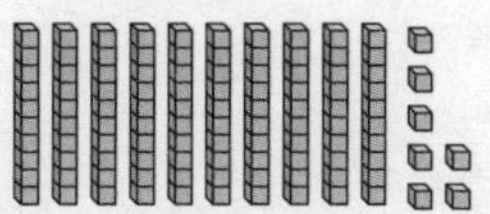 ____

2. 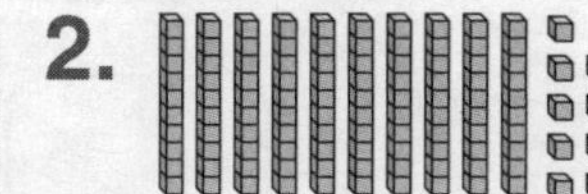 ____ 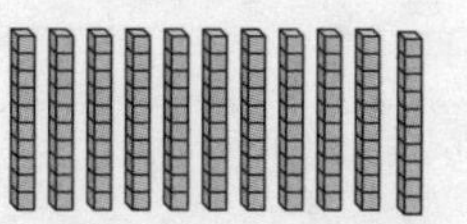 110 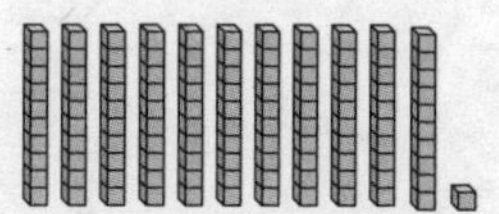 ____

Write the numbers to solve each problem.

3. Start at 118. Count forward. What are the next 2 numbers you will say?

_____ and _____

4. Start at 111. Count forward. What are the next 2 numbers you will say?

_____ and _____

5. **Look for Patterns** Sage starts counting at 99. She says, "101, 102, 103, 104..."

What number did Sage forget to say?

_____

6. **Look for Patterns** Cairo starts counting at 107. He says, "108, 109, 110, 112..."

What number did Cairo forget to say?

_____

7. **Higher Order Thinking** Write the missing numbers in the cards.

Try counting backward to find the number before 103.
103
105
108
110

8. **Assessment** Which shows the correct order for counting forward by 1s? Choose all that apply.

- ☐ 99, 101, 102, 103
- ☐ 111, 112, 113, 114
- ☐ 116, 117, 119, 120
- ☐ 108, 109, 110, 111

Name ______________________

Solve & Share

Solve

Lesson 7-3

Count on a Number Chart to 120

I can ... count on a number chart to 120.

I can also use math tools correctly.

Pick a number. Write the number in the box. How can you find the number that is 1 more? Write that number. Then write the next 3 numbers.

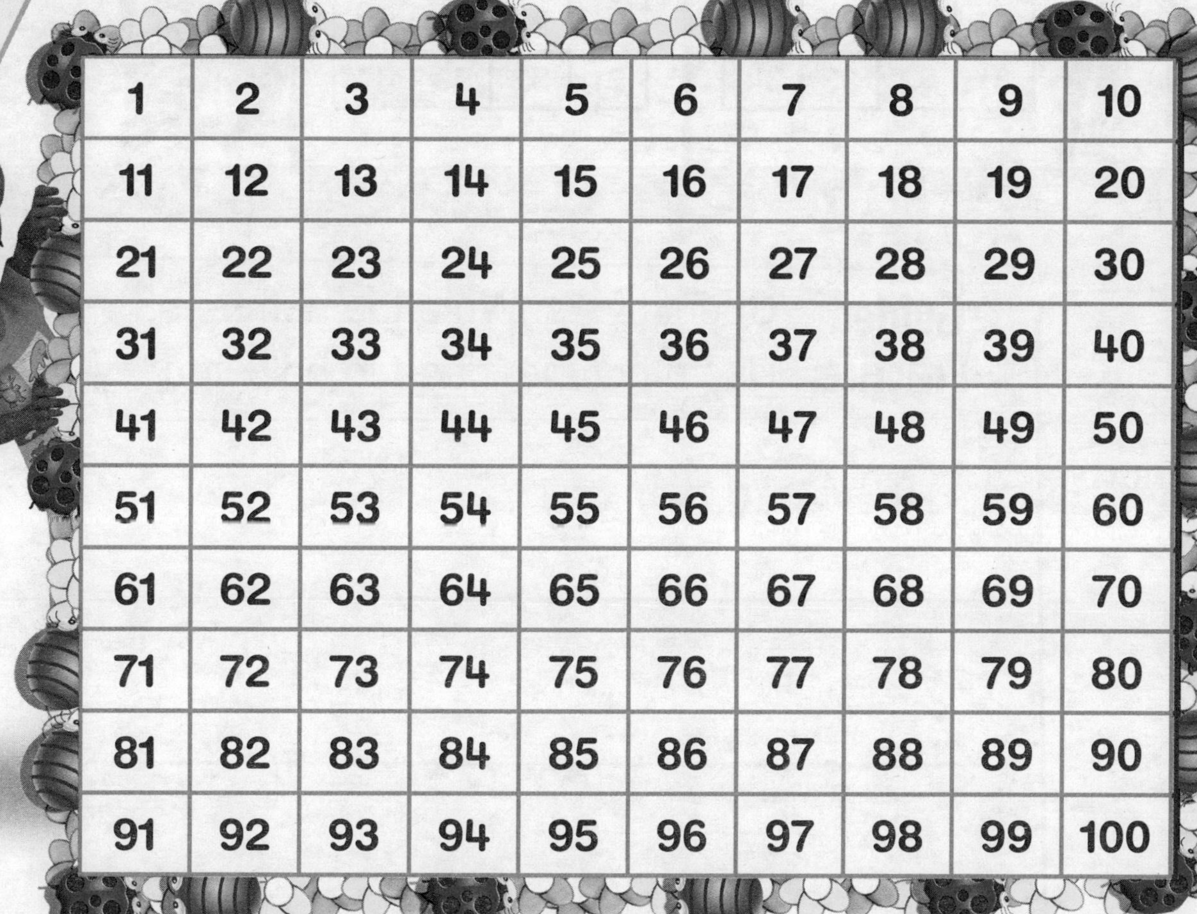

1	2	3	4	5	6	7	8	9	10
11	12	13	14	15	16	17	18	19	20
21	22	23	24	25	26	27	28	29	30
31	32	33	34	35	36	37	38	39	40
41	42	43	44	45	46	47	48	49	50
51	52	53	54	55	56	57	58	59	60
61	62	63	64	65	66	67	68	69	70
71	72	73	74	75	76	77	78	79	80
81	82	83	84	85	86	87	88	89	90
91	92	93	94	95	96	97	98	99	100

☐ ______, ______, ______, ______

A-Z
Learn
Glossary

You can find patterns when you count forward on a **hundred chart**.

1	2	3	4	5	6	7	8	9	10
11	12	13	14	15	16	17	18	19	20
21	22	23	24	25	26	27	28	29	30
31	32	33	34	35	36	37	38	39	40
41	42	43	44	45	46	47	48	49	50
51	52	53	54	55	56	57	58	59	60
61	62	63	64	65	66	67	68	69	70
71	72	73	74	75	76	77	78	79	80
81	82	83	84	85	86	87	88	89	90
91	92	93	94	95	96	97	98	99	100

The tens digit in each number in this row is 1.

1	2	3	4
11	12	13	14
21	22	23	24
31	32	33	34

The ones digit in each number in this column is 4.

1	2	3	4
11	12	13	14
21	22	23	24
31	32	33	34

A number chart can extend past 100 to greater numbers.

81	82	83	84	85	86	87	88	89	90
91	92	93	94	95	96	97	98	99	100
101	102	103	104	105	106	107	108	109	110
111	112	113	114	115	116	117	118	119	120

The numbers past 100 follow the same pattern.

Do You Understand?

Show Me! How do the numbers in a number chart change?

Guided Practice

Count by 1s. Write the numbers. Use a number chart to help you.

1. 14, 15, 16, 17, 18

2. 21, ____, ____, ____, ____

3. 103, ____, ____, ____, ____

4. ____, ____, 49, ____, ____

Name ______________________

Tools Assessment

Independent Practice Count by 1s. Write the numbers. Use a number chart to help you.

5. ____, 65, ____, ____, ____

6. ____, 52, ____, ____, ____

7. ____, ____, 83, ____, ____

8. 110, ____, ____, ____, ____

9. ____, ____, ____, ____, 79

10. ____, ____, ____, ____, 98

11. ____, ____, ____, ____, 91

12. ____, ____, ____, 102, ____

Higher Order Thinking Look at each partial number chart. Write the missing numbers.

13.

34		36	
	45		47

14.

	98		
107			110

Problem Solving

Use the number chart to solve each problem.

1	2	3	4	5	6	7	8	9	10
11	12	13	14	15	16	17	18	19	20
21	22	23	24	25	26	27	28	29	30
31	32	33	34	35	36	37	38	39	40
41	42	43	44	45	46	47	48	49	50
51	52	53	54	55	56	57	58	59	60
61	62	63	64	65	66	67	68	69	70
71	72	73	74	75	76	77	78	79	80
81	82	83	84	85	86	87	88	89	90
91	92	93	94	95	96	97	98	99	100
101	102	103	104	105	106	107	108	109	110
111	112	113	114	115	116	117	118	119	120

15. **Use Tools** Billy counts forward to 50. What are the next 5 numbers he counts? Write the numbers.

50, _____, _____, _____, _____, _____

16. **Use Tools** Sasha counts forward to 115. What are the next 5 numbers she counts? Write the numbers.

115, _____, _____, _____, _____, _____

17. **Higher Order Thinking** Pick a number from the number chart. Count forward. Write the numbers.

_____, _____, _____, _____, _____,

_____, _____, _____, _____, _____

18. **Assessment** Draw an arrow to match the missing number to the number chart.

75 100 101 114

112	113		115	116	117	118

Name ________________

   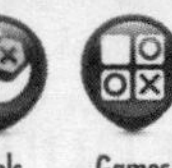
Help Tools Games

Homework & Practice 7-3

Count on a Number Chart to 120

Another Look! You can use a number chart to count forward.

1	2	3	4	5	6	7	8	9	10
11	12	13	14	15	16	17	18	19	20
21	22	23	24	25	26	27	28	29	30
31	32	33	34	35	36	37	38	39	40
41	42	43	44	45	46	47	48	49	50
51	52	53	54	55	56	57	58	59	60
61	62	63	64	65	66	67	68	69	70
71	72	73	74	75	76	77	78	79	80
81	82	83	84	85	86	87	88	89	90
91	92	93	94	95	96	97	98	99	100
101	102	103	104	105	106	107	108	109	110
111	112	113	114	115	116	117	118	119	120

What number comes after 33? 34

What number comes after 34? 35

What number comes after 35? 36

33, 34, 35, 36

HOME ACTIVITY Write the following series of numbers: 15, 16, ___, 18, ___, 20. Have your child write the missing numbers. If necessary, create a portion of a hundred chart on a sheet of paper for your child to use while filling in the missing numbers. Repeat with other numbers.

Count by 1s. Write the numbers. Use a number chart to help you.

1. 71, ___, ___, ___, ___

2. ___, ___, ___, 101, ___

3. ___, ___, ___, ___, 111

4. ___, ___, 65, ___, ___

Count by 1s. Write the numbers. Use a number chart to help you.

5. 40, _____, _____, _____, _____

6. _____, _____, _____, 32, _____

Higher Order Thinking Write the missing numbers. Look for patterns.

7.

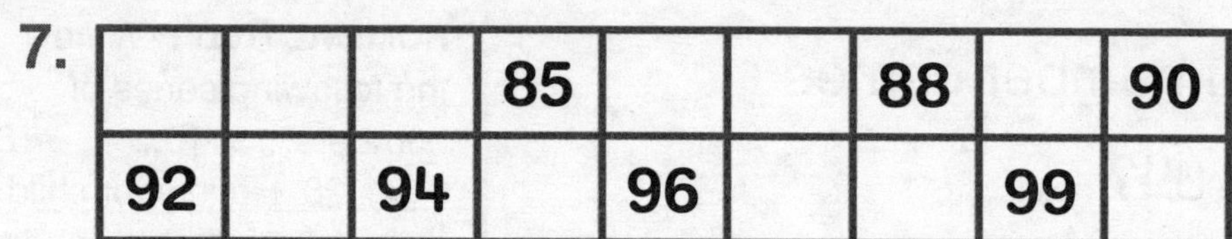

			85			88		90
92		94		96			99	

8.

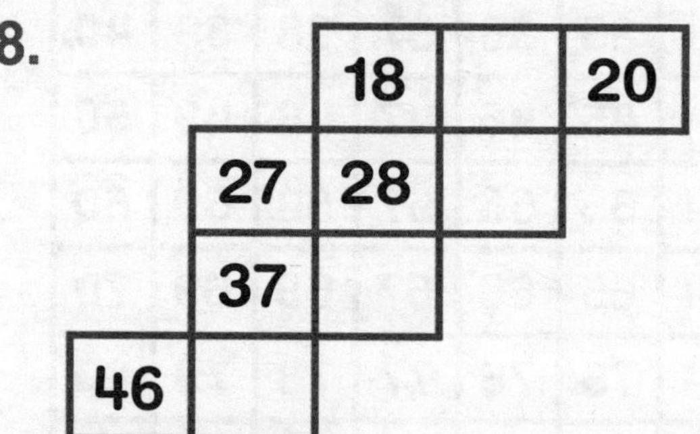

		18		20
	27	28		
	37			
46				

9. **Assessment** Draw an arrow to match the missing number to the number chart.

92	70	55	31

54		56	57	58	59	60

10. **Assessment** Draw an arrow to match the missing number to the number chart.

46	33	84	17

81	82	83		85	86	87

Name ___________________________________

Lesson 7-4
Count by 1s or 10s to 120

I can ... find number patterns on a hundred chart.

I can also look for patterns.

Solve & Share

Count by 10s, starting at 10. Color the numbers you count yellow. What pattern do you see? Count by 1s, starting at 102. Draw a red square around the numbers. Count by 10s, starting at 34. Draw a blue circle around the numbers. Describe the patterns for each.

1	2	3	4	5	6	7	8	9	10
11	12	13	14	15	16	17	18	19	20
21	22	23	24	25	26	27	28	29	30
31	32	33	34	35	36	37	38	39	40
41	42	43	44	45	46	47	48	49	50
51	52	53	54	55	56	57	58	59	60
61	62	63	64	65	66	67	68	69	70
71	72	73	74	75	76	77	78	79	80
81	82	83	84	85	86	87	88	89	90
91	92	93	94	95	96	97	98	99	100
101	102	103	104	105	106	107	108	109	110
111	112	113	114	115	116	117	118	119	120

You can count on a number chart to find a pattern.

1	2	3	4	5	6	7	8	9	10
11	12	13	14	15	16	17	18	19	20
21	22	23	24	25	26	27	28	29	30
31	32	33	34	35	36	37	38	39	40
41	42	43	44	45	46	47	48	49	50
51	52	53	54	55	56	57	58	59	60
61	62	63	64	65	66	67	68	69	70
71	72	73	74	75	76	77	78	79	80
81	82	83	84	85	86	87	88	89	90
91	92	93	94	95	96	97	98	99	100
101	102	103	104	105	106	107	108	109	110
111	112	113	114	115	116	117	118	119	120

Count by 10s.

1	2	3	4	5	6	7	8	9	10
11	12	13	14	15	16	17	18	19	20
21	22	23	24	25	26	27	28	29	30
31	32	33	34	35	36	37	38	39	40

Count by 1s from 58 to 61.

58, 59, 60, 61

41	42	43	44	45	46	47	48	49	50
51	52	53	54	55	56	57	58	59	60
61	62	63	64	65	66	67	68	69	70
71	72	73	74	75	76	77	78	79	80

Count by 10s, starting at 84.

84, 94, 104, 114

81	82	83	84	85	86	87	88	89	90
91	92	93	94	95	96	97	98	99	100
101	102	103	104	105	106	107	108	109	110
111	112	113	114	115	116	117	118	119	120

Do You Understand?

Show Me! Compare counting by 1s and by 10s. How are the patterns alike? How are the patterns different?

Guided Practice

Write the numbers to continue each pattern. Use a number chart to help you.

1. Count by 1s.

12, 13, 14, 15, 16, 17, 18, 19, 20

2. Count by 10s.

22, 32, 42, ____, ____, ____, ____, ____, ____

3. Count by 1s.

90, 91, 92, ____, ____, ____, ____, ____, ____

Name ______________________

Tools Assessment

Independent Practice

Write the numbers to continue each pattern.
Use a number chart to help you.

4. Count by 10s.

10, 20, 30, ____, ____, ____, ____, ____, ____, ____

5. Count by 10s.

35, 45, 55, ____, ____, ____, ____, ____, ____

6. Count by 1s.

102, 103, 104, ____, ____, ____, ____, ____, ____, ____, ____, ____

Number Sense Write the missing numbers on the number chart below. Then write the next three numbers in the pattern you started.

7.

	62	63	64	65	66	67	68	69	70
	72	73	74	75	76	77	78	79	80
	82	83	84	85	86	87	88	89	90

____, ____, ____

Problem Solving Solve each problem below.

8. Look for Patterns Anita walks her neighbor's dog to earn money. She starts on Day 13 and walks the dog once a day through Day 19. How many times does Anita walk the dog?

Use the chart to count.
Write the number.

1	2	3	4	5	6	7	8	9	10
11	12	13	14	15	16	17	18	19	20

_____ times

9. Look for Patterns Matt starts swimming lessons on Day 5. He goes every 10 days. How many lessons will Matt go to in 30 days?

Use the chart to count.
Write the number.

1	2	3	4	5	6	7	8	9	10
11	12	13	14	15	16	17	18	19	20
21	22	23	24	25	26	27	28	29	30

_____ lessons

10. Higher Order Thinking Anna counts to 30. She only counts 3 numbers. Did Anna count by 1s or 10s? Use pictures, numbers, or words to explain.

11. Assessment Tim counts by 10s, starting at 54.

54, 74, 84, 94, 114

What numbers did Tim forget to count?

_____

Name ____________

Homework & Practice 7-4

Count by 1s or 10s to 120

Another Look! You can count on a number chart. When you count by 10s, the number in the tens digit goes up by one, but the number in the ones digit stays the same.

21	22	23	24	25	26	27	28	29	30
31	32	33	34	35	36	37	38	39	40
41	42	43	44	45	46	47	48	49	50
51	52	53	54	55	56	57	58	59	60
61	62	63	64	65	66	67	68	69	70
71	72	73	74	75	76	77	78	79	80
81	82	83	84	85	86	87	88	89	90
91	92	93	94	95	96	97	98	99	100
101	102	103	104	105	106	107	108	109	110
111	112	113	114	115	116	117	118	119	120

What numbers will you say when you count by 10s, starting at 60?

60, 70, 80, 90, 100, 110, 120

What numbers will you say when you count by 10s, starting at 25?

25, 35, 45, 55, 65, 75, 85

HOME ACTIVITY Practice orally counting by 1s and 10s with your child. If necessary, have him or her use a number chart. Ask: "What patterns do you see when you count by 10s?"

Write the numbers to continue each pattern. Use a number chart to help you.

1. Count by 10s.

38, 48, ____, ____, ____, ____

2. Count by 1s.

66, 67, ____, ____, ____, ____

Write the numbers to continue each pattern. Use a number chart to help you.

3. Count by 10s.

17, 27, ____, ____, ____, ____

4. Count by 1s.

108, 109, ____, ____, ____, ____

5. Higher Order Thinking Vicky has baseball practice every 10 days. She starts on May 5. Will she have practice on May 19? Write **Yes** or **No**. ____

How do you know?

____

____

____

Write 2 more dates that Vicky will have practice.

____

____

Use this calendar to help you!

May

Sunday	Monday	Tuesday	Wednesday	Thursday	Friday	Saturday
	1	2	3	4	5	6
7	8	9	10	11	12	13
14	15	16	17	18	19	20
21	22	23	24	25	26	27
28	29	30	31			

6. **Assessment** What are the missing numbers?

65, __?__, __?__, 95, __?__

____

7. **Assessment** Jamie counts by 1s. He counts: 54, 56, 57, 59. Which numbers did Jamie forget to count?

____

Name ____________________

Solve & Share

Use the open number line to show how to count from 78 to 84.

78

Lesson 7-5
Count on an Open Number Line

I can ...
count to 120 using an open number line.

I can also model with math.

You can use an open number line to count on by 1s.

Count on by 1s from 97 to 103.

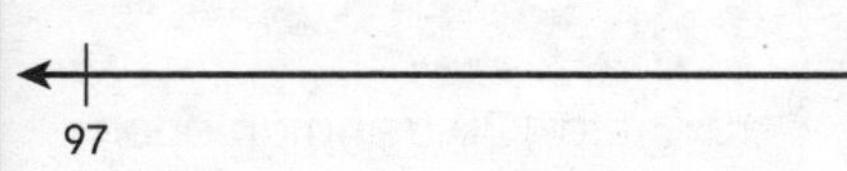

You can use an open number line to count on by 10s.

Count on by 10s from 56 to 116.

Do You Understand?

Show Me! Use an open number line. What number comes after 109 when you count on by 1s?
What number comes after 109 when you count on by 10s?

Guided Practice

Show your counting on the open number line.

1. Start at 99. Count on by 1s to 105.

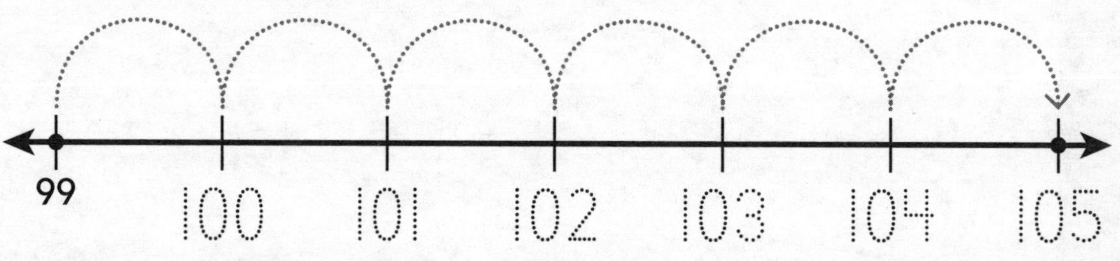

2. Start at 72. Count on by 10s to 112.

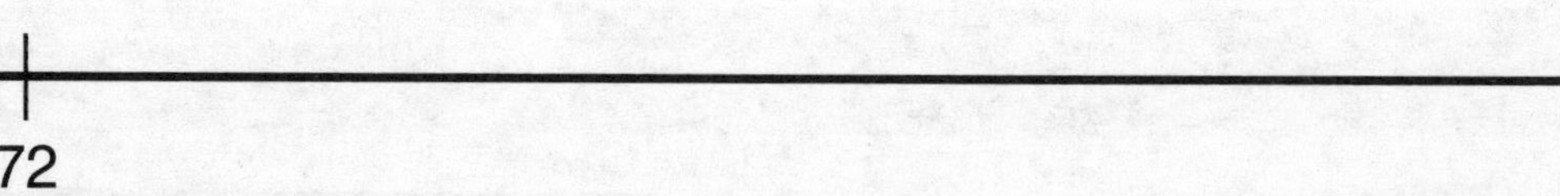

Name ______________________________

Independent Practice

Show your counting on the open number line.

3. Start at 89. Count on by 10s to 119.

4. Start at 111. Count on by 1s to 118.

5. Number Sense Teresa and Doug both draw a number line starting at 27. Teresa counts on by 1s five times. Doug counts on by 10s five times.

Will they stop counting at the same number? Use the number lines. Explain.

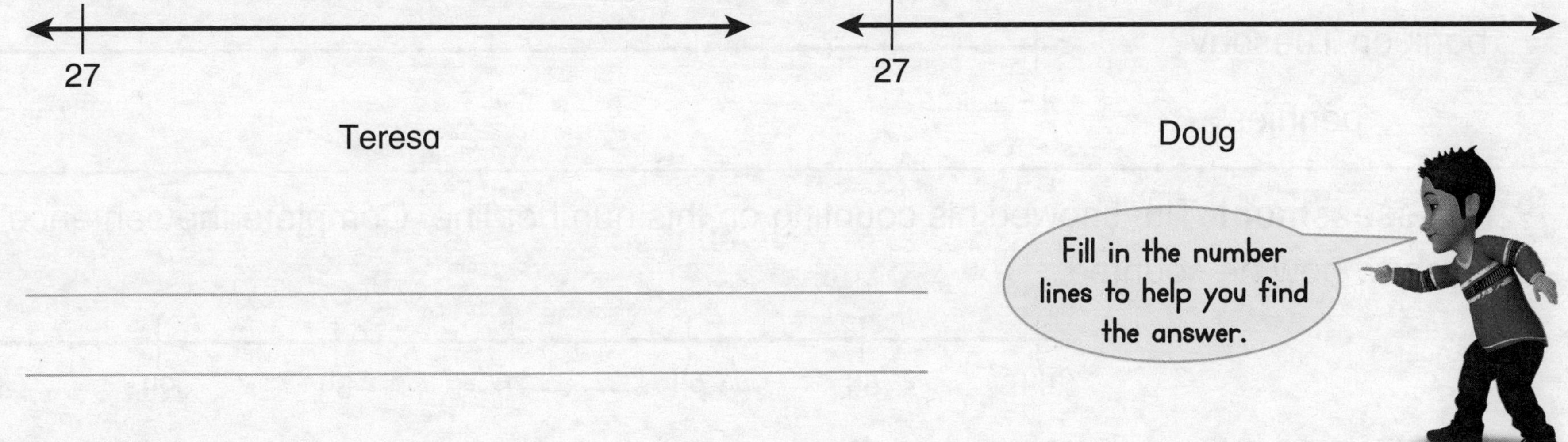

27
27
Teresa
Doug
Fill in the number lines to help you find the answer.

Problem Solving Use the number line to solve each story problem.

6. **Model** Dennis counts 41 marbles. Then he counts 8 more marbles. How many marbles did he count in all?

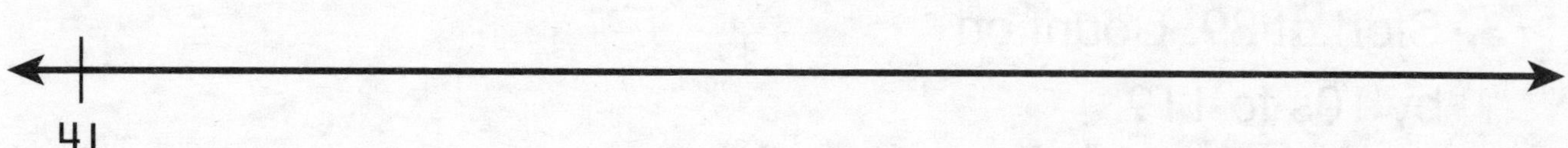

_____ marbles

7. **Algebra** Serena used the number line to count on from 12 to 15. Complete the addition equation to show what she did.

12 + _____ = _____

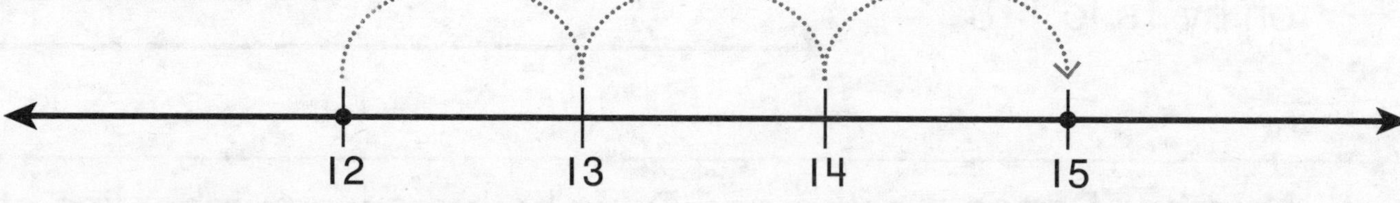

8. **Higher Order Thinking** On Monday, Kate puts 12 pennies in her piggy bank. On Tuesday, she puts some more pennies in her bank. She puts 19 pennies in all in her bank. How many pennies did she put in her bank on Tuesday?

_____ pennies

9. **Assessment** Tim showed his counting on this number line. Complete the sentence to show how he counted.

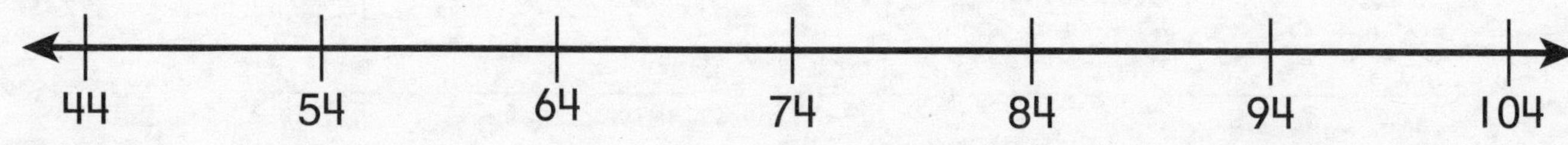

Tim counted by _____ from _____ to _____.

Name ________________________

Help Tools Games

Homework & Practice 7-5

Count on an Open Number Line

Another Look! Counting on is like adding.

Start at 87. Count on by 1s to 92.

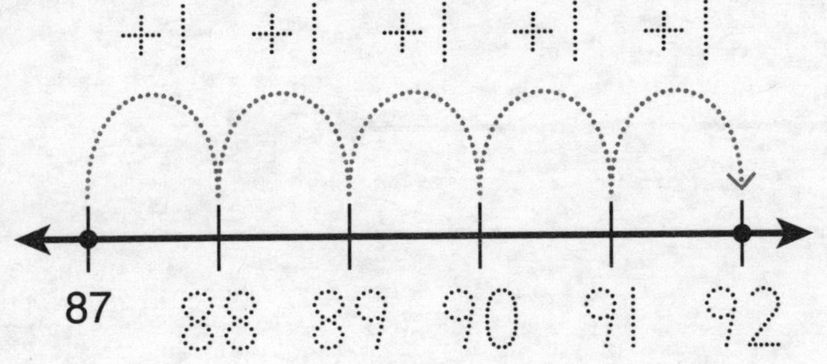

You add 1 each time you count!

Start at 62. Count on by 10s to 112.

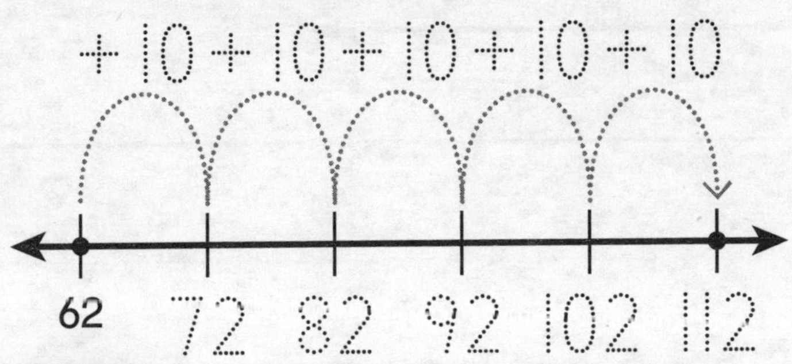

You add 10 each time you count!

HOME ACTIVITY Draw two simple number lines with no labels. Ask your child to use the first number line to count by 1s from 53 to 58. Ask your child to use the second number line to count by 10s from 67 to 107.

Show your counting on the open number line. You can use addition to help.

1. Start at 115. Count on by 1s to 120.

115

Show your counting on the open number lines. You can use addition to help.

2. **Math and Science** There are 16 baby chicks sleeping in a hen house. Outside the hen house, there are 6 more baby chicks chirping for their mothers. How many baby chicks in all?

3. Start at 18. Count on by 10s to 78.

4. **Higher Order Thinking** Lorna starts counting at 48.
She counts on by 10s four times.
Then she counts on by 1s three times.
What was the last number she said?
Tell how you know.

5. **Assessment** Ben showed part of his counting on this number line. Fill in the missing numbers. Complete the sentence.

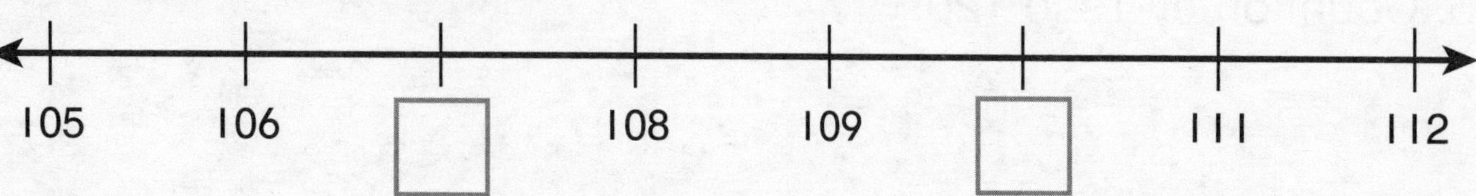

Ben counted by _____ from _____ to _____.

Name ____________________

Lesson 7-6
Count and Write Numerals

Solve & Share

Look at the oranges below. Count to find out how many in all and then write the number. Explain how you counted the oranges.

I can ...
write a numeral to show how many objects are in the group.

I can also make sense of problems.

There are _____ oranges.

How many stickers are shown?

What is the best way to count this many stickers?

You can count by 1s.

1 2 3 4 5 6 7 8 9 10
11 12 13 14 15 16 17 18 19 20
21 22 23 24 25 26 27 28 29 30
31 32 33 34 35 36 37 38 39 40
41

There are 41 stickers!

You can also count by 10s.

10
20
30
40
41

I can count 10, 20, 30, 40. Then I add the 1 left to get 41 stickers.

Do You Understand?

Show Me! Start counting at 19 and count on 6 more. Then write the numeral that you ended on.

Guided Practice

Count the objects any way you choose. Then write how many in all.

1. 46 balls

2. ______ rabbits

Name ______________________________

Tools Assessment

Independent Practice

Count the objects. Then write how many in all.

3.

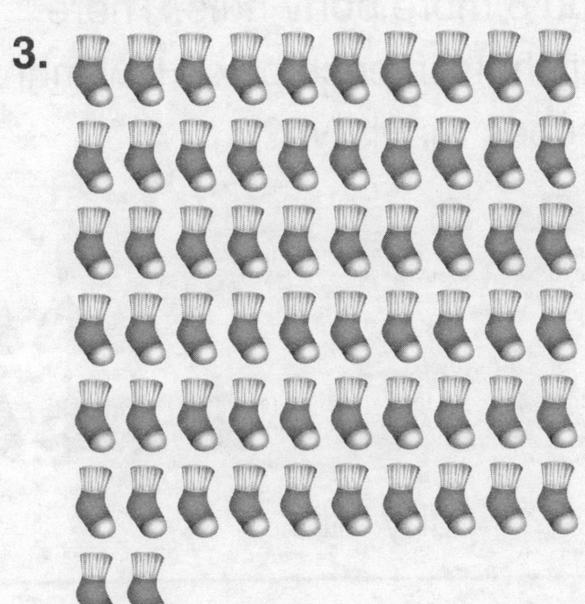

_____ socks

4.

_____ bananas

Count the tens and ones. Then write how many in all.

5.

_____ tens _____ ones

_____ in all

6.

_____ tens _____ ones

_____ in all

7.

tens _____ ones _____

_____ in all

Problem Solving Solve the problems below.

8. Reasoning Daniel finds 3 boxes of teddy bears and 4 more teddy bears. Each box holds 10 teddy bears. How many teddy bears did Daniel find?

Daniel found _____ teddy bears.

9. Reasoning Kim throws a party. She has 8 boxes and 6 more party hats. There are 10 party hats in each box. How many party hats does Kim have?

Kim has _____ party hats.

10. Higher Order Thinking Write the number of objects you see. Tell how you counted them.

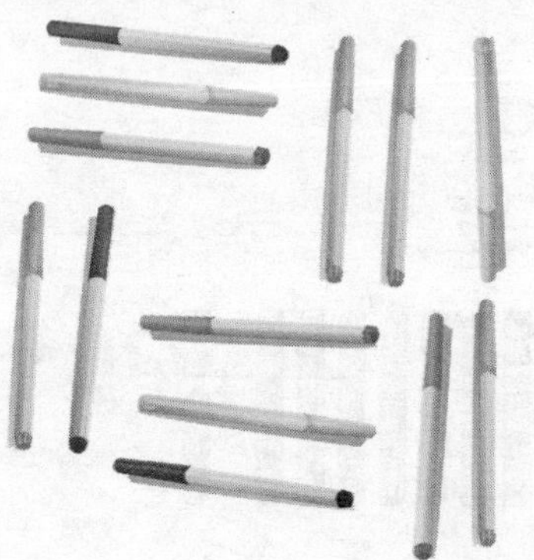

____

____

11. Assessment How many strawberries are in this set?

Ⓐ 18

Ⓑ 24

Ⓒ 26

Ⓓ 62

Name ______

Homework & Practice 7-6

Count and Write Numerals

Another Look! You can count groups of objects by 1s or 10s.

When you count by 1s, you count each object separately.

1 2 3 4 5 6 7 8 9 10
11 12 13 14 15 16 17 18 19 20
21 22 23 24 25 26 27 28 29 30
31 32 33 34 35 36 37 38 39 40
41 42 43 44 45 46 47 48 49 50
51 52 53

There are 53 buttons.

When you count by 10s, you count groups of 10, and then add the 1s.

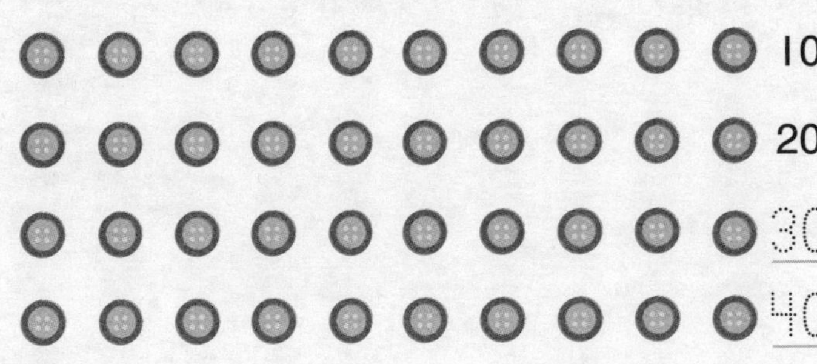

10
20
30
40
50
51 52 53

There are 53 buttons.

HOME ACTIVITY Set up a pile of between 50 and 120 small objects. Ask your child to count them in the fastest way he or she can think of. Remind your child that sorting the objects into groups or counting more than one at a time will make it easier. Repeat with a different amount in between 50 and 120.

Count the tens and ones. Then write how many in all.

1.

_____ tens _____ ones

Total _____

2.

_____ tens _____ ones

Total _____

3.

_____ tens _____ ones

Total _____

Count the objects. Show how you counted. Then write how many in all.

4. 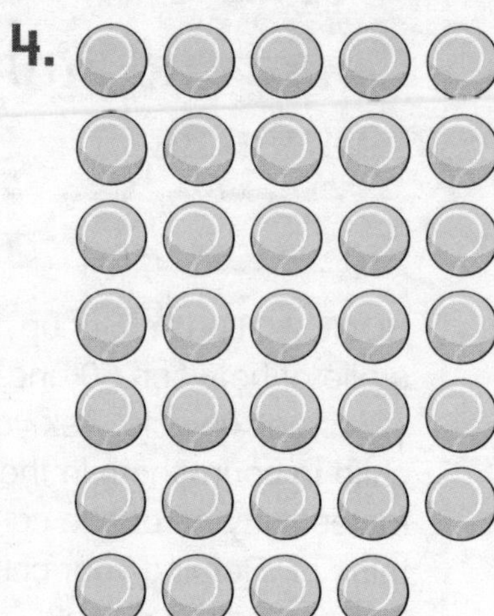

____

5. 

____

6. **Higher Order Thinking** Explain why counting by tens might be faster than counting by ones.

7. **Assessment** How many tens and ones are shown?

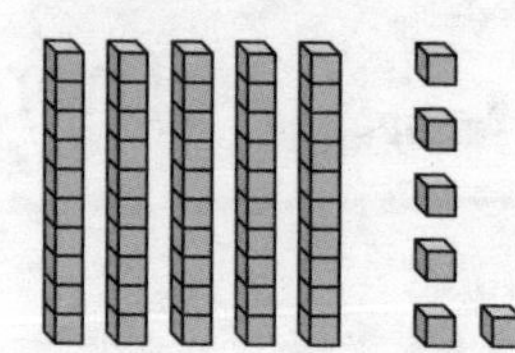

Ⓐ 4 tens and 5 ones

Ⓑ 4 tens and 6 ones

Ⓒ 5 tens and 5 ones

Ⓓ 5 tens and 6 ones

Name ______________________

Solve & Share

How can you find the number of apples on the ground without counting them one at a time? Explain your shortcut.

I counted by ______. ______ apples

Solve

Problem Solving

Lesson 7-7
Repeated Reasoning

I can ...
find better, faster ways to solve problems.

I can also count by tens and ones.

Thinking Habits

Is there a shortcut that makes sense?

What can I use from this problem to help with another problem?

Learn Glossary

Matt spills some puzzle pieces on the floor. 61 pieces are still in the box. How can Matt find the number of puzzle pieces in all?

How can you use what you know to solve the problem?

I can look for shortcuts and things that repeat.

Circle a group of 10 and count on. Repeat until there are no more groups of 10. Then count on by 1s.

61, 71, 81, 82, 83, 84, 85. There are 85 puzzle pieces in all.

71 81 82 83 84 85

Do You Understand?

Show Me! Why is counting by 10s and 1s better than counting 1 at a time?

Guided Practice

How many in all? Use a shortcut to count on. Tell what shortcut you used.

1.

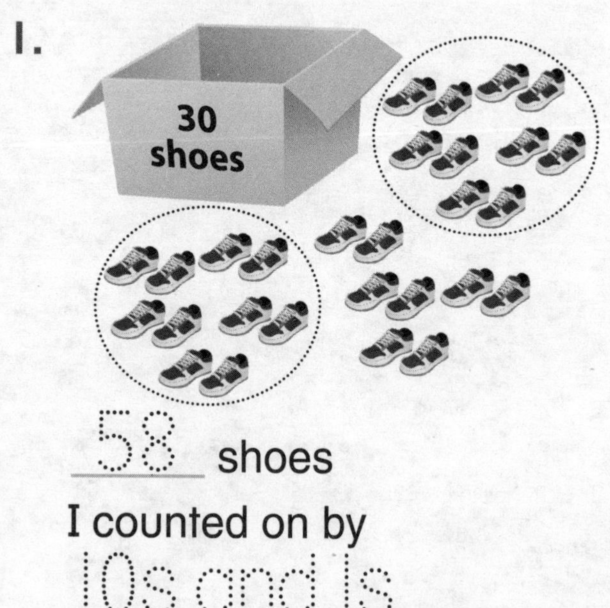

58 shoes

I counted on by 10s and 1s.

2.

_____ muffins

I counted on by _____________.

Name ______________________________

Tools Assessment

Independent Practice How many in all? Use a shortcut to count on. Tell what shortcut you used.

3.

______ watches

I counted on by ____________.

4.

______ train cars

I counted on by ____________.

5.

______ books

I counted on by ____________.

6.

______ desks

I counted on by ____________.

Performance Assessment

Students and Snowmen

62 students stay inside at recess. The rest each build a snowman outside. How can you count to find the number of students in all?

62 students

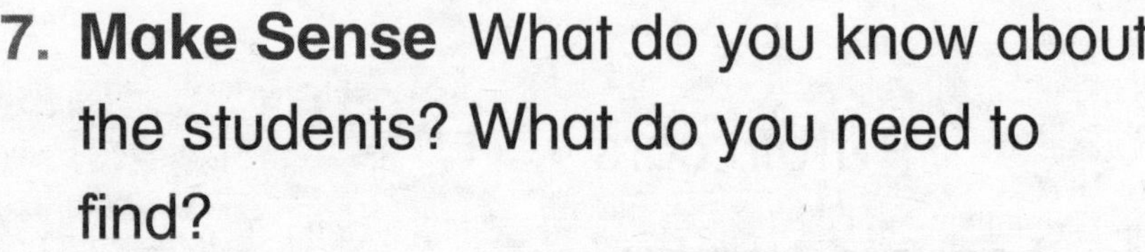

7. **Make Sense** What do you know about the students? What do you need to find?

____

____

____

____

8. **Reasoning** What does the number of snowmen tell me?

____

____

____

9. **Generalize** How many students in all? What shortcut can you use to find the answer?

____

____

____

____

____

____

____

____

____

Name ______________________

Homework & Practice 7-7
Repeated Reasoning

Another Look! Grouping objects makes it easier to count on.

Amy has some cars in a box and some on the floor.
How can she count to find how many in all?

101, 102, 103, 104

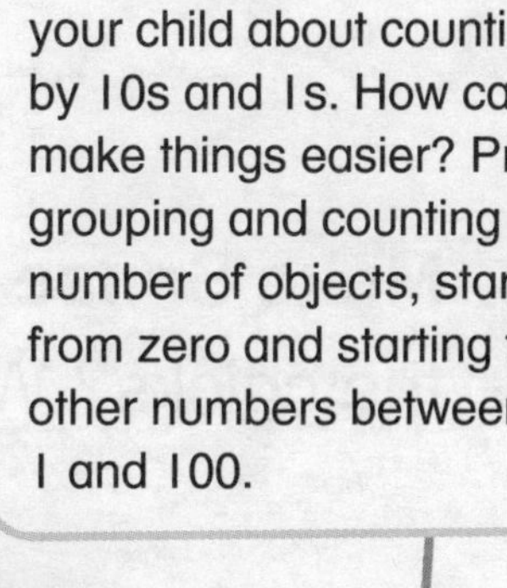

I will count by 1s with so few cars. Amy has 104 cars.

HOME ACTIVITY Talk to your child about counting on by 10s and 1s. How can it make things easier? Practice grouping and counting a number of objects, starting from zero and starting from other numbers between 1 and 100.

Generalize and count on by a number to help you find how many in all.

1. 

_____ dinosaurs

I counted on by __________.

2. 50 teddy bears

_____ teddy bears

I counted on by __________.

Performance Assessment

Baby Chicks

Kevin counts 75 chicks in the hen house. He also sees more chicks outside the hen house. How can Kevin count to find how many chicks in all?

3. **Make Sense** What do you know about the chicks? What do you need to find?

4. **Reasoning** How do the pictures of the chicks help me?

5. **Generalize** How many chicks in all? What shortcut can you use to find the answer?

Name ____________________

Fluency Practice Activity

Show the Word

I can ...
add and subtract within 10.

Color these sums and differences. Leave the rest white.

8 5 6

4 + 2	5 − 3	0 + 6	6 + 2	8 + 0	7 + 1	8 − 3	7 − 2	1 + 4
9 − 3	10 − 3	8 − 2	10 − 2	2 − 2	2 + 6	2 + 3	2 + 2	6 − 1
10 − 4	6 + 0	3 + 3	1 + 7	10 − 7	3 + 5	0 + 5	5 − 0	3 + 2
5 + 1	1 + 1	2 + 4	5 + 3	9 − 5	9 − 1	4 + 1	1 + 2	9 − 7
7 − 1	1 − 1	6 − 0	8 − 0	4 + 4	0 + 8	10 − 5	9 − 0	5 − 2

The word is

__________ __________ __________

Vocabulary Review

Glossary

Word List
- column
- hundred chart
- number chart
- ones digit
- row
- tens digit

Understand Vocabulary

1. Circle the number that shows the ones digit.

   106

2. Circle the number that shows the tens digit.

   106

3. Circle a column in the part of the hundred chart.

87	88	89	90
97	98	99	100

4. Circle a row in the part of the number chart.

107	108	109	110
117	118	119	120

5. Circle the number on the chart that is 1 more than 101.

97	98	99	100
101	102	103	104

Use Vocabulary in Writing

6. Fill in the number chart to count on from 96 to 105. Then explain the difference between a number chart and a hundred chart and label the chart using words from the Word List.

91	92	93	94	95					
					106	107	108	109	110

Name ______________________

Reteaching

Set A

You can count by 10s when you have a lot of objects to count.

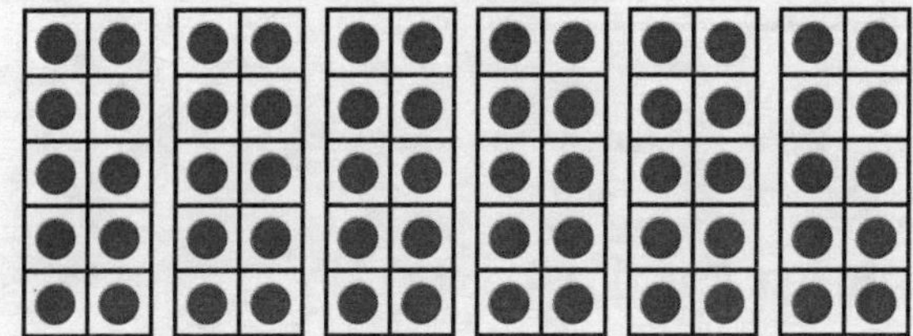

There are 6 tens.

6 tens = 60

The word name for 60 is sixty.

Count by 10s. Write the number 3 different ways.

1.

_____ tens

number: _____

word name: __________

Set B

You can use a number chart to count on by 1s or 10s.

81	82	83	84	85	86	87	88	89	90
91	92	93	94	95	96	97	98	99	100
101	102	103	104	105	106	107	108	109	110
111	112	113	114	115	116	117	118	119	120

Count on by 1s.

99, 100, 101, 102, 103

Use a number chart to count on.

2. Count by 10s.

80, _____, _____, _____, _____

3. Count by 1s.

114, _____, _____, _____, _____

Set C

You can use an open number line to count on by 1s or 10s.

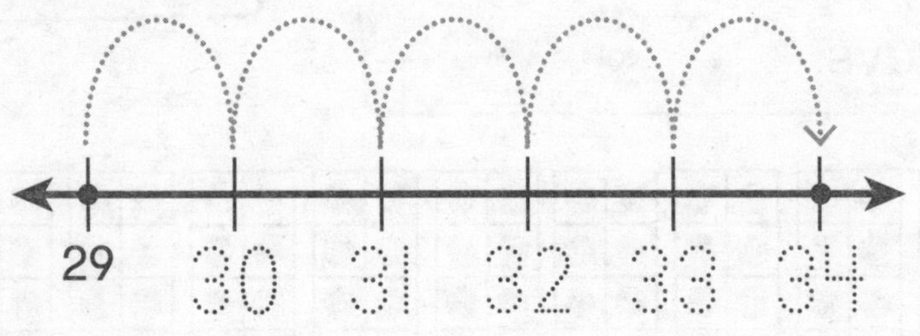

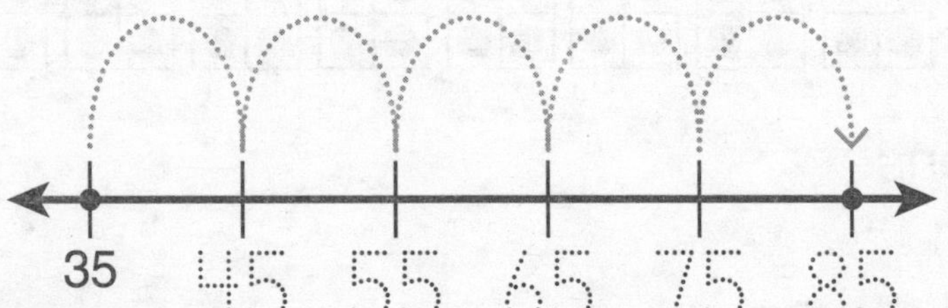

Count on using the open number line.

4. Start at 62. Count on by 10s to 102.

5. Start at 97. Count on by 1s to 101.

Set D

Thinking Habits

Repeated Reasoning

Does something repeat in the problem? How does that help?

Is there a shortcut that makes sense?

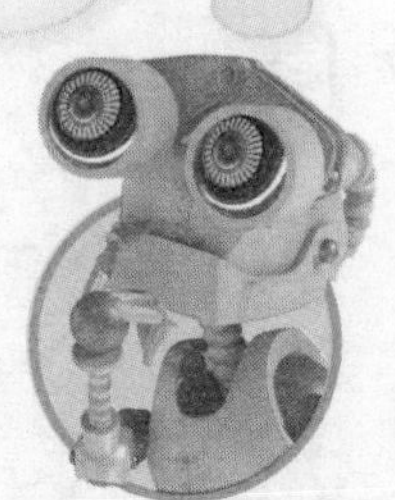

Count on by a number to find how many in all.

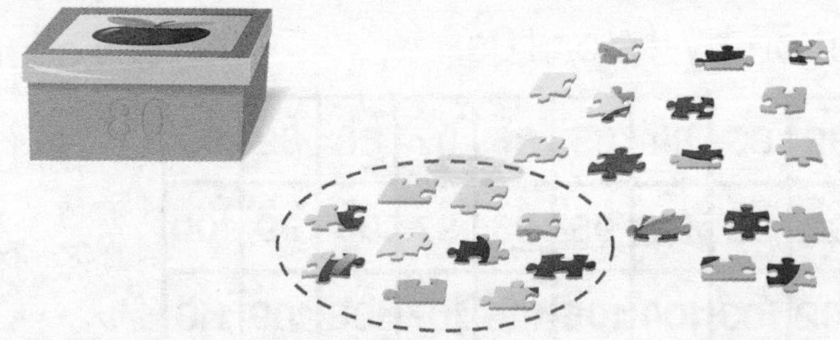

6. Sean spills some puzzle pieces. Eighty are still in the box. How many puzzle pieces are there in all?

_____ pieces

Name ______________________________

1. Count by 10s. What number is shown?
Write the number 3 different ways.

_____ tens

number: _____

word name: __________

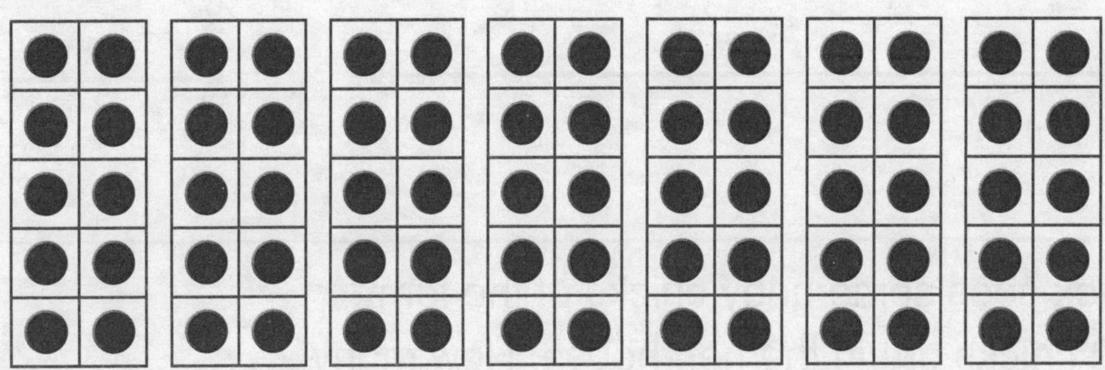

Use the partial number chart below to solve each problem.

91	92	93	94	95	96	97	98	99	100
101	102	103	104	105	106	107	108	109	110
111	112	113	114	115	116	117	118	119	120

2. Cathy counts pennies by 1s. She counts to 98. Which number will Cathy say next?

89 Ⓐ   90 Ⓑ   99 Ⓒ   108 Ⓓ

3. Sam counts by 10s. Which number did he forget to count?

80, 90, 100, 120

89 Ⓐ   105 Ⓑ   110 Ⓒ   115 Ⓓ

Show your counting on the open number line.

4. Start at 58. Count on by 10s to 98.

5. Start at 114. Count on by 1s to 118.

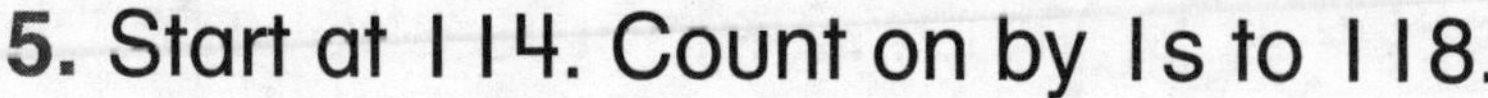

6. Alex sees some baby chicks at the farm. 50 chicks are in the hen house. How many baby chicks in all? Use the picture to solve.

Ⓐ 68

Ⓑ 72

Ⓒ 78

Ⓓ 80

7. The farm worker says there were 82 chicks this morning. How many chicks are hiding? Use the picture to solve. Then explain how you know.

Name ______________________________

Mal's Marbles

Mal collects marbles and keeps them in jars.

1. How many blue marbles does Mal have? Circle groups of 10. Then count by 10s. Write the numbers and the number word.

_____ groups of 10 marbles

_____ marbles

_____ marbles

2. Mal has some striped marbles. Use these clues to find out how many she has.

Clue 1: The number comes after 110.

Clue 2: The number comes before 120.

Clue 3: The number does **NOT** have 4 ones.

Clue 4: The number in the ones place is the same as the number in the tens place.

Mal has _____ striped marbles.

3. Mal has 105 small marbles in a jar. She puts 13 more small marbles in the jar. How many small marbles are in the jar now?

Solve using the number line or part of the number chart. Then explain how you solved.

81	82	83	84	85	86	87	88	89	90
91	92	93	94	95	96	97	98	99	100
101	102	103	104	105	106	107	108	109	110
111	112	113	114	115	116	117	118	119	120

There are _____ small marbles in the jar.

4. Mal has 48 large marbles in a jar. There are more large marbles on the floor. How can you count to find how many large marbles Mal has in all?

48 marbles

What do you know about the large marbles?

What shortcut did you use to count the marbles? Tell how you counted.

Mal has _____ large marbles in all.

Glossary

1 less

4 is 1 less than 5.

1 more

5 is 1 more than 4.

10 less

20 is 10 less than 30.

10 more

10 more than a number has 1 more ten or 10 more ones.

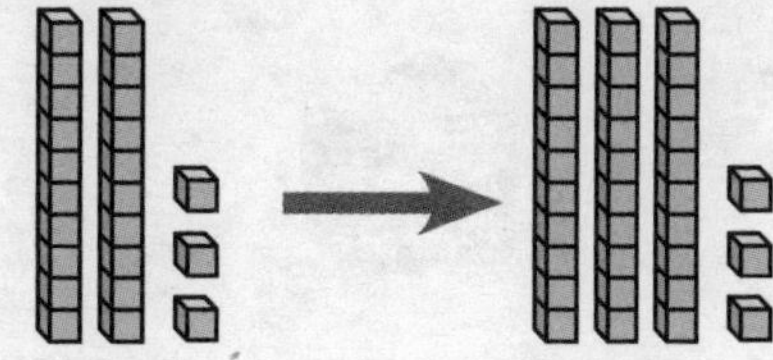

add

When you add, you find out how many there are in all.

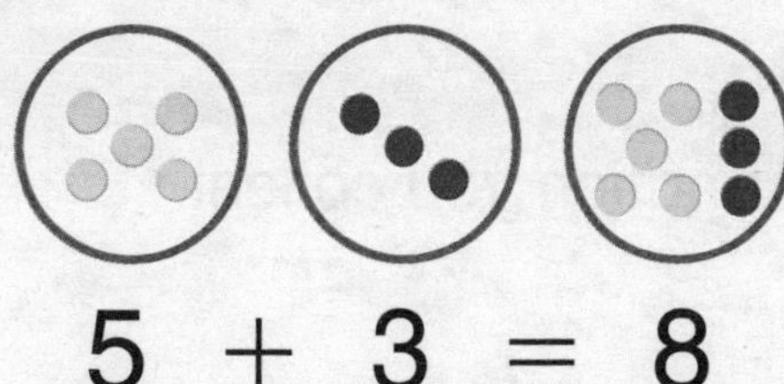

5 + 3 = 8

addend

the numbers you add together to find the whole

2 + 3 = 5

addition equation

3 + 4 = 7

addition fact

9 + 8 = 17

column

1	2	3	4	5
11	12	13	14	15
21	22	23	24	25
31	32	33	34	35

column

compare

to find out how things are alike or different

cone

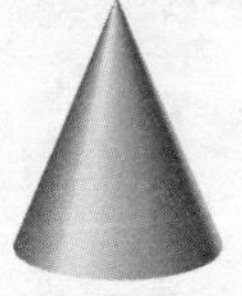

corner

count on

You can count on by 1s or 10s.

15, 16, 17, 18

20, 30, 40, 50

cube

cylinder

data

information you collect

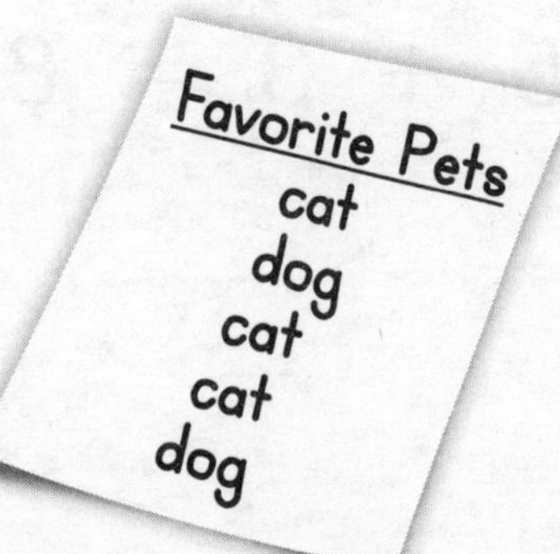

difference

the amount that is left after you subtract

$4 - 1 = 3$

The difference is 3.

digits

Numbers have 1 or more digits.

43 has 2 digits.
The tens digit is 4.
The ones digit is 3.

doubles fact

an addition fact with the same addends

$4 + 4 = 8$

4 and 4 is a double.

doubles-plus-1 fact

The addends are 1 apart.

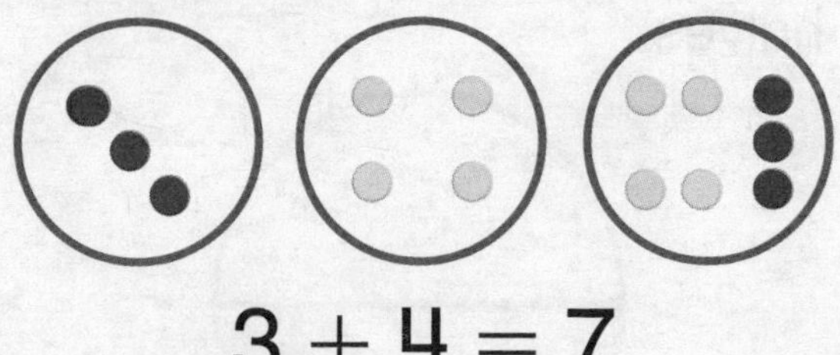

$\underbrace{3 + 4}_{\text{addends}} = 7$

doubles-plus-2 fact

The addends are 2 apart.

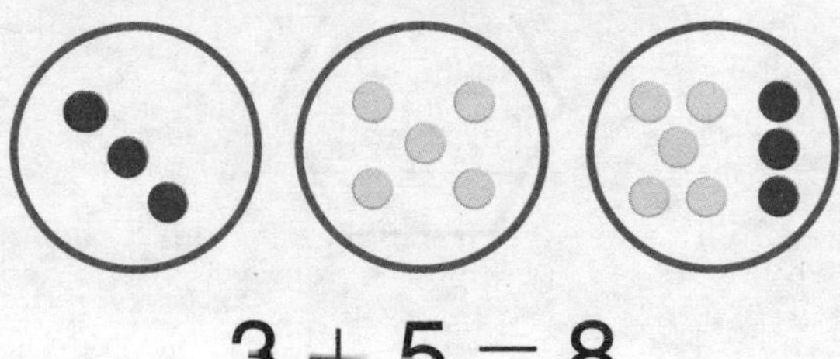

$\underbrace{3 + 5}_{\text{addends}} = 8$

edges

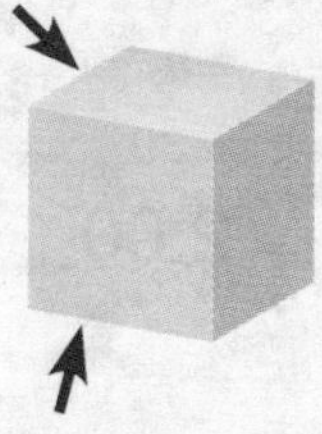

equal shares

4 equal parts

equal sign (=)

$2 + 3 = 5$

equal sign

equals

$5 + 2$ equals 7.

equation

$6 + 4 = 10$ $\quad$ $6 - 2 = 4$

$10 = 6 + 4$ $\quad$ $4 = 6 - 2$

faces

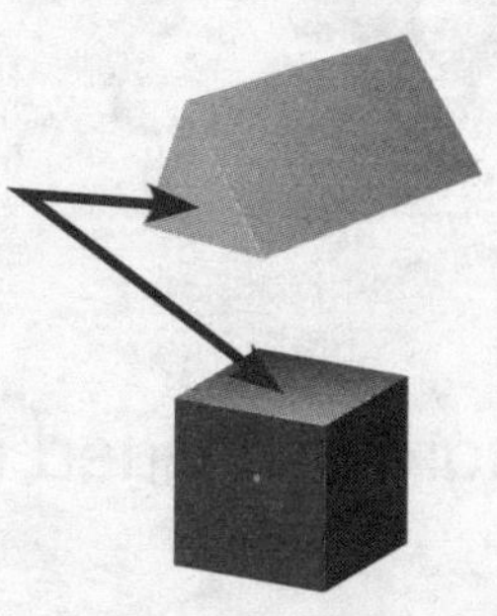

fact family

a group of related addition and subtraction facts

$3 + 5 = 8$
$5 + 3 = 8$
$8 - 3 = 5$
$8 - 5 = 3$

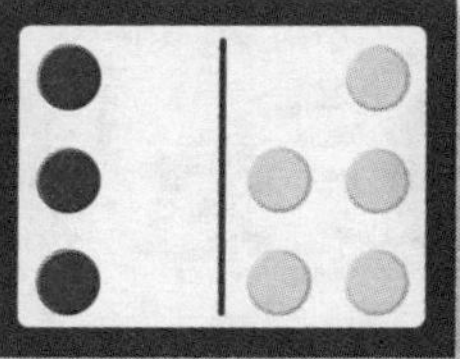

fewer

A group that has less than another group

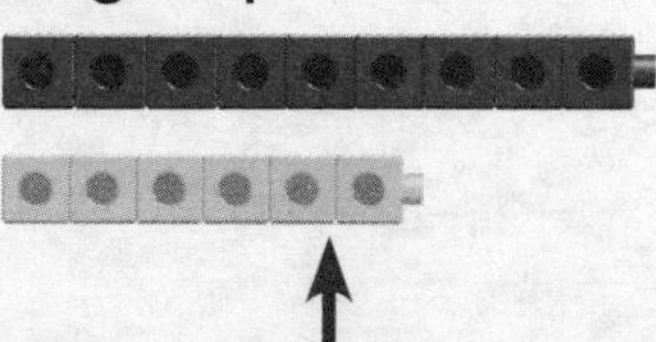

The yellow row has fewer.

flat surface

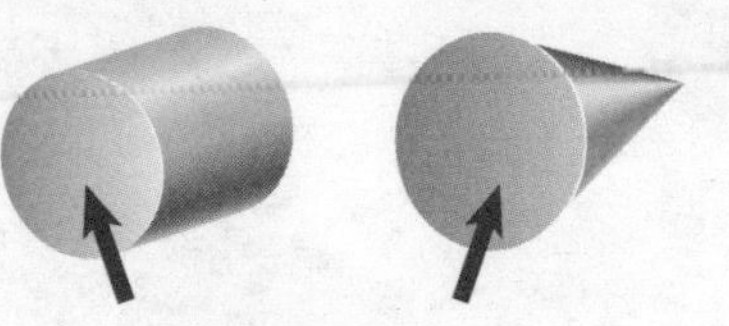

fourths

The square is divided into fourths.

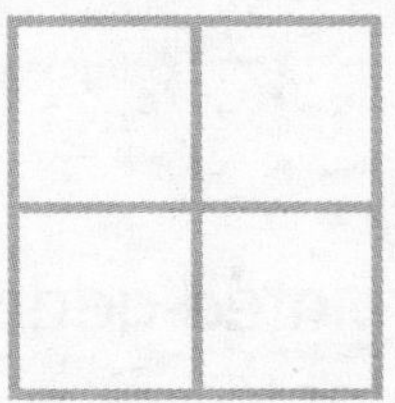

G

greater than (>)

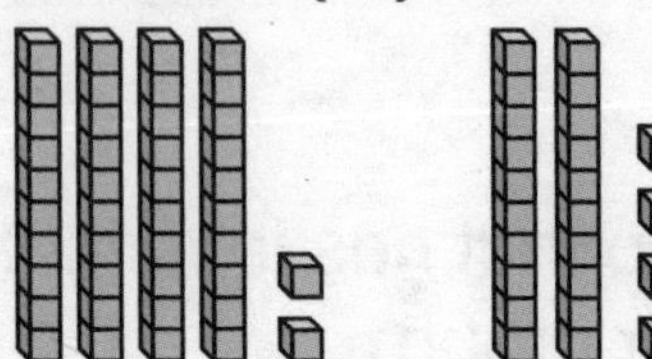

42 is greater than 24.

greatest

the number or group with the largest value

23

23 is the greatest number.

half hour

A half hour is 30 minutes.

1:30

halves

The circle is divided into halves.

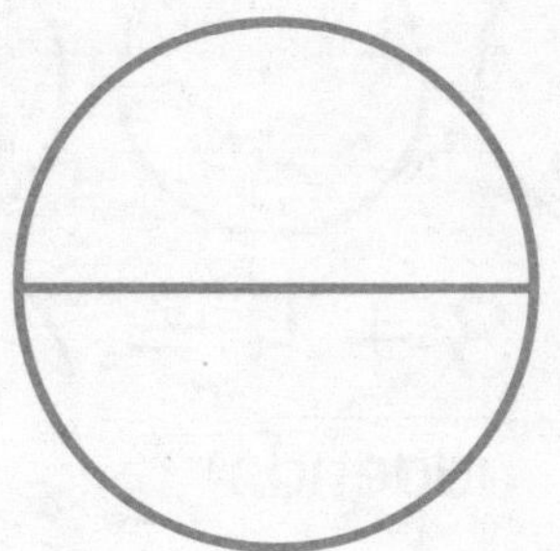

hexagon

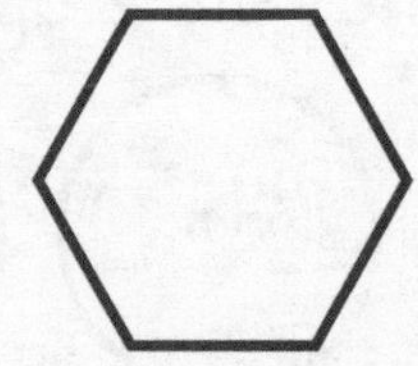

hour

An hour is 60 minutes.

2:00

hour hand

The short hand on a clock is the hour hand.
The hour hand tells the hour.

It is 3:00.

hour hand

in all

There are 4 birds in all.

inside

The dogs are inside the dog house.

join

to put together

3 and 3 is 6 in all.

least

the number or group with the smallest value

7 is the least number.

length

the distance from one end of an object to the other end

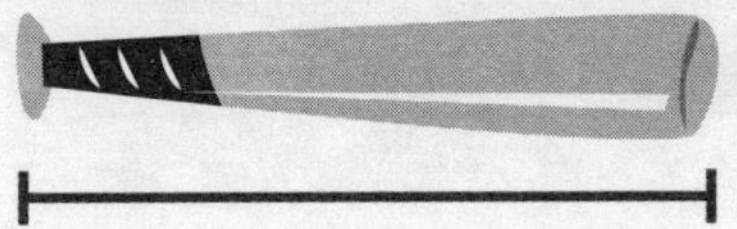

less

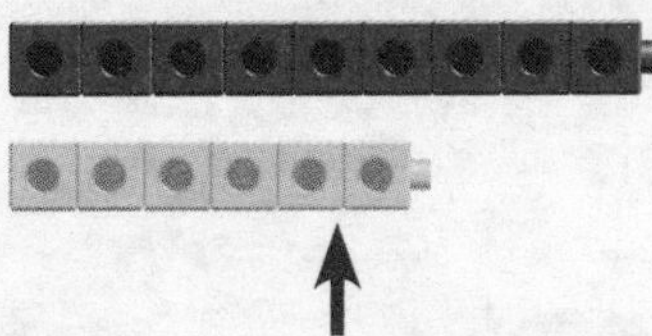

The yellow row has less.

hundred chart

A hundred chart shows all of the numbers from 1 to 100.

1	2	3	4	5	6	7	8	9	10
11	12	13	14	15	16	17	18	19	20
21	22	23	24	25	26	27	28	29	30
31	32	33	34	35	36	37	38	39	40
41	42	43	44	45	46	47	48	49	50
51	52	53	54	55	56	57	58	59	60
61	62	63	64	65	66	67	68	69	70
71	72	73	74	75	76	77	78	79	80
81	82	83	84	85	86	87	88	89	90
91	92	93	94	95	96	97	98	99	100

less than (<)

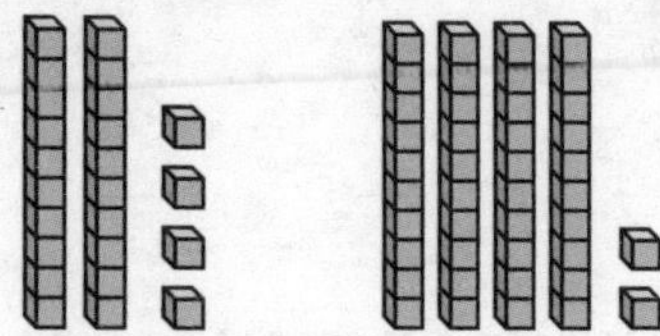

24 is less than 42.

longer

An object that is 7 cubes long is longer than an object that is 2 cubes long.

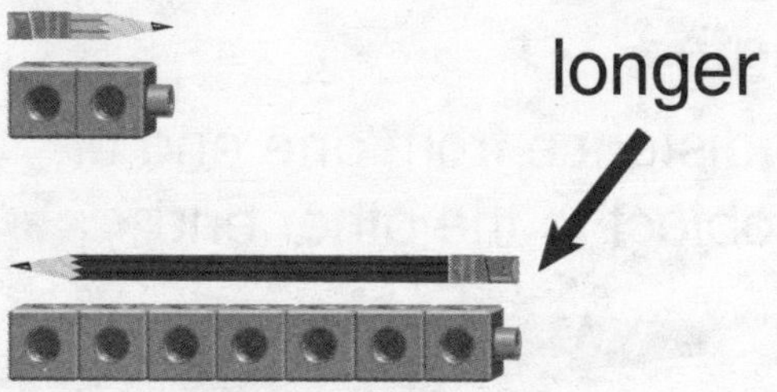

longest

The object that takes the most units to measure is the longest.

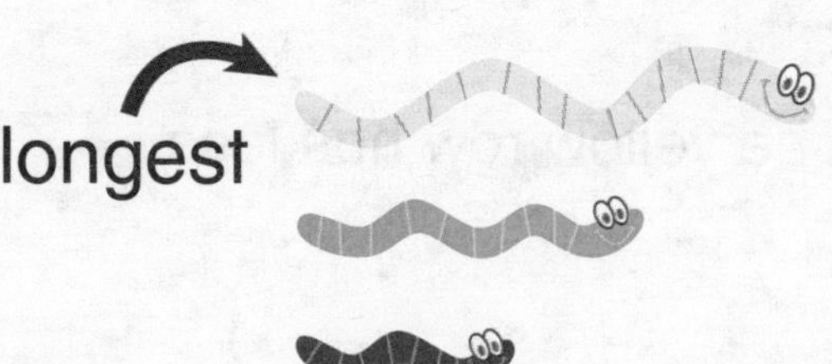

make 10

7 + 4 = ?

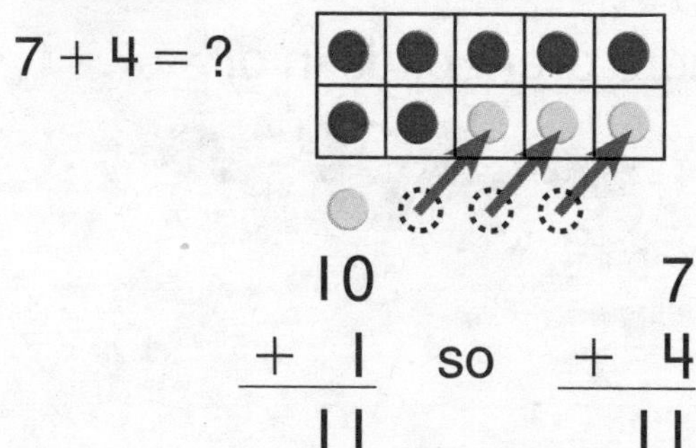

measure

You can measure the length of the shoe.

minus

5 − 3

5 minus 3

This means 3 is taken away from 5.

minus sign (−)

7 − 4 = 3

↑

minute

60 minutes is 1 hour.

minute hand

The long hand on a clock is the minute hand.
The minute hand tells the minutes.

It is 3:00.

missing part

the part that is not known

2 is the missing part.

more

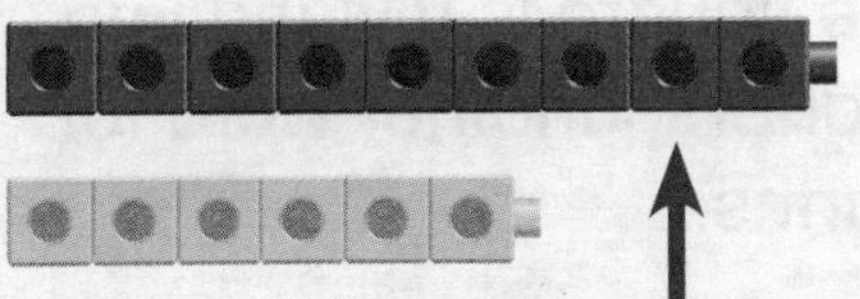

The red row has more.

near double

an addition fact that has an addend that is 1 or 2 more than the other addend

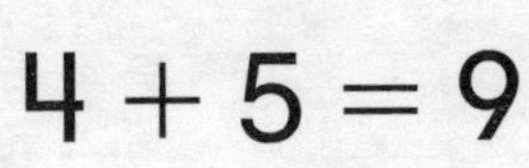

4 + 4 = 8. 8 and 1 more is 9.

number chart

A number chart can show numbers past 100.

81	82	83	84	85	86	87	88	89	90
91	92	93	94	95	96	97	98	99	100
101	102	103	104	105	106	107	108	109	110
111	112	113	114	115	116	117	118	119	120

number line

A number line is a line that shows numbers in order from left to right.

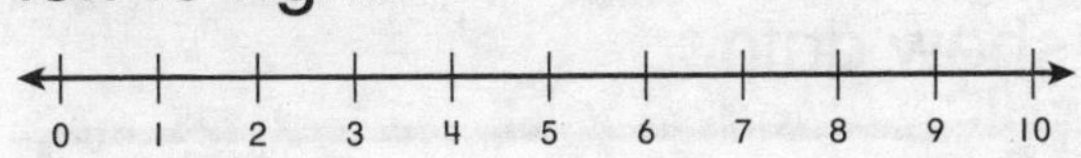

o'clock

8:00
8 o'clock

ones

The ones digit shows how many ones are in a number.

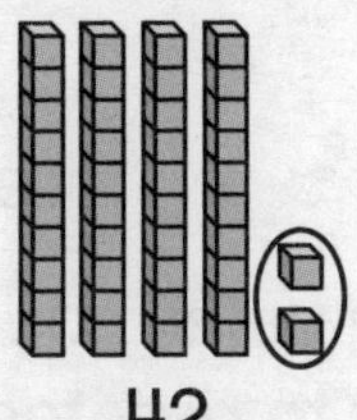

42 has 2 ones.

42

ones digit

The ones digit in 43 is 3.

ones digit

open number line

An open number line is a number line without marks in place.

order

60 61 62 63

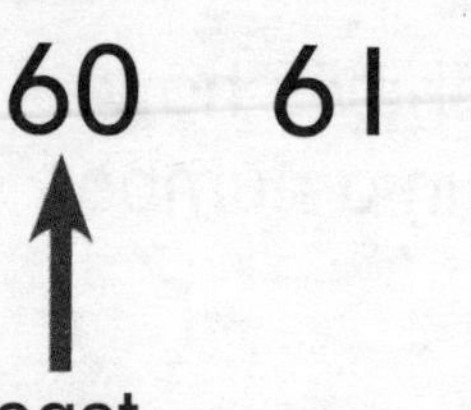

least greatest

Numbers can be put in counting order from least to greatest or from greatest to least.

outside

5 dogs are playing outside of the dog house.

part

a piece of a whole

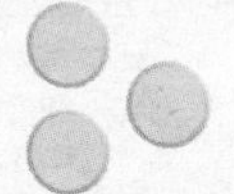

2 and 3 are parts of 5.

pattern

You can arrange 5 objects in any pattern, and there will still be 5 objects.

picture graph

a graph that uses pictures to show data

Favorite Pets			
Cat			
Dog			

plus

5 + 4

5 plus 4

This means 4 is added to 5.

plus sign (+)

$6 + 2 = 8$

quarters

The square is divided into quarters, another word for fourths.

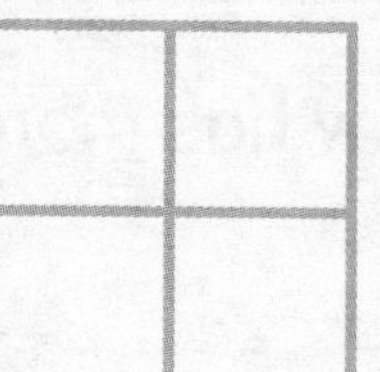

rectangle

rectangular prism

related facts

addition facts and subtraction facts that have the same numbers

$2 + 3 = 5$

$5 - 2 = 3$

These facts are related.

row

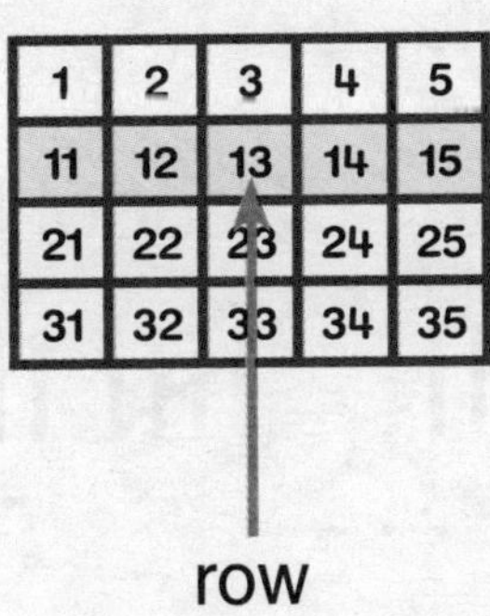

scale

A scale is used to measure how much things weigh.

shorter

An object that is 2 cubes long is shorter than one that is 7 cubes long.

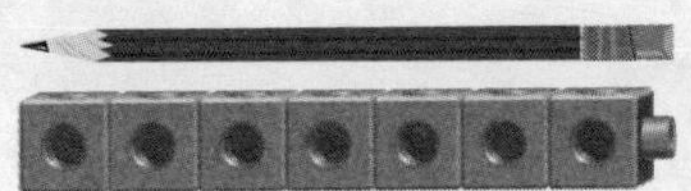

shortest

The shortest object is the one that takes the fewest units to measure.

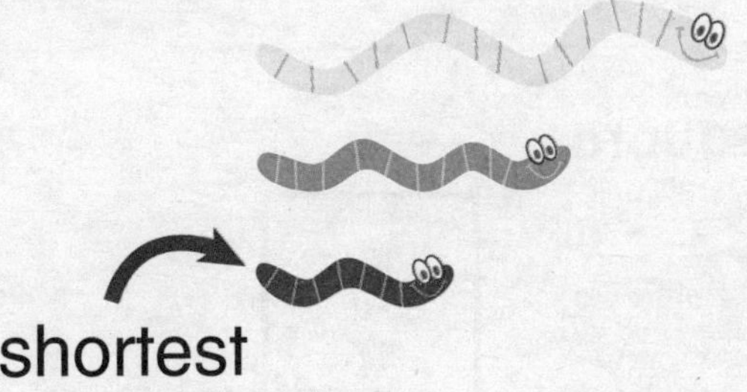

side

These shapes have straight sides.

sort

to group objects according to how they are similar

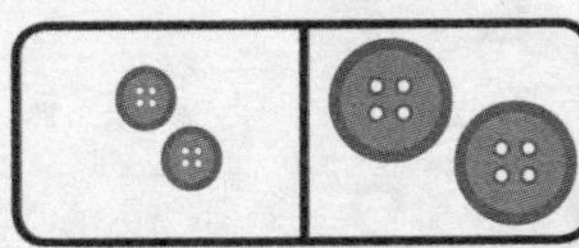

The buttons are sorted by size.

sphere

square

standard form

a number shown in digits

28

subtract

When you subtract, you find out how many are left.

$5 - 3 = 2$

subtraction equation

$12 - 4 = 8$

sum

$2 + 3 = 5$

sum

survey

to gather information

Do you like cats or dogs better?
Cats III
Dogs II

take away

Start With	Take Away	Have Left
6	3	3

$6 - 3 = 3$

To take away is to remove or subtract.

tally chart

a chart that uses marks to show data

Walk	School Bus
𝍸 II	𝍸 𝍸

tally marks

marks that are used to record data

Cats	𝍸
Dogs	II

There are 5 cats and 2 dogs.

tens digit

The tens digit shows how many groups of 10 are in a number.

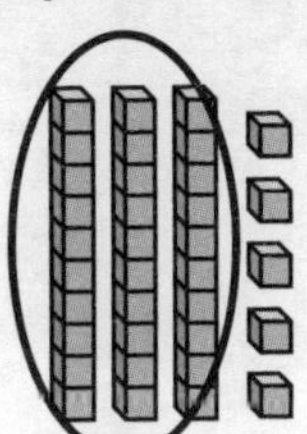

35 has 3 tens.

35

Three-dimensional (3-D) shapes

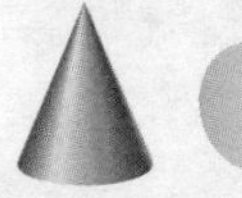   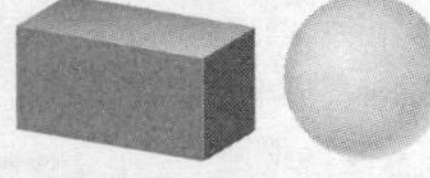

These are all 3-D shapes.

trapezoid

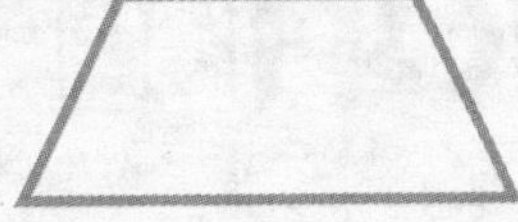

triangle

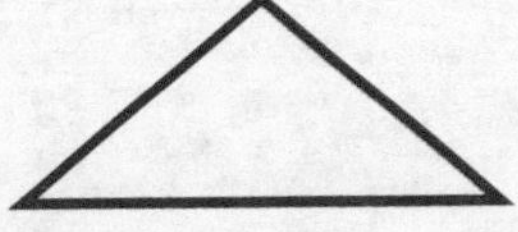

Two-dimensional (2-D) shapes

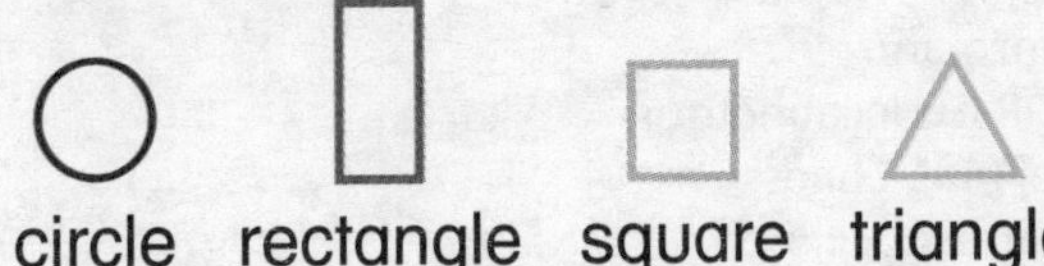

vertex (vertices)

a point where 3 or more edges meet

whole

You add parts to find the whole.

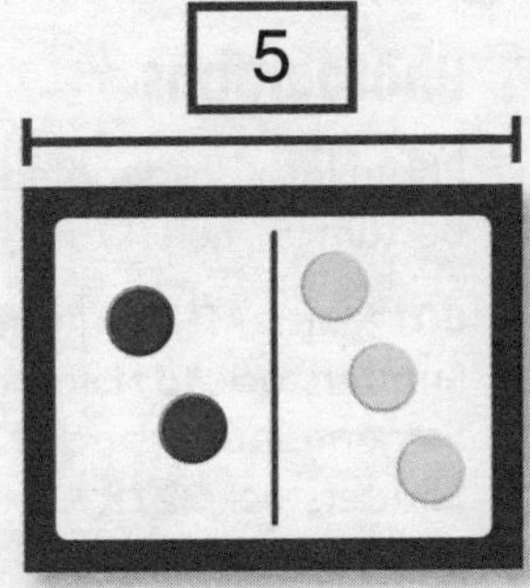

The whole is 5.

Photographs

Photo locators denoted as follows: Top (T), Center (C), Bottom (B), Left (L), Right (R), Background (Bkgd)

001 MattiaATH/Shutterstock;**075** Karen Faljyan/Shutterstock;**151L** fotografie4you/Shutterstock;**151R** Chris Sargent/Shutterstock;**227L** Galyna Andrushko/Shutterstock;**227R** Alexey Stiop/Shutterstock;**297** Willyam Bradberry/Shutterstock;**349C** Umberto Shtanzman/Shutterstock;**349L** Nick barounis/Fotolia;**349R** Gudellaphoto/Fotolia;**391** John Foxx Collection/Imagestate;**445L** Chaoss/Fotolia;**445R** Lipsett Photography Group/Shutterstock;**493** Anton Petrus/Shutterstock;**541L** Baldas1950/Shutterstock;**541R** Shooarts/Shutterstock;**609** Barbara Helgason/Fotolia;**661** Studio 37/Shutterstock;**705** Vereshchagin Dmitry/Shuhtterstock;**741** Sergey Dzyuba/Shutterstock;**813BL** Isuaneye/Fotolia;**813BR** Ftfoxfoto/Fotolia;**813TL** Sumire8/Fotolia;**813TR** Janifest/Fotolia.